The great, ugly truth about American politics today is that, even as we
champion democracy abroad, few Americans have any hope of influencing their government at home. Maybe it has to be so. Maybe, in a land
of 300 million citizens, elites must rule, and democracy can do no more
than, sometimes, throw a few rascals out. But a growing number of bold

II0663949

thinkers and activists now insist that we can do better—none more constructively than Kevin O'Leary.
—**Rogers M. Smith, University of Pennsylvania**

A provocative look at our current state of political apathy and what can be done about it. These proposals would empower the deliberations of ordinary citizens without surrendering the important features of our Constitution and our representative political system. Anyone who knows the dangers of direct democracy but who still wants to engage citizens in political decision-making should read this book.
—**Kevin Mattson, Ohio University**

Saving Democracy is a novel and promising work. It is beautifully presented and will give anyone who thinks seriously about democratic reform and innovation much to ponder.
—**Archon Fung, Harvard University**

There is nothing wrong with American democracy that a return to majority rule couldn't cure. Kevin O'Leary has a bold but realistic vision of how the restoration of real democracy could happen.
—**Jack Miles, author of *God: A Biography***

Saving Democracy

Saving Democracy

A PLAN FOR REAL REPRESENTATION IN AMERICA

KEVIN O'LEARY

Stanford University Press
Stanford, California
2006

Stanford University Press
Stanford, California

Library of Congress Cataloging-in-Publication Data

O'Leary, Kevin.
    Saving democracy : a plan for real representation in America / Kevin O'Leary.
        p. cm.
    Includes bibliographical references and index.
    ISBN-10: 0-8047-5497-7 (cloth : alk. paper)
    ISBN-10: 0-8047-5498-5 (pbk. : alk. paper)
    ISBN-13: 978-0-8047-5497-2 (cloth : alk. paper)
    ISBN-13: 978-0-8047-5498-9 (pbk. : alk. paper)
    1. Representative government and representation--United States. 2. Political
participation--United States. 3. Democracy--United States. I. Title

JK1764.O445 2006
320.973--dc22
2006017969

Typeset by Thompson Type in 10/14 Sabon

For Lita
a passionate democrat

Contents

A people, in order to preserve its liberty, must keep it firmly in its hands.

NICCOLÒ MACHIAVELLI, *1513–1517*

I hold with Montesquieu, that a government must be fitted to a nation, as much as a coat to the individual.

ALEXANDER HAMILTON, *1799*

Since all cannot, in a community exceeding a single small town, participate personally in any but very minor portions of the public business, it follows that the ideal type of a perfect government must be representative.

JOHN STUART MILL, *1865*

The essential need, in other words, is the improvement of the methods and conditions of debate, discussion and persuasion. That is *the* problem of the public.

JOHN DEWEY, *1927*

If the democratic process is not firmly anchored in the judgments of the demos, then the system will continue to drift toward quasi guardianship. If the anchor holds, the drift will stop. The problem arises because of the gap between the knowledge of the policy elite and the knowledge of ordinary citizens.

ROBERT A. DAHL, *1989*

Introduction

The Yiddish folktale "It Could Always Be Worse" tells the story of a man in a poor village who complains to his rabbi about his cramped quarters. The rabbi tells the man to bring his chickens and goose into the hut. When things get worse, the rabbi tells the man to bring in his goat as well, then the cow. Naturally, chaos erupts. At last the rabbi tells the man to let the animals out of the house, resulting in the serenity he was searching for all along.[1] Compared to most countries, the United States is politically blessed. It is obvious, given the evils and sufferings of the past century, that our political life could be much, much worse. Freedom of speech and assembly, regular elections, a rigorous legal system— these are the procedural norms of democracy that Americans take for granted and scores of nations struggle to embrace. Less obvious, but nonetheless real, is the possibility of improving democracy in America. Today it is technologically possible to make democracy more of a reality and less of an illusion. In business, we expect and demand constant improvement. Innovation is the name of the game. Yet when it comes to politics, we typically mumble Winston Churchill's refrain about democracy being a terrible system of government except when compared to everything else, and we accept what is as what will be.

Franklin D. Roosevelt's New Deal was about the government's relationship to the economy and its responsibilities to its citizens, especially those in need. Today it is democracy itself that requires a safety net. We face not a sudden economic catastrophe but rather a protracted political crisis that corrodes the civic fabric. For more than two decades, Americans have been sending a message to anyone who cares to listen, saying that they are upset and unhappy with politics as usual. The voters—and the millions more who skip elections—are unhappy with the political system itself. For many, American democracy has a hollow ring. The basic structure of American politics—the three branches of government and federalism—is sound. Yet the relationship between the political class and the public (nearly 300 million of us) is deeply problematic.[2]

Formal political inclusion is guaranteed to every adult, yet, sadly, informal exclusion remains a reality for all but a privileged few. More than 200 years after the American Revolution, we have yet to devise a method whereby people can grapple, in a thoughtful manner, with the major issues facing the nation. Our failure to imagine a better way of conducting the public's business casts a shadow on every policy decision, every congressional vote, every election.

We live in an age of instant communication and 24-hour news. Yet as congressional districts have grown enormous (once 30,000 to 1; now more than 650,000 constituents per representative) most Americans feel increasingly disconnected from their government. It is the rare citizen who has met his or her congressional representative or whose phone rings when ABC News or Gallup conducts a national poll requiring fewer than 1,000 respondents. The individual's lack of voice and power is compounded by a system of representative government that gives no institutional role to assembled citizens. Although city councils and school boards allow people to be involved at the local level, there is no similar local body that enables and empowers citizens to debate and deliberate the great issues of the day. This central weakness of our democracy grows more acute as we face complex moral problems such as those presented by global warming, the outsourcing of jobs, and the conduct of the war on terror, to name three topics high on the current agenda.[3] The Internet, magazines, newspapers, and television news shows bombard us with information. The question is, What do we, as citizens, do after we have read, watched, and digested the news?

At the nation's founding, James Madison's goal was to create a unique form of democracy—a large republic in which majorities based on a devotion to the broad public welfare are able to triumph over the selfish interests of narrow factions. That Madison and the framers of the Constitution did an extraordinary job in creating the world's leading democratic republic cannot be denied. Yet their design could not help but be incomplete and reflect the patrician outlook of the time. In particular, Madison's solution to faction in the small city state opened the door to corruption in the large republic. In a new nation of three million individuals the dilemma of scale did not exist. In a super state of nearly 300 million people—the third most populous country on the planet behind only China and India—the gulf between those who rule and those who vote threatens to undermine sovereignty and rob American democracy of its core meaning.

Today some commentators speak of the United States as the new Rome. Our military, economic, and cultural power dwarfs our nearest competitors. But empires, even democratic ones, are prone to corruption. Given the expansion of the ratio of representatives to citizens in the United States, the Madisonian system is prone to periodic outbreaks of venality, greed, and sordid behavior by office holders who give special favors to their friends and political supporters.[4] At the zenith of America's power, it is incumbent on its citizens to consider the health of the American republic. Some experts say the political system is broken. Others say the system works, but not as well as it should. What the average person knows is that American democracy today is a counterfeit of what earlier generations practiced and our most gifted thinkers intended.[5] Imagine Alexis de Tocqueville on a return visit. Could he write the same glowing portrait he did in 1835? The answer is clearly no.

Fifty years ago, political parties allowed people to participate in politics in a significant way. From the ward level up, party structures gave citizens an arena where they could exert themselves. This is no longer the case. True, some of the urban machines were corrupt and the local parties were not open, participatory mechanisms easily penetrated.[6] But they did exert power and were locally based. Together with a robust labor movement, the party structures of old gave middle- and working-class people a connection to power that they now lack. In the consultant era of Karl Rove and James Carville, local party organizations have largely vanished, narrowly focused interest groups control the policy agenda, and experiments with direct democracy, such as the initiative and recall, are burlesque caricatures of their original purpose.

On most election days in America, far fewer than half of those eligible to vote cast a ballot. This was the case on November 5, 2002, the first national election after 9/11. Both houses of Congress hung in the balance, and the Republican Party's clean sweep gave the GOP a lock on power in Washington, DC. You would think that questions of terrorism, economic recession, and corporate corruption would drive people to the polls. Think again. By contrast November 2, 2004, was an exception to the rule, as voters flocked to the polls. Turnout surged to nearly 60 percent, the largest in a presidential race since 1968, as George W. Bush claimed a narrow victory over John Kerry in a contest decided by the precincts of Ohio. The war in Iraq, economic unease, and intense passion among conservatives and liberals pushed participation well above the 54 percent turnout of 2000. Yet even as political interest surged, the yawning chasm between the public and the political elite remained. Like irksome Uncle Harry at a holiday dinner, the dilemma of scale is both obvious and little discussed. It grants the wealthy undue influence over the political process and makes robust civic life difficult.

As the U.S. population grows, it is as if politics takes place in an ever-expanding auditorium. Most of the audience is far from the stage, and only the loudest voices reach them. Realizing this, players perfect sound bites and handlers stagecraft entrances, backdrops, and messages. What matters are the sweeping gestures that reach far into the hall and the balcony. Those in the front rows—the 10 to 15 percent of the population who keep up with current events and politics—would like to be more engaged in the performance. But they are largely excluded, unless their checkbook grants them admittance backstage. And as the distance between the players and the audience grows, democracy shifts from a community of shared values and genuine debate to a hollow procedure where marketing trumps truth.

If you doubt that a huge gap exists between the political elite and the public, consider this: If congressional districts were as large in the 1790s as they are today, the early House of Representatives would have had only five members! (The U.S. population in 1790 was approximately three million people; congressional districts grew to 650,000 after the 2000 U.S.

Census.) A U.S. House of Representatives consisting of Dennis Hastert, Nancy Pelosi, and three friends is not what Madison had in mind.

The change in scale is astounding. Harvard University's Thomas Patterson writes, "The gap between the practitioner and the citizen—despite the intimacy of television and the immediacy of polling—has arguably never been greater. The world occupied by the hundreds at the top and the world populated by the millions at the bottom still overlap at points, but they do so less satisfactorily than before."[7] Early in the presidential season, the New Hampshire primary is a great political event precisely because the scale is human. Potential presidents talk with voters, and town meetings are the norm. Voters respond by being passionate about democracy. Taking their civic responsibilities seriously, more than 80 percent of adults vote.[8] In neighboring Vermont, 150 people serve in the lower house of the state Legislature. Because the Green Mountain State has a population of only 593,740, the ratio of representation is 1 to every 3,958 people. By contrast, in California, the most populous state with 35 million residents, a similar style of state government would swell its current 80-member state Assembly to 8,842 representatives!

Today many Americans appear to endorse, at least implicitly, democracy without citizens. Yet it is a mistake to expect experts, elected representatives, the press, and opinion polls to do the work of democracy for us. We can rely on experts, but many important public policy issues have moral and ethical dimensions that specialists are ill equipped to address. We can rely on elected representatives, but in the current system, presidents, governors, and members of Congress listen closely to the powerful interests that fund their campaigns. We can rely on the media, but reporters move to the next story after exposing wrongdoing, and the tabloid trend toward the sensational deflects attention from issues that matter. We can rely on polls, but rare are polls that measure the opinions of Americans who have studied and discussed an issue before being asked to summarize what they think.

We cannot expect busy adults to be public policy wonks. Still, when important issues are being decided, it is impossible not to include the public in the equation. Consider two of the most critical debates in recent years—national health care and a second war with Iraq. These two enormously complex issues could not be left to only experts and interest groups. The public had to weigh in. We have public opinion polls, of course, but they are flawed in two respects. First, they are superficial. Most respondents lack the time and inclination to make a thoughtful, informed response, what pollster Daniel Yankelovich calls a considered judgment.[9] Think of the incredibly uninformed citizens who regularly share their wisdom with *Tonight Show* host Jay Leno. No one wants these people making public policy. Second, opinion polls, scientifically valid when properly conducted, offer an illusion of participation that does not exist. Because such a small sample is needed for national polls (fewer than 1,000 respondents), having the *Los Angeles Times* or NBC News randomly select your house for a phone call is about as likely as winning the lottery. And in the unlikely event that they do call, Neil Postman captured our dilemma well: "We have here a great loop of impotence: The news elicits from you a variety of opinions about which you can do nothing except to offer them (to a pollster) as more news, about which you can do nothing."[10]

That our current system of public discussion and debate is lacking was clearly demonstrated by the run-up to the invasion of Iraq in March 2003. After six months of sustained front-page coverage of the Iraq crisis, nearly 50 percent of the American public believed that there was a direct link between Saddam Hussein and the 9/11 attacks on the World Trade Center and the Pentagon. Hussein led a brutal regime, but no evidence has been found—despite a rigorous search by U.S. intelligence and the world's best investigative journalists—showing he had anything to do with 9/11. True, the Bush administration did its best to portray Iraq as a rogue nation that might be tempted to aid terrorists. But any person who bothered to keep up with the debate knew that Al Qaeda and Saddam's Iraq were separate and distinct. Of course, you may say the gap between the mass public and the political elite has always existed and is nothing to be alarmed about. But consider this. Just days before President George W. Bush launched the second Iraq War, *New York Times* columnist Thomas Friedman told NBC's Tim Russert that "a very small group—about one hundred people in Washington, DC.—made the decision to go to war in Iraq."[11] In a robust democracy, this would not be the case.

As we begin the twenty-first century, the United States is rich, powerful, and politically troubled. Many recognize the symptoms of our democratic malaise, but because our political system is wracked by both hyperdemocracy and apathy, a solution eludes us. In some respects, the political system is more open and responsive than at any time in our history. Elected officials, barraged by e-mail, faxes, phone calls, and lobbyists, feel as though the political system is operating on amphetamines. Yet electoral participation is episodic, often dipping to near-record lows, and political knowledge is thin.[12] Beneath a veneer of surface detachment and cool cynicism, Americans remain idealists, especially about democracy. As idealists, we believe that democracy should allow for active participation on the part of interested citizens. As realists, we know that the sheer scale, rapid pace, and complexity of modern life make this impossible.

Or do they?

THE ASSEMBLY REFORM

The United States is now one hundred times more populous than at the time of its founding, yet there has not been a proportional increase in the membership of the House of Representatives. One result has been a growing sense of distance between people and their lawmakers. Another has been a breakdown in political engagement, leaving political discussion in fewer and fewer mouths. This may be good for the pundit class and the wealthy elite who control the political process, but it is not healthy for democracy in America.

Today it is possible to combine the traditional town hall and the Internet to fashion a new understanding of representative government that would empower citizens while rejecting the mass plebiscite of the initiative system. Beneath each member of Congress, we would create a one hundred-person citizen assembly whose job will be to study and discuss the great issues of the day and thereby provide us with a more deliberative and thoughtful sample of public opinion than now exists. The Assembly reform would bring our representative system closer to the people and allow more citizens to take an active role in self-government.* The average size of a congressional district has tripled in the past century. In 1900, the average district had a population of 195,000. Today, we ask members of the

---

*I will use Assembly when speaking of the national system and assembly when talking about the local delegation in a particular congressional district.

House to "represent" more than 650,000 people. And current congressional districts are not going to shrink; instead, as the U.S. population grows, House districts will inch toward 700,000 and then 800,000 and finally 1 million. This is not the "intimate" representation that Madison envisioned for the House of Representatives. To deal with the challenge of great size and population, we need to redesign the national government to provide for a smaller ratio of electors to representatives.

Grounded in American history, the Assembly builds from a synthesis of Madison and Thomas Jefferson's understandings of democracy. Under the Assembly reform, in each of the nation's 435 congressional districts, there would be a local assembly of one hundred citizens, selected by lot, who would meet and discuss the major domestic and international issues. In the first stage of the assembly reform, delegates would study and debate pressing issues—Social Security or immigration reform, for example—and then offer their opinions. Their views would constitute a second, more sophisticated, more informed measure of public opinion than traditional opinion polls. In this first stage, the Assembly has no formal power and acts strictly in an advisory capacity. Yet elected officials, the press, and the public would watch the opinions of these "super" citizens carefully, and the opinions of the Assembly would help shape the opinions of the public at large.

In the second stage, the People's House, the national network of local assemblies would gain formal power to vote yea or nay on major legislation that has passed the House of Representatives and the Senate. This veto power would allow members of the People's House to send bills back to the House of Representatives and the Senate for reconsideration, and a separate "gate-opening" power would allow the People's House to force a floor vote on certain bills heretofore stuck in committee and destined to die. Other positive powers include the authority to initiate bills in either the House or the Senate, the power to offer amendments to bills under consideration on the floor of the House or the Senate, the ability to pass formal instructions to individual representatives, and the right to draft at-large resolutions addressed to the House of Representatives or the Senate as a whole.

To avoid undue complexity, the People's House would not be involved in committee deliberations about bills. Like the Assembly, the People's House would help focus the public's attention on the most critical issues of the day and, in addition, would act either as a popular brake or accelerator on national legislation. The Federalists constructed the American system to safeguard the interests of the wealthy and powerful at the expense of participation by average citizens. A skyrocketing population accentuates this bias. The People's House would rebalance the system by injecting our national government with a dose of popular energy and common sense.

At the time of the founding, Madison and his colleagues had an excuse for their sociology. They truly believed in a wiser and more virtuous elite and were deeply afraid of laborers, particularly those who might become a powerful "faction" against the interests of property and commerce. Such were the lessons they drew from Shays's Rebellion, when debt-ridden farmers rebelled against Boston bankers, and from the Pennsylvania Constitution of 1776 with its unicameral legislature and the extraordinary Article 15, which required every bill passed by the legislature to be circulated for consideration by the people at large before becoming law in the next legislative session. Afraid of the democratic forces unleashed by the American Revolution, the Federalists worked hard to create a distant national government far from the people who gave their consent.

The world we live in is far different from 1787. Today we think of virtue and corruption as being equally distributed across the population. Today Anti-Federalists' fears about a distant and remote government ring true. And today it is within our power to add a popular assembly to the constitutional mix. Doing so would correct the flaw in Federalist thinking and help us recapture democracy's promise. In the Assembly, average citizens would have a chance to be players in the national debate. Of course, only a limited number of people could serve in the Assembly or the People's House, but everyone would have an equal chance of being chosen to be a delegate and, in the case of the People's House, an equal chance to participate in governing the nation. In addition, and just as important, the degree of separation from the federal government that each of us feels would be radically reduced. The chances of the average citizen meeting or knowing his or her congressman or congresswoman are slim when districts are 650,000 persons large. In a 6,500-person ward it would be much more likely that you, a person in your family, or a friend would actually know the local delegate. This simple dynamic would stimulate interest and conversation about the important issues of the day.

Extending representation downward in the political system and asking a cross section of citizens to take a formal deliberative role in setting national policy would both confront the dilemma of scale and help control corruption. Extending representation downward would engage voters in a way that goes far beyond the illusory participation of polling. Madison's idea of extending representation horizontally across space in *Federalist* No. 10 was a stroke of genius. It enabled the United States to build democracy on a continental scale. Today it is time to consider extending representation deeper into the population.

THREE BENEFITS

Powerful medicine, the Assembly and the People's House would strengthen American politics in three specific, critical ways. No other reform on the horizon offers so many benefits while staying true to Madison's vision.

1. This reform would give the public back its voice by creating opportunities for intelligent participation. As Harvard Law professor Mary Ann Glendon writes, "Self-government not only requires certain civic skills (deliberation, compromise, consensus-building, civility, reason-giving), but *theaters* in which those arts can be meaningfully exercised."[13] The Assembly and the People's House would drastically improve opportunities for participation and involvement in a way that is deliberative and thoughtful, not impulsive and emotional.

2. By encouraging the formation of broad-based civic majorities (Madison's goal), this reform would help curb the excessive influence of special interests that has gained strength in this era of consultant-dominated politics. The assembly reform would act as a counterweight against single interest groups that block sane solutions to pressing problems.

3. The gate-opening aspect of the People's House would give us the option of forcing a floor vote on popular bills locked in committee. Thus, a reform that improves participation also boosts legislative speed.

Locally the Assembly would add a third arena of public engagement. Today the school board and city council are platforms where citizens take turns conducting the public's business. Both Tocqueville and John Stuart Mill extolled the critical role that local participation plays in the health of democracy. The local assembly would be similar to the school board and city council in terms of its close connection to citizens and its moderate time demands on elected delegates. The difference lies in its focus on national affairs. In an increasingly cosmopolitan and global world, power long ago moved beyond city limits. The national Assembly continues the American tradition of local political engagement, while greatly expanding our understanding of what local participation means.

During the 1960s, the idea of participatory democracy energized a generation. Today, combining the traditional town hall and the Internet to fashion a new understanding of representative government would allow greater participation—and influence—by average citizens. It would help break the special interests' lock on Congress and control a sometimes imperial presidency.[14] A one-hundred-person citizen assembly in every congressional district would be a healthy antidote to the politics of plutocracy, elites, and narrow special interests. This new institution would assist us in becoming the nation that Madison and Abraham Lincoln envisioned—one where politics rises above self-interest and strives on a regular basis to reach the civic republican goal of "civic-minded" majorities, deciding issues on the basis of arguments presented, not campaign checks collected.

Serving in the national Assembly would be similar to serving on a jury; we expect people on a jury to do their best to make dispassionate decisions based on the law and the evidence presented. In the same way, in the Assembly, delegates would be asked to think beyond partisanship and self-interest to consider what is right for the community and the nation. A virtual national Assembly, built on face-to-face town halls in communities across the country, would help the United States realize its democratic promise by giving the people a greater role in public debate and increased power over their government. Updating the Athenian Assembly and the New England town meeting, the Assembly would enable citizens to discuss and shape their common future.

THE BOOK'S STRUCTURE

The chapters that follow offer a radical, yet practical, plan to give voters a true voice in national affairs and, potentially, a vote in Congress. Chapter 1 focuses on the dilemma of scale and the problem with public opinion polls.

Chapter 2 examines corruption in the large republic. Together they explain, in part, why the system is broken. Chapter 3 shows how the Assembly emerges from classic American political thought, and Chapters 4, 5, and 6 explore the Assembly proposal, its benefits, practicality, and possible objections. Chapter 7 discusses how the Assembly would give the public power and explains how the reform fits with contemporary theories of deliberative democracy. Chapter 8 addresses the reform's attraction given America's unique constitutional structure. Chapter 9 discusses the wider implications of blending participation and representation in regard to the nation's cosmopolitan diversity and America's role in the world. Together Chapters 3 through 9 explain how and why a novel reform is possible— one that builds on our political heritage while embracing our technological present.

Readers should understand that the message of the book goes beyond the specific reform presented. I offer one possible blueprint; others will offer theirs. The important thing is to generate a national dialogue about how to improve citizen engagement, deliberation, and representative government. My purpose in writing this book is threefold: first, to make an argument about why it is important and how it is practical to institutionalize deliberative democracy; second, to explain how doing so would strengthen the civic republican component of the American political tradition; and third, to develop a representative reform that would allow for a more accurate and fair aggregation of interests and preferences than the current political system. My focus is on what Yale University's Robert Dahl calls "democracy's third transformation," which arises from the pressing need to narrow the "growing gap that separates policy elites from the demos."[15]

The American political system has periodically undergone modifications while remaining true to the core of the Constitution, which is the separation of powers and federalism. The reform offered here would reinvigorate a felt sense of democratic power among citizens while staying true to the American tradition. It has an intimate connection with American political ideas and history. As such it has a greater chance of success than European transplants such as proportional representation or parliamentary democracy.[16] Following Michael Walzer, this book is a work of connected criticism rooted in our history; both the Federalists and Anti-Federalists could have comprehended and appreciated it.[17]

A century ago, the Progressives cleaned up the corrupt urban machines. Their good government crusade resulted in the initiative and primary system and city manager form of municipal government.[18] In 1920, after decades of organizing, women gained equal political and civil rights when the 19th Amendment was ratified. In the 1960s, the push continued to grant full political rights to all adults. The civil rights movement literally altered the face of America when the Civil Rights Acts of 1964 and 1965 opened doors for minorities of all colors. And, in the past three decades, mobilizing first around Ronald Reagan and then George W. Bush, the Christian right has reshaped American politics and the judicial bench. When Americans mobilize, change happens.

Looking at the political landscape, historian Arthur Schlesinger Jr. and journalist E. J. Dionne Jr. argue that a progressive era is coming our way.[19] If that is the case, questions about the quality and content of democratic participation will surely be part of the equation. Forecasting an era of reform may seem like an odd prediction in the wake of the 2004 election. Yet politics goes in cycles, and the excesses and corruption that accompany a corporate takeover of politics often produce a civic reaction. While the rich and the powerful are not going to lead a crusade to increase the participation and power of average citizens, grassroots volunteers of all political persuasions will see value in what I am proposing. Readers should understand that the reform I propose is, in fact, politically neutral.[20] A national network of citizen assemblies is neither conservative nor liberal, neither Republican nor Democrat. Being about democracy as a social norm and political institution, the Assembly operates on a different level than regular partisan politics and challenges political elites to focus less on fundraising and more on connecting with—and representing—ordinary people.

How do we bridge the great divide that now separates the broad public and the privileged class that runs the political system and the government? This book answers that question.

1.

Size and Democracy

As the population of the United States grows—from just over 5 million in 1800 to 76 million in 1900 to more than 281 million in 2000—the country's political system ratchets up and away from the average citizen.[1] The increase in population, the growth of scale, and the remoteness from power all feed estrangement from modern representative government. In little New Hampshire and Vermont, representatives in the lower house have approximately 3,800 and 4,100 constituents, respectively.[2] However, legislative districts in large states approach—and sometimes even surpass—the average size of congressional districts.[3] When Madison and the framers first introduced the idea of direct election of representatives to a national Congress, they proposed congressional districts of 30,000 constituents. At the time, these were astonishingly large districts, and many Anti-Federalists refused to vote for the new Constitution because they felt districts of this size made a mockery of representation.[4] Today, we would relish a return to such intimate scale. Madison's own electoral experience points to the startling change in scale. After co-authoring *The Federalist Papers,* he returned to Virginia to run for a seat in the new House of Representatives against another future president, James Monroe. Campaigning hard, Madison eked out a victory by 1,308 votes to Monroe's 973—a vote total far below what it takes to win a school board election today.[5]

The problem of scale is so daunting that we rarely give it much thought. The small-town society that Tocqueville admired disappeared with the industrial revolution and the urbanization of the early twentieth century. The Progressives grappled with these dramatic changes, but the full impact of massive scale was not felt until the latter part of the twentieth century. In 1950 only half of all Americans lived in major metropolitan areas; by the mid-1990s four in five did. The number of people who live in towns and rural areas fell from 44 percent in 1950 to 20 percent in 1996. At the same time, the proportion living in central cities has remained steady—averaging 32 percent across the last half of the twentieth century. The greatest increase came in the suburbs where the population exploded from 23 percent in 1950 to 49 percent in 1996.[6] In 2000, 85 million Americans lived in urban centers, 140 million lived in metropolitan suburbs, and 56 million lived outside the big metropolitan areas—23 million in cities and 33 million in rural areas.[7]

For those living in giant metropolitan regions, the dilemma of scale is that much more real. We know some of our neighbors, but not all, and some of our best friends may live a time zone or two across the country. Beyond the community association and local school board, our connection to political power can be faint. In Houston, a city council of 14 represents 4 million people. In Los Angeles County, 5 county supervisors represent 9.5 million people. In New York, 62 state senators represent 19 million constituents. In Florida, the population jumped from 9.7 million in 1980 to 16.3 million in 2001 while the number of state legislators remains constant at 160.[8]

In the beginning, the national numbers were small. Just after the American Revolution, the newly established United States' population stood at 2,780,400. By the 1830s, when Tocqueville visited and penned *Democracy in America,* the population had grown to more than 15 million. When Lincoln addressed the fallen at Gettysburg, the combined population of North and South totaled roughly 33 million. When Theodore Roosevelt discovered the bully pulpit and spent New Year's Day shaking hands with as many White House visitors as wanted to greet him, the head count was more than 80 million.[9] At the start of the Jazz Age, the total stood at 106 million. When Franklin Roosevelt took the oath of office during the Great Depression, 127 million Americans looked to him for guidance. By the Korean War, our numbers totaled 151 million. At the end of the 1960s, the numbers reached 203 million, then 226 million in 1980, and 248 million in 1990; at the start of the new millennium, the U.S. Census counted 281,421,906 Americans.[10] The Census Bureau estimate for 2010 is 308,936,000. [11] We are, in many respects, a long way from the Revolution.

Globally, the numbers are staggering. In 1925 there were approximately 2 billion people on planet Earth; by 1975 that number had doubled to 4 billion; by 1990 we had reached 5.3 billion; by 2006 the number of mouths to feed reached 6.5 billion.[12] In 1800, there were only six cities that had more than half a million people: Beijing, Canton, Istanbul, London, Paris, and Tokyo. By 1990, approximately 800 cities had surpassed the half-million mark. At least 270 cities had more than 1 million residents, and 14 topped 10 million.[13] The demographic volcano and the accompanying dilemma of scale have many repercussions. If we do not keep the world economy growing as rapidly as the population, we risk a dramatic rise in famine, nation-state breakdown, and terror. If we do not figure out how to deal with environmental challenges such as global warming, we could destroy the earth's thin ecosphere. And if we do not take steps to deal with the challenge that scale presents to government, popular sovereignty could become a relic of the past.

But is the dramatic increase in scale really a problem for democracy? At the beginning of the twentieth century, only a few nations were democratic, and even those restricted the franchise to men. Today, 122 nations meet the criteria of allowing all adult citizens to vote in regular elections.[14] It is not hard to hold elections, but it is hard to make democracy meaningful. The challenge is to construct a political system that supports and sustains a robust civic culture. Civil society and democratic institutions are intimately related. Elections have been held in post-Saddam Iraq, but few would call Iraq a democracy. Real democracy has a qualitative dimension. As Tocqueville recognized, democracy is most importantly about mores, those habits of thought and action that sustain civic involvement. In other words, the global expansion of democracy is one thing; the quality of the democratic experience is another. After the struggles of the twentieth century, American politics finally opened its doors. Women and minorities have fought hard to gain equal standing with white Anglo-Saxon males. American society has become much more inclusive, yet the political philosopher Sheldon Wolin makes a telling observation when he says, "Americans no longer feel democracy in their bones."[15] In certain respects, our current political life is only a shadow of what it was in Abraham Lincoln's day when the United States was a nation of small towns, and our population was approximately a tenth of what it is today.

As scale grows, our grasp of "reality" becomes twisted. Today a large part of what we know is filtered and experienced through television and other media. In the 1920s, Walter Lippmann famously wrote about the "world out there and the pictures in our heads." Today, multinational corporations and mass marketing have helped create a celebrity culture where Hollywood stars have the glamour, money, and image to become governors and even president. Daniel Boorstin warned about a society dominated by pseudo-events—events such as photo ops and press conferences that are manufactured solely to be reported—and coined the contemporary definition of celebrity as "a person who is known for his well-knownness."[16] Mid-twentieth-century writers fretted about mass society, but at the beginning the twenty-first-century Americans are not as isolated and alienated as some social critics feared. Most people are ensconced in routines, families, and friends. "Fears that city life produces larger numbers of relatively isolated, alienated individuals lacking strong ties and a sense of community" were exaggerated.[17] Alienation and anomie are not the problem; the challenge of scale is. In their book, *Size and Democracy,* Dahl and Edward Tufte write:

> As the inexorable thrust of population growth makes a small country large and a large country gigantic, demands are often heard for bringing government closer to the people, for grassroots democracy. Small units are often said to facilitate democracy better than larger units; hence the larger units must be broken up into smaller units, where grass-roots democracy is possible—regions, states, cities, neighborhoods. At the same time, there are complaints that the smaller units are incapable of handling their problems, and demands are heard for larger units such as metropolitan areas, a United States of Europe, a world federation.[18]

This, in a nutshell, is the dilemma of scale.

Today, with one national government, 50 state governments, and 87,849 local governments—3,043 counties, 19,431 municipalities, 16,506 townships, 13,522 school districts, and 35,356 special districts—the United States has a decentralized form of public administration.[19] We have plenty of chances to participate and influence events, locally. Traditionally, average citizens have participated in "self-rule" through the city council and school board. Yet, this approach is no longer adequate.[20] As public problems grow beyond local capacities, critical decisions get pushed to the state and national level. School funding decisions too often depend on the governor's budget. Local economic growth waxes and wanes with regional and global investment decisions. Transnational corporations generate neighborhood environmental hazards, and cleanup depends on federal budgetary priorities. "Think globally, act locally" only goes so far.

The United States, the most populous Western democracy, has just 535 federal legislators in Washington, DC, who represent nearly 300 million people. This ratio is extremely low. With one member of the House of Representatives for every 650,000 Americans, our connection with the federal government is stretched thin. The number of representatives in the House has not changed since 1910, when the 435 members each represented approximately 200,000 constituents.[21] Of course, one way to increase representation would be to increase the size of the House of Representatives. But unless we quadruple the size of the House to nearly 2,000 members, constituents in the home districts will not notice a difference. And radically increasing the size of the House would make it wildly unwieldy and difficult to run. In contrast to the 100-member Senate, it is already hard for House members to get to know many of their fellow politicians.[22] As any recent visitor can attest, Capitol Hill, especially on the House side, is a maze of offices crowded with staff.

For some, the issue of scale is moot.[23] After all, what are we supposed to do? Ask people to stop having children? For most Americans, questions about the public schools, taxes, economic growth, the environment, civil rights, and health coverage are front and center. Yet, our ability to make genuine progress on issues such as these is related to how well the public understands the challenges the nation confronts, which, in turn, is connected to the problem of scale and how we conduct politics in a mass society.

THE RATIO OF ELECTORS TO REPRESENTATIVES

The crucial question is precisely how to fashion the connection between elites and regular citizens. Today, we rely on voting, which has been slipping for four decades; opinion surveys, which measure off-the-top-of-the-head reactions; and interest groups, which focus on a narrow agenda with little regard for the big picture. All are inadequate. How can the connection between political elites and citizens be strengthened? Is it possible to improve the pattern and character of political discourse and its ties to rational government? These are critical questions for the future of democracy in the United States.

The connection between political elites and the public is problematic, in large part, because we have a high ratio of electors to representatives. The high ratio, first and foremost, transforms national legislators into a special elite class—economically and socially—living at great remove from those who vote for them. The 535 members of Congress are a breed apart. As one political scientist has written—they are *the* Washington establishment with longevity that outlasts presidents and their administrations.[24] Even state representatives, at least in large states, are elected royalty, with fawning personal staffs and a frenetic professional life in which they are in constant motion, running from one meeting to the next, whether chairing the subcommittee on banking or speaking to a high-tech lobby group or dining with wealthy donors. Within their world, legislators are the center of attention, the star attraction, the king or queen of their domain. It is not so much that national legislators are economically and socially part of the upper strata—though many are, given the cost of winning a seat in Congress. What is more important is the psychological distance that gradually grows between them and their constituents. True, successful politicians develop what Richard Fenno calls a "home style" for dealing with constituents back in the district.[25] But this technique masks the psychological distance that naturally grows when elected officials take up residence in Washington, DC or the state capital and become players in the capitol scene. Representatives, like all of us, are creatures of habits and time constraints. House members meet with constituents back home, but often these are people who constitute the politician's political base. Core supporters have access; people from the opposition are a nuisance. It is human nature; put yourself in the shoes of your congressman or congresswoman. After a tough week in Washington, DC, and a red-eye flight back home, whom would you want to have breakfast with on Saturday morning?

The great distance—physical and psychological—between national legislators and voters makes it hard for the representatives to know the lives and the problems of their constituents. And it makes it more difficult for constituents to hold their representatives accountable. A century ago, Roberto Michels made an argument that organization inevitably leads to oligarchy. When you have a representative structure of governance, said Michels, those elected to office and those who vote cannot help but develop different perspectives, wants, and needs. Michels developed his "iron law of oligarchy" in regard to labor unions and political parties, but his argument takes on additional force when examining the U.S. national system where many senators are millionaires and each House member "represents" 650,000 constituents.[26]

Obviously, competitive elections and retirements mean we get a circulation of elites, so we are not dealing with a rigid, static oligarchy. Thus, in one sense, Michels is wrong. Such is the argument that democratic theorists such as Joseph Schumpeter and Dahl use to refute Michels.[27] But, in another sense, Michels is right. That national elected officials are an elite political class, largely separate and distinct from everyday voters, remains a very real problem for modern democratic states—especially large ones such as the United States. Of course, it was widespread resentment of the politicians as a segregated and privileged class that fueled the drive for term limits on legislators in the early 1990s. Term limits is an ill-conceived reform, yet the impulse is understandable. Granted, Americans are not going to give up on representative government; participatory democracy is clearly utopian, and authoritarian politics is not an option. So the question becomes, Can we do something about the absurdly high ratio of electors to national representatives that now exists?

Setting a lofty standard, our goal should be to make it within reach for Americans to govern themselves as much as possible and not be governed by others, no matter how well-intentioned. This was Jefferson's aim, and it should be ours.[28] Any other perspective leads down the road to guardianship—benign or brutal. So argues Dahl, the leading democratic scholar of the postwar era.[29] But how? Radicals of the 1960s insisted on "participatory democracy." Direct democracy, inspired by Rousseau, can only be a romantic reaction against the modern nation-state and the reality of great size and complexity.[30] Burned out by the struggle for civil rights and protests against the Vietnam War, 1960s radicals ran into the brick wall of scale and never figured out how to marry participatory democracy to representative government.[31] The early Students for a Democratic Society (SDS) was inspired by Jefferson, John Dewey, and C. Wright Mills, not Mao. But the SDS and other activists of the 1960s never reconciled their anti-elite rhetoric with the necessity of representative government. It was never quite clear how the participatory democrats proposed to run a society based on complex institutions, and Dahl made precisely this point in *After the Revolution?* (1970). As David Brooks explains in *Bobos in Paradise,* the college rebels of the 1960s succeeded in transforming American society. Today, the American upper middle class is a blend of bohemian and bourgeois values.[32] Culturally, the 1960s generation won. Politically they lost.

True, the 1960s resulted in an opening up of institutions, a more critical attitude toward those in authority, and an expansion of direct mass democracy in terms of the presidential primary system and state initiatives. The attack on the old regime blew apart the traditional party system. But these changes are not all positive. More to the point, the push for participatory democracy ran aground. In most respects, politically we are no closer to participatory democracy than we were in 1959. Suspicious of elites and hierarchy, participatory democrats of the 1960s and 1970s idealized New England town meetings, small cooperatives, and workplace democracy—situations where small scale made versions of participatory democracy possible.[33] As such, the hard work of actually crafting a feasible plan for allowing greater participation in the national representative system was deferred.

A big, complex society requires elites. Some commentators, such as Lippmann in the 1920s and *Newsweek International* Editor Fareed Zakaria, today say we should delegate authority to elites and experts who know what to do.[34] Obviously, we must do this to a certain extent. But many important issues are not just technical; they involve fundamental political and moral choices. To argue that technocrats and the elite political caste have the expertise and the wisdom to do the right thing is to delegate a significant chunk of popular sovereignty. In sum, neither the participatory nor the elitist options are satisfactory.

In a massive country such as the United States, polling is the primary means by which we gauge what the public thinks. A presidential pollster explains polling this way: "It defies logic that interviews with 800 Americans will accurately mirror the opinions of 250 million of their countrymen. But the laws of science seem crazy . . . I've seen it time and again."[35] The latest poll numbers trumpet from the media on a daily basis. Opinion surveys, conducted by CNN, Zogby, Gallup, or any of a dozen highly esteemed polls, are widely accepted as legitimate expressions of the public's voice.[36] Yet, a number of academic researchers now question "their usefulness as mirrors of the public mind."[37]

Public opinion research is not flawed; rather, the substance being measured presents the difficulty. Practitioners have long recognized problems with how question order, wording, sampling errors, and nonresponses can skew conclusions. But the real conundrum is the public's low level of political knowledge, its uneven distribution, and people's willingness to spew out opinions when they know next to nothing about what is being asked. Scott Althaus says the problem is "so pervasive as to call into question whether opinion surveys can tell us reliably what the people really want."[38] On the one hand, modern polling gives us a scientifically valid measure of what the public is thinking. Statistical sampling and margins of error allow political scientists and pollsters to accurately gauge what the public is thinking at any one time. If we lacked random sampling, a perfectly credible and widely accepted method of measuring preferences, our knowledge of the political universe would be severely curtailed. On the other hand, there is the old problem of "garbage in, garbage out." If most of the public pays little attention to public affairs, and a majority of those polled know very little about, say, the situation in Iraq or the major planks of the president's energy initiative, having an accurate picture of their views, while a good thing, does not change the fact that scant knowledge and minimal thought lie behind the answers. Princeton's Larry Bartels states the problem succinctly: "Citizens have attitudes but not preferences."[39] The people who are polled are statistically representative of the mass public and, sadly, its ignorance.[40]

Political scientist Samuel Popkin, a veteran of Democratic presidential campaigns, says voters may not be well-informed, but that, working from cues, stereotypes, and information gathered from daily life, they make rational choices when it come to politics. Voters, Popkin says, neither form opinions irrationally nor change them capriciously. They do, however, employ information shortcuts. Following Anthony Downs's analysis of how people make efficient use of information, Popkin argues that citizens take cues from bits of information and then use their own life experience to "complete the picture." Most Americans possess only rudimentary civics knowledge, but, says Popkin, working from what they know they can "read" presidential candidates fairly well.[41] A key part of what the average voter does is to look to pundits, political elites, and politically sophisticated friends for help.

> Most citizens don't study the details but look at the bottom line. Are we at war? Is the economy healthy? Most people entrust the rest to experts and specialists. What is important is that there are perhaps five percent who are activists and news junkies who do pay close attention. If they see that something is seriously wrong in the country, they sound the alarm and then ordinary people start paying attention.[42]

The increased education level of citizens means more people follow national and international issues, but Popkin says whatever education level they have, voters use "information shortcuts and cost-saving devices . . . to assess ideology, platforms, individual competence and character."[43] As a result, presidential campaigns work hard to win the contest of short-cut symbols—Willie Horton in 1988, health care and welfare reform in 1992, and the contest over John Kerry's Vietnam service in 2004, for example. A single appearance can be critical if it crystallizes an impression of the candidate—Clinton's comment on Sister Soulja in 1992, Howard Dean's scream speech after the Iowa Caucuses in 2004, and President Bush's edginess and apparent discomfort in the first 2004 presidential debate.[44] It is far easier to develop a narrative about the kind of person Candidate X or Y is than to evaluate the candidate's policy recommendations.

While Popkin focuses on presidential campaigns, John Zaller examines mass opinion from a wider perspective. In his influential *The Nature and Origins of Mass Opinion,* he looks at how individuals convert political information and argument into political opinions.[45] The prevailing view of many citizens and political observers is that citizens have preferences about major policies and that these preferences then largely determine the actions of politicians and governments. But Zaller views public opinion as a function of elite debate. His working assumption is that "elite communications shape mass opinion rather than vice versa."[46] Citizens have preferences, but their opinions are the product of the deliberation and argument among the elites.[47]

Ordinary citizens are often said to have a strong voice on major policy, while lobbyists, interest groups, policy experts, and government officials prevail on issues of low visibility.[48] There are two important caveats to this received wisdom. First, even on major issues, the public's opinion is very much a reflection of elite debate. If there is elite consensus about national or international policy, says Zaller, "the public can do little more than follow the elite consensus on what should be done." The early stages of the Vietnam conflict fit this pattern, as did the 1990 Persian Gulf War. The Bush Sr. administration's mobilization of public support for the first Gulf War was a striking example. "When Iraq invaded Kuwait in August 1990 only a small fraction of Americans were aware that Kuwait existed. Yet within two weeks, public support for the use of American troops to prevent further Iraqi aggression was topping 80 percent in the polls." When elites divide, the public splits as well, following elites who share their general ideological position.[49] Second, increasingly, politicians and their top strategists use polls to "find the most effective ways to move public opinion closer to their own desired policies." The politicians' own policy goals, and those of ideological activists, drive policy initiatives. More and more, polls are used not to find out what the public wants, but to identify the best arguments, symbols, and buzz words by which to "sell" the policy.[50] The research forces us to reevaluate how much independence and autonomy the mass public has from elite opinion. Zaller sums up the gist of his argument thus:

> People are continuously exposed to a stream of political news and
> information, much of it valenced so as to push public opinion in

one direction or the other. But, owing to the generally low levels of
attention to politics in this country, most people on most issues are
relatively uncritical about the ideas they internalize. In consequence,
they fill up their minds with large stores of only partially consistent
ideas, arguments, and considerations. When asked a survey question, they call to mind as many of these ideas as are immediately
accessible in memory and use them to make choices among the options offered them. But they make these choices in great haste—typically on the basis of one or perhaps two considerations that happen
to be at the 'top of the head' at the moment of response.[51]

For example, if asked about defense spending, most people would answer
the question based on the latest news item on that topic—say a nightly
news story on a defense procurement scandal. "The psychological literature on opinion change lends great support to the notion that individuals
typically fail to reason for themselves about the persuasive communications
they encounter. Instead, people rely on cues about the 'source' of a message
in deciding what to think of it."[52] As to why this is the case, Zaller argues
that this is what we should expect given how unusual it is for the average
person to be asked his or her opinion on a matter of public importance.
The phone rarely rings with the ABC News or the *New York Times* pollster on the other end of the line ready to listen to our words of wisdom.

Historian Robert Wiebe cautions that opinion polls in the large nation
state are no substitute for more vigorous democracy. Even when the public is paying attention, polls often are "pseudoparticipatory proxies that
create an illusion of citizens actually having a say in their government."[53]
We give polls too much credence when we treat them as serious measure-
ments of public opinion. If opinion surveys actually worked the way they
are advertised—if they actually counted people's thoughtful consideration
of an issue rather than being off-the-cuff reactions—then the magic numbers generated would command respect. As it is, public opinion polls are
inaccurate because much of what they measure is so ill-considered; they
are fraudulent because they give the public a sense of participation that
can best be described as mythical.

Polls do not engage us; they do not cause us to think; they do not ask
us to grapple with the issues at hand, to weigh competing demands, to

ponder tradeoffs and the possible consequences of different courses of action.[54] Public opinion surveys are the political equivalent of game shows. Being called to the stage and asked whether the prize is hidden behind door 1 or door 2 is such a random occurrence that there is no reason for us to prepare for the contest, much less take the experience seriously. The contestant wants to win the prize, but there is no ongoing purpose to the experience; it is separate and apart from daily life.

COLD WAR HANGOVER

Another, less visible, but critical reason why Americans feel lost in the large republic is a change in the very language of democracy. Today, politicians, journalists, and citizens continually talk about the "democratic process." It is so ingrained in our political consciousness that we rarely reflect on why we speak about democracy this way. We just accept it. But there is a reason—the fear of communism during the Cold War. The great struggle with the Soviet Union dominated American life for nearly half a century.[55]

Nearly two decades after the fall of the Berlin Wall, we remain imprisoned inside a Cold War view of democracy and its possibilities. Facing the Marxist-Leninist threat, Americans spoke of democracy in a new way, not so much as shared values and citizen participation but as a set of formal rights and procedures.[56] This was no accident. The shift—from a demanding ideal that no country has yet achieved, to institutional procedures that ensure free and fair elections—fit an ideological need. The new definition made the choice between East and West stark and simple—elections or Stalin.[57] The procedural account of democracy does not aspire to educate citizens or to encourage greater participation. Instead, discussion, deliberation, and political give-and-take are left to interest groups and a specialized, technically informed elite.[58]

Fighting the Soviet Empire required a simple concept of democracy that could be applied to many countries and would allow the United States to present itself as the paragon of democracy. Schumpeter supplied the tool by redefining democracy as a "political method" in which the political elite is forced to compete for mass favor in periodic elections. The leading Western economist of his generation after Keynes, Schumpeter developed the "democratic process" as a powerful weapon—an ideological combination punch when combined with George Kennan's strategy of geopolitical containment.[59] After his *Capitalism, Socialism and Democracy* (1942), Western nations with competitive elections and procedural norms came to be seen as fully democratic, and the meaning of democracy was abridged to individual freedom as communist regimes were sharply criticized on procedural grounds.[60]

In arguing for his "realistic" understanding of democracy, Schumpeter says the democratic method is that "institutional method for arriving at political decisions in which individuals acquire the power to decide by means of a competitive struggle for the people's vote."[61] Competition for leadership becomes the distinctive feature of a democratic political system. Thus, if the electorate has the power of eviction, then a political system is democratic: "democracy does not mean and cannot mean that the people actually rule in any obvious sense of the terms 'people' and 'rule.' *Democracy means only that the people have the opportunity of accepting or refusing the men who are to rule them.*"[62] Schumpeter drew an explicit parallel between democratic politics and economics. His analogy can be briefly stated: competitive struggle between potential leaders/firms for votes/profits has the indirect effect of producing legislation/goods for citizens/consumers. In Schumpeter's economic theory, the entrepreneur is presented as the dynamic force in the system. Likewise, in his democratic theory, the leader plays this role while the voter becomes a consumer who can only accept or reject what the political entrepreneur has to offer.[63] For Schumpeter and his followers, politics is just another market, another aspect of the division of labor, something we can safely delegate to special pleaders, consultants, and the political class.[64]

Confronting the totalitarian regimes of Nazi Germany, the Soviet Union and Communist China, a majority of Americans came to accept this more restricted, more cautious, less ambitious view of democracy. Hitler's rise to power led many in the West to think twice about the wisdom of mass participation; the logic of the postwar confrontation between the United States and the Sino-Soviet empire necessitated an identification of American democracy with freedom, individual rights, and private enterprise. At the same time, cold warriors downplayed the central democratic values of equality and community. The reason was simple: equality and fraternity, unlike liberty, are key values in socialist as well as democratic thought.[65]

Faced with an imminent loss of basic liberties and freedoms, Americans shifted to a tough but meager understanding of democracy based on rights and processes. Almost imperceptibly, in a short space of time, Americans accepted a radically reductionist understanding of democracy quite different from the democratic vision of Jefferson, Lincoln, and Progressive thinkers such as Herbert Croly and Dewey.[66] As the meaning of democracy was reduced to individual freedoms and regular elections between competing elites, an important beginning stage of democracy was crystallized into the ideal itself. In the 1950s, Louis Hartz warned that communism was being allowed to redefine "the issue of our internal freedom in terms of our external life."[67] Unfortunately, that process continues today—accentuated by America's imperial status and the global war on terror.[68]

With Carthage defeated, the question facing us modern Romans is, Do we continue to hold a minimal definition of democracy, one that accepts a growing gap between citizens and the political elite as being of little consequence, or do we work to articulate and put into practice a more demanding understanding of democracy?

Clearly, democracy as "competitive elites" is preferred over more authoritarian forms of politics. Yet it is severely reductionist and teaches us to tolerate—and gradually accept as normal—an enormous gap between the political elite and the public and a great deal of inequality, apathy, and lack of community. These may not be problems for the procedural view, but they are problems for us. The Cold War's hidden cost is the chill it put on democracy in America. Redefining democracy as the "democratic process" was akin to chemotherapy. It helped slay the communist cancer abroad, but left politics in a weakened condition at home at a time when new challenges demand, not languor, but democratic vitality.

DIRECT DEMOCRACY TRAP

A final reason we have such a difficult time dealing with the problem of scale is the habit of thinking of democracy primarily in two ways—direct democracy and standard representative government. Schumpeter and Jean-Jacques Rousseau are the seminal writers on modern representative and participatory democracy, respectively, and most institutional thought about democracy hovers around these two poles. Schumpeter says people have the right to accept or reject those who make the decisions, but that between elections the public should stay quiet. Participation, civic virtue, and vigorous democratic dialogue are of little consequence. Madison, the original theorist of modern representative government, is also elitist, but Schumpeter pushes this stance to the limit.

On the other democratic extreme, we find Rousseau, the eighteenth-century author of *The Social Contract* and patron saint of modern participatory democrats.[69] He famously favored tiny republics filled with virtuous citizens and gave modern articulation to the ancient Greek understanding of democracy.[70] In contrast to Schumpeter, Rousseau insists that political power exercised by individual leaders must be directed by and under the authority of "the freely expressed will of the people as sovereign."[71] A radical direct democrat, Rousseau says that representation is the death of democracy: "The English people thinks it is free. It greatly deceives itself; it is free only during the election of the members of Parliament. As soon as they are elected, it is a slave, it is nothing . . . the instant a people chooses representatives, it is no longer free; it no longer exists." [72]

Given his controversial, complex, and radical views, some wonder whether Rousseau was a democrat at all.[73] But it is a serious misreading of Rousseau to deny his commitment to democracy. He is an exhilarating, idealistic, penetrating, and most uncompromising thinker. Reading Rousseau and James Miller's masterful *Rousseau: Dreamer of Democracy*, it is hard not to feel the sense of excitement, fulfillment, and possibilities to be found in the ideal of direct democratic participation.[74] Ironically, Rousseau is difficult to fathom because he is unrelenting and absolute in his pursuit of freedom and democracy.

At bottom, Rousseau's philosophy is not about democracy but about freedom. The *Social Contract* opens with the famous statement: "Man was/is born free, and everywhere he is in chains." Man was born free before civilization existed, and every man or woman is born with a natural freedom to choose whether or not to obey others. "And everywhere he is [in] chains," questions the legitimacy of every government— whether constitutional democracy or authoritarian dictatorship. Rousseau's project is to show how individuals can indeed maintain their freedom in society—a very difficult task, but a possible one in the perfect social order. For Rousseau, democracy and freedom are undeniably linked because a democratic social order is the only one where freedom is possible. A guide to the philosophically pure, Rousseau says that if a people truly want to be free and if they prize human freedom above all other goods, they must follow a strict regimen.

In book III, chapter IV: "On Democracy," he writes:

> Consider how many things that are hard to combine are presupposed by this form of government. First, a very small State where the people is easily assembled and where each citizen can easily know all the others. Second, great simplicity of mores, which prevents a multitude of business and knotty discussions. Next, a great equality of ranks and fortunes, without which equality of rights and authority could not subsist for long. Finally, little or no luxury, because either luxury is the result of wealth, or it makes wealth necessary. It corrupts both rich and poor, the one by possessing, the other by coveting. It sells out the homeland to indolence and vanity; it deprives the State of all its citizens by enslaving some of them to others and all of them to opinion.[75]

It is clear that Rousseau is writing a treatise on the principles of democracy "fit for but a few times and a few places."[76] Three paragraphs after listing the above conditions he states, "If there were a people of Gods, it would govern itself democratically. Such a perfect government is not suited to men."[77]

Rousseau's vision stands in stark contrast to two basic realities of modern society. In his democracy, representative government is not allowed and, thus, the citizen body must be very small for citizens to assemble and directly decide laws and policy. In addition, Rousseau's citizens must be radically similar—not diverse—to ensure that they will have harmonious interests and can agree on a general good. On both counts, size and diversity, the United States is fundamentally unsuited for his philosophy.

In many respects, Rousseau's philosophy was a radical rejection of modern life and, thus, his most passionate followers are often viewed as hopeless romantics.[78] This raises the question, If Rousseau is so unsuited to modern life, why is he so important to us as a philosopher of democracy? First, we all live in the shadow of his dream. He is the writer most responsible for igniting the French Revolution—the greatest of the democratic revolutions—and spreading its message. Before Rousseau, aristocracy and feudalism were the norm. After Rousseau, popular sovereignty is the starting point, and the question becomes how much aristocracy we are willing to tolerate in a democratic society. By transforming the meaning of sovereignty from something that endowed kings with special powers to something that belonged to the people, he became the rare political theorist who did, in fact, change history. Second, Rousseau combines the modern era's yearning for individual freedom with the ancient Greek understanding of democracy as direct participation of citizens in shaping their common life. He argued that freedom is the greatest good and that democracy is the only government capable of protecting and perfecting it.[79] These ideas are commonplace conjecture in the modern world—consider President Bush's justification for the war in Iraq—but Rousseau, in large part, helped make it so. Third, emerging from the French Revolution three paths all owe a debt to Rousseau. Representative democracy requires the abolition of feudal privilege and the idea of equality before the law—two goals Rousseau sought. Dictatorial democracy of the modern totalitarian type concentrates the powers of the government in "enlightened leaders" who are willing to force people "to be free." And direct democracy aims to realize lawmaking "as an activity undertaken by the people themselves."[80]

Of course, few political thinkers take as extreme positions as Schumpeter and Rousseau and, in fact, most political theorists take a middle position. Still, in the United States most discussion about democratic institutions remains focused on either small-scale participatory democracy or full-scale representative government. In fact, only with the Progressive reformers early in the twentieth century do we find sustained democratic inventiveness in the middle of the spectrum. The 1960s experiments with small-scale direct democracy expired when the protests over the Vietnam War and civil rights ended. Most Americans have never doubted that traditional representative democracy is the only possible way to operate a modern society. The overwhelming majority of Americans understands that, except in very small communities, democracy must mean representative government. Totalitarian regimes and radical fundamentalists present the most serious challenge to modern democracy, not romantic dreamers of pastoral democracy.

OUR CHALLENGE

Our challenge is to develop and operate from a more flexible institutional outlook than those offered by Schumpeter and Rousseau. At the beginning of the twentieth century, the Progressive reformers devised the initiative and the mass primary by taking the basic principle of direct democracy—every citizen should have a vote on policy—and pushing the town meeting to a grand scale. Yet, government by mass direct democracy—witness California's destructive obsession with initiatives—is problematic, to put it mildly.[81] First, hot-button propositions are not instruments of sound public policy. They are campaign weapons. Designed by political consultants to appeal to specific groups in the electorate, many initiatives are flawed and incoherent. They make bad law. Second, the primary system opens up the selection process for candidates, but unless practiced on a scale such as New Hampshire—where the running joke is that voters feel deprived if they've only met the presidential candidates twice—the average voter has no clearer picture of the candidates than in the general election. And scheduling all the major primaries between the end of January and the beginning of March biases the presidential system toward super fund-raisers and the super wealthy. The evidence is in: mass direct democracy is anemic. Voters are uninformed, manipulated by slanted television ads, and rarely determine the agenda on which they vote. The juggernaut of ballot initiatives in states across the nation during the past three decades seems to have as its goal an "automatic pilot system" of government, writes Peter Schrag, with scant involvement by the electorate "beyond occasional trips to the polls to vote on yet more initiatives."[82]

If traditional representative government is unsatisfactory, because it allows for little participation and deliberation by average citizens, and traditional direct democracy is inadequate, because it is focused only on small communal settings, what can we do? Confronting this dilemma early in the twentieth century, the Progressive reformers thought they had the answer when they invented *direct mass* democracy. At the start of the twenty-first century, having exhausted the direct mass democracy option, it is time to reexamine representative democracy. Is there another way to reach the middle ground between small-scale participatory democracy and traditional representative government? In the twenty-first century, fruitful reform will start and unfold from the representative pole. Table 1 displays the choices before us.

Table 1

Schema No. 1

	DIRECT DEMOCRACY	MIDDLE GROUND	STANDARD REPRESENTATIVE GOVERNMENT
18th century	Rousseau		Madison/Schumpeter
20th century		**initiative primary** direct mass democracy	
21st century		???????????????????????	

2.

Corruption in the Large Republic

The terms *liberal* and *republican* have distinct democratic meanings. When we talk about American politics, people usually speak in the rhetoric of public policy and party ideology. We understand that President George W. Bush is a conservative Republican and that Senator Edward Kennedy is a liberal Democrat. Yet, it is well-known that *liberal* and *republican* have philosophical meanings as well, and here we will use the terms philosophically rather than ideologically. At bottom, philosophic liberals follow the seventeenth-century English philosopher John Locke in viewing government as an instrument and not as an end in itself. They see politics as a necessary evil; individuals must look to business and private life for fulfillment. By contrast, civic republicans follow Aristotle, Niccolò Machiavelli, and James Harrington in viewing politics as a worthy end in itself—certainly not the only one, but an important one. While liberals emphasize individual rights and are skeptical of collaborative efforts, republicans stress civic virtue and believe collective deliberation is essential in defining the common good.

Once it could be claimed that the American Revolution was all about Locke—life, liberty, private property, and the right to rebellion. True, Jefferson's *Declaration* reads as a gloss of Locke's *Second Treatise,* but now we know that Americans are not only Lockean liberals but Machiavellian republicans as well. Today, it is common knowledge that ancient Rome and the civic republican tradition heavily influenced the views of the founders. Following Bernard Bailyn, we recognize republican ideas as the sparks that ignited the American Revolution. From J. G. A. Pocock, we understand how Machiavelli and the Italian Renaissance saw the duel between civic virtue and corruption as the key to whether republics succeed or fail and how republican concepts and language became an intricate part of Anglo-American political thought. And from Gordon Wood, we grasp how these republican ideas were modernized and transformed by the American experience during the nation's early years.[1]

When the Constitution was debated, the country faced a choice between two understandings of politics. The liberal conception of the Federalists won the day with a focus on a strong national government, institutional protections against tyranny, and a representative system designed to keep the people at arm's length from their government. The liberal framework of the American government is supported by accounts of politics that focus on rights before duties and individual freedom before the common good.[2] As Hartz asserted long ago, the liberal tradition in America is wide and deep with only those on the fringe, such as communists or reactionary racists, rejecting its claims.[3] For example, President Bush and Senator Kennedy are the standard bearers of the Republican and Democratic parties, respectively, but both are committed liberals in the philosophic sense of the word.

Although dominant, liberalism is not the totality of American political ideas. The civic republican tradition is, as Cass Sunstein has written, an "enduring legacy." Its main commitments remain current, especially the focus on deliberative democracy and republican liberty—a sophisticated understanding of what citizenship can and should mean.[4] Indeed, the republican tradition of Rome, Machiavelli, and the Italian city-states provides us with a theory of politics with contemporary relevance. Republican liberty insists that political participation is essential to the defense of liberty and demands that liberty be concerned about domination and power.[5]

There are two major schools of republican thought. For neo-Aristotelians, character development and moral excellence are the goal of the demos and participation as a citizen is the highest good. However, in our complex, varied and pluralist world, few see politics as a good to be pursued above all others.[6] Liberals are correct when they say we cannot go home again—meaning to Athens. Hannah Arendt and Alasdair MacIntyre present an arresting critique of modernity and liberal democratic politics; yet, as a practical option, the idea of a polity built on the participation of all citizens united by a common vision of the good life is an impossible goal.[7] By contrast, the republican tradition of Rome and Machiavelli finds many goods in life outside the political arena—excellence in business, the arts, and friendship, for example. Still, while not expecting or demanding full participation in politics, modern republicans hold with the Greeks and the Romans that the public happiness found in political association is a desirable good.

Of what does this public happiness consist?[8] It is a dialogue with one's fellow citizens about the goals and aspirations for the community that they share together. For republicans, politics and government are not mechanical devices that aggregate private wishes. Instead, dialogue and discussion among citizens shape and change preferences. In the give and take of public speaking, minds are changed, listeners inspired, and the course of the republic is set. Thus, the ideal model for republican governance is the one hundred-member Senate and the New England town meeting. Public business—*res publica*—is what *republic* means.[9]

For democracy to have substance as well as process, the public must be able to form its own values and judgments on the important issues of the day. To do this, the public must be able to talk to itself. When the Anti-Federalists attacked the proposed Constitution, they did so based on republican principles. Sunstein writes, "They believed that the Constitution would destroy the system of decentralization on which true liberty depended. The citizens would lose control over their representatives; they would also be deprived of the opportunity to participate in public affairs, and thus the principle of civic virtue would be undermined. Rule by remote national leaders would . . . rupture the alliance of interest between the rulers and the ruled." [10] In sum, the Anti-Federalists understood that the "removal of the people from the political process, the creation of a powerful and remote national government, the new emphasis on commerce—all threatened to eliminate the 'public happiness' for which the American Revolution had, in part, been fought."[11]

The Anti-Federalists and contemporary republicans understand that the combination of large scale, extremely high ratios of electors to representatives, and a procedural understanding of democracy bleeds democracy dry of its meaning. For republicans, simply voting every four years is not enough. For republicans, the political system exists for the citizens. What is to be feared is a political system dominated by money and powerful interests where average people have little clout. When corruption of civic character continues unabated, it can, eventually, spell the death of the republic. Such was the experience of Rome, the first, and until recently, the only republic ever to rise to a position of global power.[12]

Raised on the classics, the founders—both Federalists and Anti-Federalists—understood that, in setting up their republics, the Romans and the Italian city-states had two goals. The first was to create a system in which the people had a voice. The second was to divide the state's power among people and groups in order to keep any single individual from acquiring too much power. As citizens, Romans "proudly boasted of the values that distinguished them from slaves—free speech, private property, rights before the law." They understood that a "free city was where a man could be most fully a man." And for more than 400 years, the citizens of the Roman republic demonstrated that they would sacrifice everything to preserve their city's freedom. For the citizen of Rome, the only alternative to liberty was slavery or death.[13] Thus, when Patrick Henry stood and shouted, "Give me liberty or give me death!" he was speaking words Cicero and Machiavelli understood and passionately believed. He was demanding the core republican belief—that citizens have a strong and continuing role in ruling themselves. This is the essence of the republican tradition.

CORRUPTION IN THE LARGE REPUBLIC

But what about the republican tradition when transferred from a city-state to a large nation? In the single most important of *The Federalist Papers,* No. 10, Madison turned the tables on Montesquieu and the republican tradition by arguing that great size, instead of being a fatal flaw, was actually necessary for democracy to flourish. Although city-state democracy, Madison wrote, "can admit no cure for the mischiefs of faction," a representative democracy "opens up a different prospect, and promises the cure for which we are seeking." The larger the size, the greater the "variety of parties and interests," and hence the less probability "that a majority of the whole will have a common motive to invade the rights of other citizens."[14] Suddenly, smallness became a vice and large size a virtue.

In dealing with faction, Madison believed he had solved the major problem facing republican government. Unfortunately, he was wrong. As faction is the curse of small city states, corruption is the bane of large republics. Focused as he was on replacing the Articles of Confederation with a stronger national government, living at a time when the nation's population stood at fewer than 5 million, Madison failed to think about the long-term consequences of citizens being less effective and officials more remote in a very large democracy.[15]

As used here, *corruption* has a special civic republican sense signifying the loss of public virtue, widespread apathy, and the pursuit of private gain over the public good. Being closer historically to the Progressive reformers than the founders, we tend to think about political corruption in monetary terms: lining one's pockets, kickbacks, and sweetheart deals.[16] George Plunkitt of Tammany Hall gave this thumbnail definition of graft: "I saw my opportunities and I took 'em."[17] The older republican notion of corruption seems quaint by comparison. Aside from sex scandals, no one gets investigated today for the loss of public virtue, much less sent to prison. Yet the older republican understanding of corruption remains important because it captures an often overlooked, yet critical, dimension of public life. More than a few observers believe it is precisely this kind of corruption from which we are suffering today, and their jeremiads implore us to restore civic virtue and engaged norms of public participation.[18] It is this deeper current of corruption—apathy, loss of public virtue, and the aggressive pursuit of private advantage over the public good—that fosters the individual scandals (such as those involving Jack Abramoff, Tom DeLay, and the like) that make headlines.

The vices of a large commercial republic sprout like weeds in an abandoned garden. In contrast to the excess of democratic passions feared by the Federalists, outside of participatory surges such as the 1960s, we struggle with a widespread retreat from political involvement. Government is distant, voter turnout episodic, newspaper readership plunges, and moderate voters feel ignored as rigid partisans take control. As attack advertisements become the rule of thumb, the focus of the political power struggle shifts from elections to tit-for-tat investigations.[19] In this climate, the partial success of a Ross Perot and the election of an Arnold Schwarzenegger reveal a frustrated public willing to flirt with what George F. Will calls a "watery Caesarism."[20] Patriotism surged following the terror attacks of September 11, but people remain wary and distrustful of the political process and those elected to high office.[21]

Also, there is the background issue of rampant consumerism as the economic wants and needs of the world's most advanced and dynamic capitalist economy routinely crowd out other concerns—whether they be education, the arts, family and friends, or civic involvement. David Ricci argues that the question is whether economic enterprise can be confined to civilized limits. Can we restore the understanding that freedom means "a citizen's ability to join others, when necessary, in creating decent conditions for social life rather than a consumer's capacity, on occasion, to buy either a blue or pink cellular phone?"[22]

Republics suffer, depending on the circumstances, from either faction or corruption. In *Federalist* No. 10, Madison defines faction as "a number of citizens, whether amounting to a majority or a minority of the whole, who are united and actuated by some common impulse of passion, adverse to the rights of others, or the permanent and aggregate interest of the whole."[23] Similarly, we can define *corruption* with precision. Corruption is the disaffection of a large portion of the public from politics, combined with a loss of faith in public institutions and a growing gap between the political elite and the masses, encouraging self-interested activity by many parties.

In eras when corruption is high, selfish individualism grows, narrow interest groups trump the pursuit of the common good, and zero-sum politics makes partisans ever more zealous and less open to compromise. As the political world shrinks, it becomes win or lose. The lower-class faction that Madison feared usually occurs during periods of intense political activism, especially during revolution, when fundamental principles are up for debate. Corruption, on the other hand, is common during periods of "normal politics," when a great many people are passive and few issues mobilize the masses. Because the evil of faction is visible and its consequences apparent, it is easier to discuss the damaging effects of faction on small republics than it is to talk about the corruption that periodically plagues a large republic. Corruption—the absence of civic spirit—is fundamentally a moral problem found as much in men's souls as in their deeds. When factions emerge, political malcontents are hard to ignore. By contrast, "habits of the heart," such as civic virtue and apathy, are notoriously difficult to pinpoint with social science measures.[24] Apathy is a gradual fading away of civic engagement: people retreat into private pursuits, leaving actions not taken—ballots not marked, conversations avoided, precincts unwalked.

Tocqueville, a cultural detective, saw how republican beliefs, habits, and values temper individualism and nourish democratic community. In contrast to Madison, who blended republican and liberal attitudes in creating a constitutional structure that forces political leaders to build civic majorities, Tocqueville approached the problem from a different direction. Instead of focusing on elites, he examined the mores of the ordinary citizen. The key to democracy in America, Tocqueville discovered, was an ethic of "self-interest properly understood," summarized as "they therefore do not raise objections to men pursuing their interests, but they do all they can to prove that it is in each man's interest to be good."[25] While Madison worried about the danger of faction in the legislature, Tocqueville fretted about corruption in the culture at large. The danger looms when people become so absorbed in their private lives that they expect others to guard their liberties. Functioning purely as individuals, they forget that they are citizens with responsibilities to the community. At the end of *Democracy in America,* Tocqueville warns that democracy begins to erode when possibilities for meaningful civic association diminish and citizens become increasingly materialistic and self-involved.[26]

Granted, Americans continue to be vigorous joiners of multitudes of civic associations. The problem lies in our tenuous connection to the national (and state) government far from the local arena. Our distant relationship with our representatives, in turn, creates ample opportunities for what Dennis Thompson terms "mediated corruption." This occurs when public officials help constituent cronies, such as saving and loan tycoon Charles Keating, achieve unwarranted business opportunities in return for political cash to the office holder's campaign war chest. Observers agree that the behavior of the Keating Five was morally indistinguishable from that of most other politicians.[27]

Corruption, in the special republican meaning of the word, often runs rampant in postwar America—whether the economy is running full throttle or is stuck in a recession. In the large republic, corruption has two distinct yet connected dimensions: a disaffected public and a political system skewed in favor of the rich and elite. Here we examine each in turn.

DISAFFECTED, CRITICAL CITIZENS

The United States witnessed a major upswing in voter interest and turnout in 2004. It was a passionate election with the nation evenly split on whether President George W. Bush deserved a second term. Driven by the war in Iraq, by Mr. Bush's persona and political agenda (people seem to either love him or hate him), and by the intense mobilization effort made by both parties knowing the election was going to be close, millions of voters who previously stayed away cast ballots. The cover headline of one political magazine summed up the result: "Election 2004: Big Money, Big Turnout, Little Change."[28] It would be a good thing if more active political involvement and increased voter turnout were to continue. But the increase in turnout is probably short-lived because the factors specific to 2004 do not constitute long-term trends. Since John Kennedy's election in 1960, the voting rate had fallen in nearly every presidential election. At that time, 68.8 million citizens voted, and 40.8 million stayed home. By contrast, in 1996, 96.3 million cast a ballot, and 100.2 million did not. In 2000, turnout only reached 51 percent. Overall, 105.4 million people cast a ballot while 100.4 million decided they had better things to do in early November than to participate in the single most important ritual in American public life.

Until 2004, the past 40 years had seen the longest downturn in voting in the nation's history. What makes these numbers particularly disturbing is that the decline in participation occurred despite growing college enrollments, the women's movement, the collapse of racial barriers, and more open registration laws. All of these trends should significantly boost turnout. Instead, we witnessed a decline in "virtually every area of election activity, from volunteers who work on campaigns to the viewers who watch televised debates."[29] In certain battleground states, such as Ohio, there was a push for strong grassroots involvement in 2004. Such vigorous activity, however, did not endanger the spectator status of voters living in states either bright blue or deep red.

Turning our backs and focusing our attention elsewhere is one defense against a hollow democracy in which elites only need us to sanction their appointment to power. Covering the 1996 presidential election, Jonathan Schell began to wonder: "Isn't there something grotesquely unbalanced, even farcical, about a system in which tens of thousands of highly paid, highly trained, hyperactive, technically over equipped professional courtiers are trying with all the vast means of modern communications to provoke a response from a sovereign who is at best half asleep with boredom and at worst turned wholly away in an angry sulk?"[30] Patterson makes a similar observation and indictment: "The great tools of democracy—its electoral institutions and media organizations—have increasingly been used for private agency. Personal ambition now drives campaigns and profit and celebrity now drive journalism. Candidates, public officials, and journalists operate in a narrow professional world that is largely of their own making and that is remote from the public they serve."[31] Michael Kinsley refers to the public as "big babies" because "the people," via focus groups and opinion polls, are forever telling the politicians to "lower taxes and fix the deficit but don't cut my favorite programs."[32] Obviously, the public would rather heap tough choices and blame on the politicians rather than take the time to understand trade-offs or consider long-term consequences. Yet as William Greider points out, "If citizens sometimes behave irresponsibly in politics, it is the role assigned to them. They have lost any other way to act, any means for influencing the governing process in positive and broad-minded terms."[33]

The public may act disengaged because no process or institution exists to allow it to act otherwise. In a *New York Times* story about the 2000 presidential election, even in Washington, DC—where many people are consumed by politics—"neither Mr. Bradley, Gov. George W. Bush of Texas nor Vice President Al Gore has a headquarters where an interested citizen could volunteer to, say, stuff envelopes."[34] Writing a check was the only participation encouraged.[35] Of course, if you tell people they are powerless enough times, they eventually believe you.[36] Corruption becomes a particular danger for republics in those periods when people are focused on their private lives and businesses, when no major issue galvanizes the public's attention and energy, and when the passive public becomes more resigned still in the face of public scandal (President Clinton's affair) and reports about the power of cold cash (George W. Bush's raising $193 million as a Texas governor in his 2000 presidential campaign) in the political process. Deep apathy is more worrisome still when major issues exist that could well energize the public—the war in Iraq, for example, in 2006—but the public, by and large, is passive.[37]

In apathetic eras, a vicious cycle ensues as citizens pay less attention to public affairs and an increasingly jaded and cynical political class begins to dismiss them as hopeless boobs. Still, "the people" decide elections; therefore, the manipulation of crude public opinion based on emotions and prejudice becomes the key to political success. However, this portrait of the public can be overdrawn. The shrinking universe of citizens who continue to vote and pay attention to public affairs is fairly sophisticated. They are able to make nuanced judgments given the limited amount of information fed to them by consultants and politicians.[38] V.O. Key's observation remains relevant: "The perverse and unorthodox argument . . . is that voters are not fools. To be sure, many individual voters act in odd ways indeed; yet in the large the electorate behaves about as rationally and responsibly as we should expect, given the clarity of the alternatives presented to it and the character of the information available to it."[39]

A recent study of the issue by scholars divides nonvoters into four groups. An estimated 35 percent of nonvoters, or approximately 17 percent of all adult Americans, fall into the apathetic category. According to the Vanishing Voter Project conducted by Harvard's Shorenstein Center, these include those who "have no sense of civic duty," "aren't interested in politics," and "have no commitment to keeping up with public affairs." A second group totaling 14 percent of nonvoters are the aged, handicapped, and recently moved. These people are functionally unable to vote. The remaining 51 percent of nonvoters—nearly a quarter of all adult Americans—are not apathetic. They are either alienated ("the angry . . . so disgusted with politicians and politics that they've opted out") or disenchanted (not so much "repelled by politics as they are by the way politics is practiced"). The disenchanted "are the nonvoters who have been spawned by the political gamesmanship and negative news that dominated late-twentieth century politics. Many of them express interest in public affairs, talk occasionally about politics, and keep up with the news." More than 70 percent of all nonvoters were, in fact, registered.[40]

In sum, many nonvoters are disaffected, critical citizens who often choose the exit option. This disaffection reflects "not apathy but increasingly critical evaluations of government" as a well-educated middle class has become disenchanted with the tension between democratic ideals and current political reality.[41] Is government worse than before or have people's expectations been rising? Social science research suggests the latter. Examining data in advanced industrial nations, sociologist Ronald Inglehart reports that recent trends erode respect for authority, but increase support for democracy:

> The same publics that are becoming increasingly critical of hierarchical authority are also becoming increasingly resistant to authoritarian government, more interested in political life, and more apt to play an active role in politics. Although hierarchical political parties are losing control over their electorates, and elite-directed forms of participation such as voting are stagnant or declining, elite-challenging forms of participation are becoming more widespread . . . And though they tend to distrust political authority and big government, the publics of advanced industrial societies value democracy more, not less, than the publics of economically less secure societies . . . support for democratic principles is rising.[42]

Pippa Norris argues that these global trends signify the growth of "critical citizens" who want to "improve and reform the institutional mechanisms of representative government."[43]

Occasionally, a crisis at home or a war abroad arouses the mass public from its slumber. Such was the case with the September 11 terrorist attack and its aftermath. Suddenly, terrorism threatening the homeland; Islamic fundamentalism, and war in the Middle East dominated conversation. Dutifully, people watched the president and his advisers prepare for a new kind of war as they devoured the news screaming from newspaper headlines and blaring from television sets; and people talked to co-workers, family, friends, and neighbors eager to share their reactions and emotions. Beyond their social sphere, people wrote letters to the editor, e-mailed their congressional representatives, or joined chat rooms on the Internet. Some attended forums at local colleges. Others listened to town hall meetings on National Public Radio programs. Yet, the question arises, beyond these inchoate ways: How does the public talk to itself in an organized, deliberate manner? Unfortunately, the United States, an advanced technological nation, is primitive with respect to the mechanisms and designated public spaces where people can speak to one another as citizens and as citizens to their government. This void becomes acute during a national crisis. We make do, but civic republicans recognize our sense of isolation as another aspect of corruption.

THE INSIDIOUS INFLUENCE OF MONEY

Not surprisingly, the second face of corruption is a policy process that favors the interests of the wealthy and powerful. "Wealth Buys Access to State Politics." Headlines like this routinely appear in newspapers around the nation. Fat cats, we call them: "They can pick up the phone and get the political leader of their choice on the line. They can cook up bills or initiatives to boost their interests. They can kill measures that threaten them. They are the state's largest campaign donors and they are relatively few."[44]

Here, Madison's Constitution acts as a spur rather than a rein. Madison was so focused on the danger of working-class faction that he avoided the problem of excessive influence by the rich and powerful. By protecting the well-to-do from class warfare of the type seen in Shays's Rebellion, when debt-ridden Massachusetts farmers revolted against upper-class bankers, Madison opened the door to what may be called "Hamiltonian corruption."[45] Alexander Hamilton, George Washington's choice as treasury secretary and Jefferson's archrival, is famous for his willingness to use government power to help the well-to-do increase their fortunes. Hamiltonian corruption is not the kickbacks and slush funds that actually land politicians and their cronies in jail. Instead, it is the insidious influence of big money on the political process that makes a mockery of political equality. Individuals with the means and willingness to make large donations to parties, Political Action Committees, and politicians are the VIPs of the political process. The rest of us resent their special status and the way politicians fawn over them.

Specifically, Hamiltonian corruption occurs when the wealthy aggressively pursue policies that increase economic inequality and their economic power dominates public debate. In a nation that combines political democracy with the most dynamic economy the world has ever known, this is a recurrent problem. Our political system is relatively unprotected against Hamiltonian corruption precisely because Madison and Hamilton designed the Constitution with a bias toward electing representatives who are prominent, well-connected individuals in the community.[46] As Bernard Manin writes, "More than any other Federalist, Hamilton was prepared to advocate openly a certain role for wealth in the selection of representatives."[47] This problem is not just a contemporary concern. As Madison witnessed the triumph of Hamilton's ideas, he became less of a nationalist and more of a Jeffersonian republican.[48] Originally, the better men were gentry; then well-to-do merchants and lawyers. Today, these men and women—CEOs, high-tech millionaires, and upper-middle-class professionals—are members of what journalist Michael Lind calls the "overclass."[49] In *Wealth and Democracy*, Kevin Phillips defines plutocracy as "the determination and ability of wealth to reach beyond its own realm of money and control politics and government as well."[50] Phillips is well-known for his observation that periods of Republican hegemony begin with presidents focused on the well-being of the middle class, a Lincoln or a Nixon, followed by presidents whose actions primarily benefit the rich, a Reagan or a George W. Bush, who govern during an era when fortunes skyrocket, economic power is concentrated, taxes on the wealthy are slashed, and the wages of blue-collar and middle-class workers decline or remain stagnant. For anyone paying attention, it is clear that we are living through America's second Gilded Age. Phillips writes:

> Between 1979 and 1989 the portion of the nation's wealth held by the top 1 percent nearly doubled from 22 percent to 39 percent. By the mid-nineties, some economists estimated that the top 1 percent had captured 70 percent of all earnings growth since the mid-seventies. In 1999, the *New York Times* reported that within the most prosperous fifth of U.S. households, national income growth was shared so unevenly that *some 90 percent of that fifth's gain went to the top 1 percent.* No one, then, should regard the

$90,000-a-year accountant or $125,000-a-year lawyer—members of the top 5 or 10 percent—as fellow riders on the same glittering escalator as the investment banker making $1.5 million or the corporate CEO collecting $40 million in annual compensation.[51]

Concentrated wealth has a large political impact. "Money is the mother's milk of politics," said Jesse Unruh, the one-time boss of California politics. In the 1996 congressional races, candidates who raised the most money won 92 percent of House races and 88 percent of Senate races.[52] Former U.S. Senator Bill Bradley spelled out the political impact of Hamiltonian corruption this way: "Money not only determines who is elected, it determines who runs for office. Ultimately, it determines what government accomplishes—or fails to accomplish. Congress, except in unusual moments, will listen to the 900,000 Americans who give $200 or more to their campaigns ahead of the 259,600,000 who don't."[53] *New York Times* investigative reporter David Cay Johnston says that whether a family makes $30,000 or $300,000 a year, most Americans are being robbed by the IRS and other institutions that have been systematically corrupted, under both Republican and Democratic administrations, to serve the needs of the super rich. "Since at least 1983 it has been the explicit, but unstated, policy in Washington to let the richest Americans pay a smaller portion of their income in taxes and to defer more of their taxes, which amounts to a stealth tax cut, while collecting more in taxes from the middle class."[54]

In the early stages of the 2000 presidential race, then Texas Governor George W. Bush announced that having raised $37 million, he would forgo federal matching funds and avoid spending limitations. He went on to raise and spend an unprecedented nearly $70 million to capture the White House. In reaction, Senator John McCain decried the U.S. system of campaign finance as "an elaborate influence-peddling scheme in which both parties conspire to stay in office by selling the country to the highest bidder."[55] McCain stunned Bush in little New Hampshire, but Bush won the Republican nomination using his cash power and organizational strength to crush McCain's insurgent campaign.

McCain's criticism is telling when one considers that when wealthy Republicans wrote George W. Bush $2,000 checks during the 2000 campaign they knew this was an investment that might result in significant savings for their bottom line. Although the Bush Administration touts its tax cuts as being "fair" to average Americans and necessary as an economic stimulus, the alternative interpretation is to see them as a "quid pro quo for the many millions in party donations."[56] There are a good number of extremely wealthy individuals living in the United States. Add up the 400 richest Americans, the 3,000 to 5,000 U.S. centimillionaires (assets of $100 million or more) and the 270,000 decamillionaires (assets of $10 million or more), and it is not hard to see why the forty-third president can fly from city to city raising $1 million dollars or more at a single fundraising event.[57]

Republican domination of the White House and often the U.S. Senate since 1968 and of the House of Representatives since 1994 has resulted in a dramatic shift in the tax burden. In 1960, corporate taxes as a percentage of total receipts stood at 23.2 percent while payroll taxes (Social Security and Medicare) were 11.8 percent. In 2000, corporate taxes had dropped to 10.2 percent, and payroll taxes had risen to 31.1 percent.[58] At the same time, compensation of America's ten most highly paid CEOs jumped dramatically. In 1981, these chief executives were paid an average of $3.5 million; by 1988, the average was up to $19.3 million; and by 2000, the average annual pay of the top ten captains of industry was a staggering $154 million. Paul Krugman, *New York Times* columnist and Princeton economist, writes that the wages of ordinary workers roughly doubled during those years, though the bulk of that gain was eaten up by inflation, while the earnings of the nation's top CEO elevated 4,300 percent.[59]

Is it surprising that the well-to-do influence affairs of state? Of course not. Like every group, the wealthy should have a voice in government. The question is, are upper-class and business interests unfairly advantaged in the American system? A good argument can be made that this is indeed the case. It is obvious that the well-to-do have access, organization, and money—all critical assets required to influence the political system. In addition, business interests are protected in two other crucial ways. First is the privileged position of business. In his modern classic, *Politics and Markets,* Charles Lindblom explains how two sets of elites—governmental officials and business leaders—dominate liberal market societies.[60]

With analytic precision, Lindblom shows why business is not just another interest group. He explains that business would have significant clout in Washington, DC, even if corporate CEOs never placed phone calls to the president and business lobbyists never prowled the halls of Congress. The logic of the privileged position that business enjoys is as follows: Politicians are attentive to business needs because, while the electorate expects politicians to make sure the economy stays healthy, corporate executives are the ones who actually make investment and employment decisions for the entire society. Ever since the Great Depression, politicians have lost elections when the economy fails to perform. Mindful of this, elected officials craft public policies that take care of business. Democratic socialists who gain power—Francois Mitterrand in France and Felipe Gonzalez in Spain are telling examples—quickly learn to listen to the markets. In essence, the privileged position of business protects capitalism from the encroachment of social democracy. Any market society that increases taxes or embarks on redistribution is subject to capital flight and disinvestment. This, in turn, causes the economy to slow, seriously endangering politicians seeking re-election.[61] True, corporations continue to face off against unions and environmental groups, and industries complain how difficult it is to gain favorable treatment from the government on specific issues. But business is different than other interest groups. Even without lobbying, business gets favorable treatment. Only business, taken as a whole, enjoys this privileged position in democratic market societies. Always has, always will.

A second way business interests are advantaged in the political game is peculiar to the United States. The Hamiltonian influence can be tempered when political parties are strong and the middle and working classes are well represented. Historically, this has been true in many European nations. But in the United States, the two major parties are umbrella organizations. Although labor and working-class issues sometimes dominate the Democratic Party, often they do not.[62] There are decades, such as the New Deal period, when the Democratic Party strongly represents the interests of blue-collar workers, but this is more the exception than the rule.[63] With his encyclopedic knowledge of American political history, Michael Barone makes a convincing argument that cultural, rather than economic, factors usually dominate and shape our politics.[64] Refashioned by President Clinton, today's Democratic Party projects an upper-middle-class suburban bias similar to that of the Republican Party. In both parties, professional, suburban elites watch out for themselves and their families at the expense of the middle and working classes.[65] As the greatest middle-class society in history, the United States has traditionally had a class structure that resembles a football—fat in the middle and small at both ends. However, particularly in times of downsizing, outsourcing, stagnant wages, and growing inequality, this class structure begins to take on the shape of an hourglass. The Hamiltonian danger grows when U.S. income stratification begins to resemble Third World nations such as Brazil.[66]

We might expect economic booms, such as the late 1990s, to alleviate the gap between the classes, and to some degree they do. But the economic benefits of the growth in recent years have gone largely to the top 20 to 30 percent of the income ladder. According to government and private industry research reports, income inequality has risen substantially over the past quarter century. Theoretically, a surging economy lifts all boats, but many Americans—especially those whose economic fortunes are not connected to the most dynamic sectors of the economy—have seen their standards of living decline since the 1970s.[67] Granted, considerable truth exists about the trickle-down effect of a surging free-market economy. Journalist Gregg Easterbrook points out that those on the lower end of the economic scale have seen bigger jumps in "life span, education, standards of living, health-care quality, job safety and increased leisure time" during the twentieth century than those at the top.[68] True, but the sore point about economic power too easily translating into political clout remains.

Enron and other companies famous for their political contributions to both Republican and Democratic politicians lobbied heavily for deregulation. With weak oversight and strong incentives to cheat, corporate banditry was inevitable. But corruption extends well beyond the Enron collapse, no-bid billion-dollar contracts to oversee rebuilding in Iraq, and the Abramoff scandal that threatens to engulf the Republican leadership in Congress. What make the corruption of the George W. Bush years rank with the Gilded Age are not the individual scandals. Instead, says Phillips, it is the "vast, relentless takeover of U.S. politics and policymaking by large donors to federal campaigns and propaganda organs."[69] As *The New Republic*'s Jonathan Chait wrote, "if you look at the economic issues of the Bush presidency, in every instance Bush's position has been identical to that of whatever interest group applied the heaviest political pressure."[70] During the past quarter century there has been a strong up tick in the power of Washington's crony capitalists. *Washington Monthly* Editor-in-Chief Paul Glastris writes, "the K Street lobbying community, which once played (and corrupted) both sides of the political aisle, has in the last few years formed a virtual phalanx around the GOP and George W. Bush, and the lobbyists' wish list form the essence of that party's agenda."[71]

Modern civic republicans do not have trouble with capitalism as long as the poor and working class benefit when the rich grow richer.[72] Republican democrats—be they liberal or conservative—are not against commerce or capitalism. The United States has never been Sparta; we have always been a commercial republic. But republicans are mindful of Aristotle's (and Locke's and Adam Smith's) teaching of moderation. Walzer gives moderation a modern republican definition when he speaks of the importance of maintaining a wall of separation between different spheres of activity.[73] In the business sphere, we want people to be as successful as possible. But it is a mistake for business success to automatically translate into influence and power in other endeavors—whether it is love, art, or politics. In today's political game, economic inequality plays havoc with the civic equality necessary for political participation.[74]

PERFECT STORM AND CORRUPTION ANTIDOTE

The two sides of corruption—apathy and Hamiltonian "juice"—feed off one another. On the one hand, seeing wealthy donors buying access and clout leads more people to give up on a corrupt political process. On the other hand, political withdrawal by the average citizen allows the political process to be dominated by upper-middle-class professionals and the wealthy. Because the mass public is ignorant about policy details, a president with an amiable image can maintain popularity with the public while his administration pursues policies that a majority of the public opposes. The George W. Bush administration, for example, does this in two ways. On major issues, they often say one thing but do another. Examples include homeland security, where the president posed with firemen and emergency workers at Ground Zero, promised assistance to first responders but then provided little money; and the economy, where the Republican tax cut was touted as helping the average American, but relatively little tax relief reached the bottom 60 percent of workers. On more obscure issues, such as eliminating workplace ergonomic standards or supporting tougher bankruptcy standards on consumers, the administration pursues an under-the-radar strategy, knowing that public outcry is unlikely. Former Harvard President Derek Bok describes the modern Washington, DC, dynamic thus:

> Once elections are over and winning candidates take office, apathy enhances the power of lobbyists and their clients. As fewer people pay attention, interest groups have an easier time affecting legislative deliberations. Carefully orchestrated, well-financed grassroots campaigns have greater influence on policy than they should. With few people voting, lawmakers must be more careful not to offend organizations that are capable of mobilizing their membership to vote against unfriendly legislators and defeat them in future campaigns.[75]

The problem, of course, is that democracy begins to decay if powerful interest groups continually subvert the public interest.

Corruption's perfect storm is created when apathy and upper-class greed are joined by the desire and ability to manipulate and systematically mislead the public. This was the case when the Bush administration pushed deep tax cuts through the GOP-controlled Congress. As Jacob S. Hacker and Paul Pierson detail with precision in *Off Center,* the selling of the tax cuts systematically misled the public as to the real winners and losers of this major restructuring of the nation's fiscal house and tax burden.[76] Both the tax cut proposals and the Bush administration's run up to the Iraq War are clear instances of what Zaller labels elite domination of public opinion.[77] This occurs when *"elites induce citizens to hold opinions that they would not hold if aware of the best available information and analysis."*[78]

Is there a way to systematically uproot corruption and the pernicious influence it has on democratic politics? The causes of corruption cannot easily be removed. Similar to Madison's famous argument about faction, two impractical ways may eliminate the causes of corruption. The first is by creating a fully participatory democracy wherein the people are the government, and there is no gap between representatives and citizens. Yet, we can't force people to be politically involved. Even with the Internet, it is not possible to have anything like a fully participatory democracy in a modern nation-state such as the United States. Another impractical solution eliminates economic and political inequality, thereby stopping the well-to-do from pursuing policies that benefit their class at the expense of the middle and working classes. In a society in which everyone is middle class, class envy and political alienation might magically disappear. Yet, this is both highly improbable and unwise. Trying to eliminate corruption in this way would trample on basic civil and economic liberties. Our goal is to create a more republican polity, not to level the bourgeoisie in a Marxist purge or force people to be "free."

As with Madison, relief is to be found in controlling effects. We need to think of ways to limit the degree of corruption to the lowest practical level. In addition to bringing about significant campaign finance reform, we need to foster civic majorities (voting blocs concerned with the broad general good) and intelligent participation. The framers' dilemma was a formidable one. Madison and his colleagues sought "such an arrangement of political power as ensures the existence and security of the government, even in the absence of political virtue," without at the same time abandoning republicanism altogether.[79] Overall, they were exceptional political architects. However, on the point of corruption, their design is weak and incomplete. Our democracy is prone to periods of deep passivity during which wealthy political contributors (individuals and PACs of various political hues and agendas) have disproportionate clout in determining public benefits. The founders failed to provide an institutional means whereby the public, as opposed to legislative bodies, could participate in the formation of civic majorities via the method of deliberative democracy. In the past, we have relied on elections to control elites. However, in this new political era, elections may not be "sufficient to render elites responsive and accountable."[80] We may need to supplement elections with other mechanisms that strengthen the connection between citizens and their government.

In 1787, the framers established a strong central government while maintaining a federal system of state power. Today, our challenge is different. Harvard University's Jennifer Hochschild takes issue with those who say that our main problem is gridlock, excessive bureaucracy, and incapacity to govern. Instead, she says, "Americans have a different set of problems." One is a lack of a "unified political will" across the nation to solve problems, and another is a "lack of definition of what those problems consist of." Dahl insists there is a moral dimension to policy issues that simply cannot be delegated to experts. On issues ranging from nuclear weapons to international trade to health care reform to poverty, he says elected officials need input about how ordinary citizens understand the moral and ethical dimensions of the problem. Clearly, ordinary public opinion surveys cannot fulfill this function.[81]

Having examined the problems posed by scale and corruption, let us turn our attention to a possible cure.

3.

Building on the Founders

The most promising road to genuine political reform follows from a re-consideration—and extension—of Madison's political thought. Madison's goal was to find a constitutional structure that would provide the right mixture of scale, diversity, and social peace. His genius was to see that a large, commercial republic was indeed possible; his flaw was to freeze an aristocratic understanding of representation in the Constitution. Writing a brilliant set of essays with Hamilton and John Jay that became *The Federalist Papers,* Madison explained how and why a national republic was possible.[1] He and his fellow framers were responsible for a major advance in constitutional design, yet their thinking was not entirely modern. The product of an age that was not yet comfortable with democracy as we know it, they pointedly rejected the Articles of Confederation and state constitutions such as the Pennsylvania Constitution of 1776, with its uni-cameral legislature and its extraordinary Article 15 requiring that "every bill passed by the General Assembly be printed for consideration of the people at large before it could become law in the next legislative session."[2] Afraid of the democratic forces unleashed by the Revolution, the signatories of the Constitution created an elitist national government consciously removed and insulated from the people. Examples of their fear of popular sovereignty include the Electoral College system for electing the president, indirect election of senators, and enlarging the size of congressional districts as a way to filter the better men from the masses.

In drafting the Constitution, the founders abandoned the language of civic virtue and concentrated instead on creating liberal institutions that could function without common goals or intense political participation. Still, Madison had a particular goal for the House of Representatives. In *Federalist* No. 52, he wrote that the House of Representatives was to be the one institution of the new federal government that would remain in "intimate sympathy with, the people."[3] The modern understanding of democracy is far less patrician than that held by the founders, yet our supposedly "intimate" connection with the federal government is increasingly remote. Do we really want such a distant form of popular sovereignty?

To grasp the difference between then and now, picture in your mind California and compare our most populous state with the thirteen original states. Obvious and dramatic differences exist, but consider the similarities: size, a heterogeneous population, a diverse economy, coastal geography, and a north-south regional rivalry. One critical contrast: The population of California (35 million) is more than 10 times that of the first thirteen states. Next, put social change and economic differences to one side. Just focus on the constitutional structure and political culture; the first can have a profound effect on the second. There are striking differences between California and the original American nation on both counts. Even after the Revolution, Americans continued to demonstrate active political involvement for much of our history. Yet in *The Almanac of American Politics,* Barone finds postwar California a "profoundly apolitical commonwealth. Busy in their work, intense in their pursuit of pleasure, people . . . take government for granted and have no time for politics."[4] Think about the structure of early American government, and mentally lay it over the map of California. Modern California government consists of a governor, a legislature, county supervisors, and city councils. By contrast, the original United States-with roughly equal geographic area and *less than one-tenth* the population-gives us thirteen governors and, very important, thirteen legislatures—*thirteen* miniature parliaments where representatives debate the issues of the day, respond to constituent requests for assistance, and deal with the give-and-take of lawmaking. Is it any accident that contemporary citizens of California are apolitical? And California, on this point, is not atypical of the United States as a whole. Today, House members represent more constituents than did U.S. senators in years past.

Gradually, we have democratized the Constitution. Today, we elect senators directly, use primaries to nominate presidential candidates, and think of the popular vote for president as being just as important as the Electoral College. Yet, the House of Representatives has increased in aloofness as congressional districts have grown in size along with the nation's population. It is no secret that Madison's goal in proposing large congressional districts was to help ensure the election of republican gentlemen, the "natural aristocracy," as opposed to shop owners, laborers, and small farmers.[5] In *Federalist* No. 10, Madison writes: "the number of representatives . . . being proportionally greatest in the small republic, it follows that if the proportion of *fit characters* be not less in the large than in the small republic, the former will present a greater option, and consequently a greater probability of a fit choice."[6] Today, this aristocratic understanding of representation remains petrified in the Constitution. Two hundred years after *The Federalist Papers,* the most important strength in Madison's thought is his emphasis on deliberative democracy, the careful consideration of arguments and options before making a decision. And the greatest weakness is an outdated elite sociology. Our challenge: Promote the first, escape the second.[7]

MADISON'S CONSTITUTIONAL VISION

Madison boldly argued that it was indeed possible to extend the scope of democracy geographically across a continental nation. Earlier political thinkers—from Aristotle to Montesquieu—insisted that democracy could only exist on the scale of a city-state. It had to be small. But Madison knew that small republics suffer from the kind of nasty infighting between cliques and rivals made famous by Shakespeare in *Romeo and Juliet.* He set out to show how a large republic would escape this danger. *Federalist* No. 10 is today the most famous essay in American politics. This was not always the case. Largely ignored during the nineteenth century, it was rediscovered with a vengeance by the Progressive historian Charles Beard. He saw Madison's reference to the defense of property as being the key to the Constitutional Convention and the motives of the founders. With its focus on the ever-present struggle between the rich and the common man, Beard's *An Economic Interpretation of the Constitution of the United States* shaped the study of American history for much of the twentieth century.[8]

Today, although we recognize the elitist tinge in Madison's argument, we also admire his lofty idea of deliberative democracy. Famously, Madison argues for an extensive republic as a way to control the vices of faction. Not as well understood is how his constitutional scheme has as its aim a deliberative democracy focused on attaining the public good. Madison's constitutional vision has three elements at its core: (1) extend the scope of representative government so as to require coalition building and the creation of civic majorities; (2) establish an institutional structure that encourages a deliberative approach to public policy; and (3) make the people, not government, sovereign.

Just how to "secure the public good, and private rights against the danger" of narrow selfish action by factions, whether they be majorities or minorities, was the puzzle Madison set out to solve.[9] Together, he and Hamilton sought a constitutional design that would force public decisions to be based on sound reasoning rather than quick judgments, unreflected self-interest, and brute political muscle. Madison's aim was a government where "no man is allowed to be a judge in his own cause; because his interest would certainly bias his judgment."[10] In other words, no one should be able to craft public policy without giving good reasons why such a policy would benefit the community at large. This goal lies at the heart of Madison's audacious gamble of an extended national republic.

Madison writes that if you "*extend the sphere* [the size of the republic], and you take in a greater variety of parties and interests, you make it less probable that a majority of the whole will have a common motive to invade the rights of other citizens."[11] In a small democracy, differences of opinion can lead to strife, whereas in an extended republic, diversity and pluralism no longer hinder republican community. Instead, they assist in the formation of tolerant, broad-minded majorities who, first by necessity and then by habit, incorporate the needs of minority voices into their plans. At the end of *Federalist* No. 51, Madison makes clear his support of positive government by multi-interested majorities. He believes they will preserve republican rights and liberties while pursuing policies in the public interest. "In the extended republic of the United States, and among the great variety of interests, parties and sects which it embraces," Madison writes, "a coalition of a majority of the whole society could seldom take place on any other principle than those of justice and the general good."[12] Instead of being factious, such a broad coalition is what Samuel Beer calls, in a felicitous phrase, a "civic majority."[13]

Influenced by the English thinkers Harrington and David Hume, Madison articulates a distinctly modern understanding of civic virtue. In doing so, he turned away from the ancient understanding of civic virtue as a commitment to the common good that subdues and overrides private interests. Instead of relying on sterling character to preserve a republic, Harrington and Madison focus on designing good institutions and, in doing so, they accept as fact that most people are motivated by self-interest.[14] Instead of stern morals and self-sacrifice, for Harrington and Madison virtue is "the power of reason to discover by discussion a common interest that embraces and reconciles private interests."[15] Instead of asking people to practice altruistic self-denial, Madison and contemporary republicans ask people to participate in a process of discussion and decision that results in action in the broad public interest.

The second part of Madison's plan involved institutionalizing deliberative democracy. For Madison, the task of government is not simply to aggregate individual interests but to devise a structure of discussion where people discover and promote common concerns. He understood that politics is by nature deliberative. Dialogue and open discussion among citizens, as well as among elites, are critical features of the governing process. This is a far richer notion of democracy than simply voting. In the pluralism of the large republic, Madison saw the prospect of broad coalitions focused on justice and the common good. Democratic government would be majoritarian, but the governing majorities would be civic majorities. He hoped, "the judgments of the extended republic will be more just because they will be more general, and they will be more general because, perforce, they must include a greater variety of interests."[16]

As Joseph Bessette writes, there are two types of public voice. "One is more immediate or spontaneous, uninformed and unreflective." The other is "more deliberative . . . resting on a fuller consideration of information and arguments."[17] Madison sought to promote the second type of public decision making by filtering popular views "through the medium of a chosen body of citizens." He pushed for a representative scheme in which voters in large electoral districts were likely to elect men "whose enlightened views and virtuous sentiments render them superior to local prejudices and to schemes of injustice."[18] Madison hoped that the best sort of men would be elected to Congress and, once there, they would focus on attaining the public good. Yet he did not rest his hopes on traditional civic republican expectations that an upper-class gentry would do the right thing. Institutionally, they are encouraged to do what they ought to do because, in an extended republic, they must form broad-based civic-minded majorities to accomplish their goals. Madison believed, rightly, that "representatives were better qualified to make laws than voters, not because of their superior virtue *but because of their position in the structure* of deliberation, which enabled them to be better informed . . . than did the constituents themselves."[19]

The extended sphere and deliberative democracy form the core of Madison's constitutional vision. The separation of powers and federalism, institutional mechanisms there for everyone to see, act as insurance plans in case the first two methods fail to achieve a just and well-reasoned polity.[20] Overall, he envisioned a system promoting public rather than selfish interests. The idea of deliberative democracy is sound and Madison's goal noble—"to refine and enlarge the public views, by passing them through the medium of a chosen body of citizens, whose wisdom may best discern the true interest of their country, and whose patriotism and love of justice, will be least likely to sacrifice it to temporary or partial consideration."[21]

Yet, however innovative, Madison was a prisoner of his time. He believed that only upper-class gentlemen could carry out the public's business in a calm, dispassionate, and fair manner. Most of the writers he relied on, including Hume and Harrington, were elitists who shared with their upper-class peers a deep fear of the masses. For Hume, the constitutional provision for popular power in the Roman republic was its central flaw.[22] For Harrington, the people as a whole are unfit for political debate, and only an aristocracy of the wise was "intellectually capable of discovering what is best for the commonwealth."[23] The consequences of Madison's romantic hope of an elite gentry running the national legislature remain with us today. For us, representative government has become inseparable from democracy.

The early inventors of representative government in the United States and Europe saw representation as an alternative to popular self-rule. In his incisive *The Principles of Representative Government* Manin writes: "What today we call representative democracy has its origins in a system of institutions (established in the wake of the English, American, and French revolutions) that was in no way initially perceived as a form of democracy or of government by the people."[24] Today, our enormous congressional districts are based on an antiquated social theory. It is impossible for an enlightened upper-crust elite to speak for the rest of us. The egalitarian, pluralistic republic Madison helped create will not allow it.[25] Social forces unleashed by the Revolution rapidly moved American society away from notions of hierarchy and "social betters." The idea of a virtuous upper-class guiding the uneducated masses faded by Jefferson's election in 1800, and by the Jacksonian era it was dead. As Tocqueville clearly saw, the United States was not Europe.

After civic majorities and deliberative democracy, the third essential part of Madison's constitutional design is the sovereignty of the people. In England, sovereignty lay with the king. Under the Articles of Confederation, U.S. sovereignty was vested in the legislative assemblies of the individual states. But in the Constitution, the framers took the radical but logical step of saying that sovereignty rests with the people. According to Madison, "In the United States . . . The People, not the Government, possess absolute sovereignty."[26] Yet, as with his idea of the "better men" being elected to the new national government, so Madison's idea of sovereignty is both cautious and elitist. The Federalists knew they faced a difficult problem. Wood, in *The Creation of the American Republic, 1776-1787,* writes: "Only a new continental republic that cut through the structure of the states to the people themselves, and *yet* was not dependent on the character of the people, could save the American experiment with republicanism."[27] True, the Federalists placed sovereignty with the people. Yet, fearing that extensive democratic activism would lead to both social unrest and legal attacks on property, they fashioned the new Constitution to hold the people at arm's length. In contrast to the direct democracy of the ancient republics, under Madison's plan, American government provides for, as he writes in *Federalist* No. 63, "total exclusion of the people, in their collective capacity."[28] Beer notes that this is a startling statement but argues that it does not mean that Madison favors aristocracy; just that he favors multiple, indirect elections as the best way to deal with a public whose passions and virtues cannot be trusted to follow the wisest course of action.[29]

Madison and his colleagues were fearful of the political turmoil of the post-Revolutionary period. In Shays's Rebellion, they saw the possibility of intense local participation spinning toward anarchy. Mass participation seemed the norm in the revolutionary era in which they lived. Facing an excess of political excitement, they sought mechanisms to contain and channel popular enthusiasms. This resulted in a *distant* form of representative government at the federal level, combined with strong state and local governments. The practical result of the Federalist Constitution is captured by Bruce Ackerman's distinction between constitutional moments and normal politics.[30] Madison's constitution is a political system that can function at a high level of efficiency without mass participation and in the absence of civic virtue. In periods of "normal" politics most people, most of the time, can pursue their individual goals and leave the government to interest groups and experts. Yet, in special politicized eras—when political matters begin to command the attention of a majority of the population and interest-group politics no longer seems legitimate—we can say that "we the people" are again speaking as the sovereign voice of the nation. The Civil War, the Progressive Era, and the New Deal are examples of periods of institutional and constitutional change that we deem legitimate precisely because of the public's high level of political awareness and activism.

Madison's critics, the Anti-Federalists, had an excellent understanding of the dangers and problems posed by a large republic. True, they were romantics in defending small-scale politics based on civic virtue sans institutional checks and balances. The state governments of the Articles of Confederation period vested nearly all power in a single-house legislature. Still, their central criticism of the Federalists hits home. As Wood explains:

> The Anti-Federalists thus came to oppose the new national government for the same reason the Federalists favored it: because its very structure and detachment from the people would work to exclude any kind of actual and local interest representation and

prevent those who were not rich, well-born, or prominent from exercising political power. Both sides fully appreciated *the central issue* the Constitution posed . . . whether a professedly popular government should actually be in the hands of, rather than simply derived from, common ordinary people.[31]

Anti-Federalist objections to elite representation are as valid today as when they were first voiced. Patrick Henry said the Constitution "presupposes that the chosen few who go to Congress will have more upright hearts and more enlightened minds than those who are members of the individual legislatures." In his *Letters from the Federal Farmer,* Richard Henry Lee went to the core of the issue: "Every man of reflection must see that the change now proposed is a transfer of power from the many to the few."[32]

Since Jefferson's election in 1800, Americans have maintained a democratic, egalitarian understanding of American society and politics. Over time, we have gradually democratized the federalist Constitution. Today we elect U.S. senators directly and use primaries to nominate presidential candidates. Yet, with our enormous congressional districts, our political structure guarantees an ever-increasing distance between the government and the people. Is it possible to expand our idea of representative government and involve more citizens in the act of governing?

EXTENDING MADISON

Madison's constitutional scheme has as its objective a deliberative democracy focused on attaining the public good. In a nation that has grown enormously large—a population *nearly 100 times as large* as when Madison and his fellow delegates met during that hot summer in Philadelphia in 1787—how might we attain that end? Given their goals, the framers achieved success beyond their wildest dreams. Still, Madison and his colleagues could not do everything. They created a "partial constitution," to use Sunstein's apt phrase, biased toward a liberal conception of politics.[33] This approach was understandable given their upper-crust social standing, their bias toward protecting the status quo, and their practical struggle to create a federal Constitution to correct the weaknesses of the Articles of Confederation. Even if Madison had been a closet Jeffersonian, he could not argue for institutions to encourage local participation; to do so would have vitiated his argument for a strong national state and yielded too much to the Anti-Federalists. The battle over ratification was too close a contest for such concessions.

Madison sought a solution to the endemic divisiveness of small republics. By contrast, our generation confronts the cancer of corruption in the large republic. To win this battle it is necessary to return to Madison and extend his argument. He spoke of *horizontally* extending the sphere of the American republic; we should consider extending representation *vertically*—downward—to reconnect the American people to their government. Doing so would remedy the hollowness of modern procedural democracy by encouraging engaged and intelligent participation. Living in an era of intense political engagement, Madison failed to comprehend how his large legislative districts would fuel political alienation in less active periods of "normal" politics. More than 200 years later, to alleviate widespread alienation and to combat upper-class faction, civic majorities must be allowed to find their voice.

In arguing for an extensive republic, Madison followed the argument laid out by Hume in his 1752 essay, "Idea of a Perfect Commonwealth."[34] There Hume sketched a "form of government, to which," he claimed, "I cannot, in theory, discover any considerable objection." [35] What excited Madison was that Hume presented a plan that allowed for republican government based on the consent of the people and, at the same time, minimized the danger of the factionalism that plagued city-state republics of Renaissance Italy and ancient Greece. In so doing, Hume rejected the argument of Montesquieu in *The Spirit of the Laws* [1748] that a large republic was simply not possible. Instead, Hume argued, that while founding a free state in a large territory was indeed difficult and would require a leader with the vision and virtue of a Solon or a Moses to suppress his personal ambition for power, once founded a large republic would be more stable and secure.

> We shall conclude this subject, with observing the falsehood of the common opinion, that no large state, such as FRANCE or GREAT BRITAIN, could ever be modeled into a commonwealth, but that such a form of government can only take place in a city or small territory. The contrary seems probable. Though it is more difficult

to form a republican government in an extensive country than in a city; there is more facility, when once it is formed, of preserving it steady and uniform, without tumult and faction.[36]

In Hume's plan, the national legislature would consist of a smaller, indirectly elected senate and a larger, directly elected branch. The senate would meet in the national capital and exercise executive as well as legislative power. The members of the more popular branch would meet in separate assemblies in the counties from which they had been elected. Hume writes:

> Let GREAT BRITAIN and IRELAND, or any territory of equal extent, be divided into 100 counties, and each county into 100 parishes, making in all 10,000 . . . Let all the freeholders . . . meet annually. . . and choose by ballot, some freeholder of the county for their representative, whom we shall call the county representative . . . Let the 100 county representatives . . . meet in the county town, and choose by ballot, from their own body, 10 county magistrates and one senator . . . *There are, therefore in the whole commonwealth, 100 senators . . . and 10,000 county representatives . . . Let the senators meet in the capital* [London], *and be endowed with the whole executive power of the commonwealth . . . Let the county representatives meet in their particular counties, and possess the whole legislative power of the commonwealth; the greater number of counties deciding the question . . .* Every new law must first be debated in the senate, and though rejected by it, if 10 senators insist and protest, it must be sent down to the counties . . . Whether the law be referred by the senate to the county magistrates or representatives, a copy of it, and of the senate's reasons, must be sent to every representative eight days before the day appointed for assembling, in order to deliberate concerning it.[37]

In arguing for a bicameral division of power, Hume agreed with Harrington's analysis of political power.[38] "All free governments must consist of two councils, a lesser and a greater; or, in other words, of a senate and a people," Hume writes. "The people, as HARRINGTON observes, would want wisdom, without the senate: The senate without the people, would want honesty."[39] Both Hume and Harrington were elitists, as were most of the writers of their day. But they saw the people as a check against the abuse of power and corruption that would inevitably take place if the senate or nobility were left to their own devices. Although Hume thinks the "lower sort of people and small proprietors" are "wholly unfit" for the higher offices of the republic, he believes they are good judges. And against the belief that the people will act as a "mere mob," Hume holds that although this possibility may be true in a large assembly of 1,000 or more, "divide the people into many separate bodies; and then they may debate with safety." In addition, he defends the ability of ordinary citizens to debate and reason together. "Though every member be of only middling sense, it is not probable, that any thing but reason can prevail over the whole. Influence and example being removed, good sense will always get the better of bad among a number of people."[40] Thus, by dividing the government into a senate and a representative body of the people meeting separately in the towns and villages across the nation, Hume believed he had created an institutional structure that would support a large republic.

Seeking to ensure rational deliberation by forming small assemblies of 100 members each, Hume thought that entrusting national legislation to these small representative assemblies would protect the public interest against narrow special interests focused on their own agendas. Beer writes,

> While the two branches of the national legislature were institutionally separate, in the exercise of their power they were interdependent. Proposals of legislation moved from the senate to the more popular assemblies, which had the final say. The decision was made by a majority of the counties . . . the equal apportionment of voters to legislators and the equal electorates of each county meant that a vote by the majority of the counties also embraced a majority of the legislators representing a numerical majority of the national electorate.[41]

Madison built on Hume's ideas and in *Federalist* No. 10 proposed a compound republic extending across continental space. Yet Madison neglected to follow Hume in one crucial area: he did not include local popular assemblies in his political vision for the United States. Although members of the senate met together, Hume's representatives were never assembled as a single legislative body. Instead, the representatives convened in their own counties, and each county was to have one vote.

Republican government without a true popular branch opens the door to the scandals that often consume Washington, DC, and our state capitals. In large republics, corruption becomes dangerous when the formation of civic majorities becomes difficult, when wealthy individuals and powerful corporations have undue influence on policy, and when average citizens become so involved in their private lives that they forget they are citizens with responsibilities to the community.

Is any of this an accident? One can argue that a national political system carefully constructed to keep the government at arm's length from its citizens is fated to at least a low level of endemic corruption. Because Americans have liberal as well as republican norms, corruption is to be expected. But the dramatic increase in scale—particularly as it affects congressional representation—makes the increase in corruption a political crisis without an easy cure. Can the civic republican prescription of greater involvement by average citizens alleviate the problem? Perhaps. To give citizens both a reason and a mechanism by which they can form civic majorities on key issues is a tall order, but it is probably the best way to control corruption and keep alienation and avarice in check.

Extending representation downward in the political system and asking a representative slice of the population to deliberate and debate questions of national policy would both confront the dilemma of scale and help control corruption. Extending representation deeper into the population would engage voters in a way that goes well beyond the illusory participation of traditional public opinion polling. It would enable us to foster civic majorities focused on the broad common good. Madison's idea of extending the republic horizontally across space in *Federalist* No. 10 was critical in the development of the United States. The questions facing us are: Is it time to consider extending representation vertically in the political system? Why must the state capitals and Washington, DC, monopolize legislative power?

How exactly does the preceding argument modernize Madison? Let's return to the three elements at the core of his constitutional vision. First, he argued that by extending the scope of republican government we make it more difficult for factions to organize and achieve their injurious purposes. However, given modern communications, factions do quite well at the national level. Mancur Olson's classic work on free riders explains why motivated factions often achieve their aims when pitted against a public good broadly felt, but lacking in energy. "The best lack all conviction, while the worst are full of passionate intensity" continues to be a problem in the large republic.[42] Yet Madison's idea of using civic majorities to counter factions is a good one. The challenge is to devise a mechanism that better allows civic majorities to form and exert democratic power. Second, to revive intelligent political discussion while living in the age of "reality TV," talk radio, and 30-second political commercials, we should consider creating an institutional structure that encourages a deliberative and thoughtful approach to politics. Third, if we want to make the people sovereign in a fashion that does not passively accept the "total exclusion of the people, in their collective fashion," we must rid Madison's idea of sovereignty of its elite bias. In sum, extending representation downward in the nation's congressional districts and including more people in the decision-making process (1) increases our chances of blocking factions and fostering civic majorities on the major issues of the day, (2) offers the possibility of deliberative forums in every community in the nation, and (3) promotes a modern idea of popular sovereignty.

Americans in the twenty-first century have the opportunity to follow Hume's logic and have not only national and state representative assemblies but local representative assemblies as well. In 1790, the United States had a tiny population (3.9 million for the thirteen states; the largest cities, such as Boston, held 35,000 residents), strong local communities, and vigorous local politics. The lack of local assemblies was not an impediment to a vital, robust democracy. Today, with nearly 300 million people, a postindustrial economy and fifty states spread over a continental nation, the reverse is true. Fortunately, it is now possible to make the idea of a national virtual assembly on Hume's model a reality. This possibility is due in part to technological advances. It is also true because the problems that vexed Madison's generation have been solved. For example, today, Americans accept our national identity as having priority over the states. Few, if any, would now choose to fight for Virginia against the Union, as did General Robert E. Lee in the Civil War. Today, the United States has a strong federal government and the world's leading economy. As such, a reform based on Hume's vision would not sabotage the Federalist goal of a strong

central government that provides uniform rules for economic development and commerce.

It is sometimes said that the sign of a mature individual is the ability to
hold two contradictory ideas at the same time. This was true in the particular case of Thomas Jefferson, and it is true of Americans in general. Jefferson's synthesis of the liberal and republican understandings of democracy
offers an important clue to how Americans have maintained loyalty to two
conflicting democratic ideologies.[43]

In writing the Declaration of Independence, Jefferson relied on the rhetoric of Locke to justify and defend the American rebellion. Lockean liberalism is famous for its commitment to individual rights and private
property. Immortalized in Jefferson's famous phrase, "life, liberty and the
pursuit of happiness," the essence of Locke's philosophy has been passed
on to each generation of Americans. Yet Jefferson is equally famous for
writing about the special virtue of the citizen farmer and the importance
of political participation. After the American Revolution, Jefferson increasingly shifted to a modern republican understanding of politics, which
champions civic virtue and political participation and rejects social hierarchy in favor of equality.[44] His one full-length book, *Notes on the State of
Virginia* [1787], contains this celebrated passage filled with republican
fears of moral decline:

> Those who labor in the earth are the chosen people of God, if He
> ever had a chosen people, whose breasts He has made His peculiar
> deposit of substantial and genuine virtue . . . Corruption of morals
> in the mass of cultivators is a phenomenon of which no age nor na-
> tion has furnished an example . . . It is the manners and spirit of a
> people which preserve a republic in vigor. A degeneracy in these is a
> canker which soon eats to the heart of its laws and constitution.[45]

In the first case Jefferson is a liberal; in the second he is a civic republican. In the Declaration, he is concerned with protecting liberty from external tyranny. In *Notes on Virginia,* he wants to protect civic virtue from
internal decay.

By following two strategies, Jefferson is able to employ both the republican and liberal traditions. The first strategy is to shift emphasis from one to the other, depending on the needs of the moment. Against the external threat of corrupt British power, Jefferson uses the Lockean principles of individual rights and the right to revolution. Alternatively, Jefferson draws on the civic republican tradition as he works to construct a new political order dedicated to the ideas of public happiness and political participation. He envisioned the United States as based on more than individual self-interest; the new democracy will be a true political community that will enrich the lives of the citizens. Private life and commerce will be important, but so will an active public life and civic spirit. His second tactic was to modernize the ancient model of civic republicanism by dropping the classical norms of hierarchy and adopting the modern liberal norm of equal rights for all citizens. In this way, he succeeded in harmonizing liberalism and republicanism. How was this possible? Briefly, Jefferson's generation expanded the idea of classical citizenship, saying all yeoman farmers were entitled to full citizenship. The Jeffersonians sought to make a clean break from a social and political order grounded on hereditary privilege and worked to establish a new social system based on individual equality and talent. Yet, at the same time that the Jeffersonians abandoned the distinctly elitist aspects of the classical republican doctrine, they never broke with the concern for public happiness and political participation. As republicans, they continued the classical insistence on public duties as well as private rights, on politics as well as commerce.[46]

Jefferson and his followers helped Americans become liberal-republican democrats. Jeffersonian republicans were Lockean liberals in the sense that they understood and used the language of individual rights and political equality. They were liberals in their optimism about the future and their emphasis on private and voluntary associations. Lockean liberal attitudes, shared by all contemporary Americans from House Speaker Hastert on the right to Senator Barbara Boxer on the left, have a different focus than does the republican tradition. At the same time, Jefferson did not think self-interest a sufficient basis for citizenship. He and his followers did not regard the government as existing solely to protect the private pursuit of happiness, nor were they totally comfortable with the greed and wealth generated by the new capitalist economy. These were republican attitudes. Finally, Jeffersonian republicans think of liberty not only as freedom from restraint but also as the freedom to participate actively in politics. Jefferson understood that intelligent, passionate participation is what keeps political liberty alive. This attitude is republican to its core.[47]

The Jeffersonians quarreled with the Federalists, in no small part, because many of the Federalists were democratic elitists who wished to banish ordinary people from active participation in politics. Afraid of mob action and working-class control of the legislature, the authors of the Constitution played it safe with democracy. After the Revolution, many of the Federalists expected that the new American political institutions would function within the old assumptions about a politically active elite and a deferential, compliant electorate.[48] The Federalists tried to channel the civic spirit that the Revolution unleashed into private activities, instead of devising some means of perpetuating it.[49] This was the key difference between Jefferson and Federalists such as George Washington and Alexander Hamilton. Today, this difference over the relative importance of public life is *the* major dividing line between today's republican democrats (whether conservative, moderate, or progressive) and those satisfied with a political system dominated by a political elite and big money.

JEFFERSON'S WARDS UPDATED

"We are all Republicans, we are all Federalists." With these words the third president of the United States sought to heal the political wounds that divided the two major political parties that had battled in the presidential election of 1800. Yet these words have a deeper meaning than just a conciliatory gesture. They are a succinct expression of Jefferson's democratic philosophy, premised on active participation by all adult citizens while at the same time accepting representative government on a continental scale.[50] Jefferson's goal was to add the town-hall meeting to the Constitution. More than any other Revolutionary leader, he struggled with the problem of how to keep the spirit of the revolution alive. He understood that the Constitution protected our rights, but he understood that it also kept citizens at bay and turned them toward private life. The problem, as Jefferson saw it, was that there was no constitutionally protected *space* where average people could regularly exercise their political freedom.[51]

Jefferson understood that if people were only provided the opportunity to participate in public life during infrequent elections, democracy would become, in Arendt's telling phrase, a "mechanism of government administration" through which rulers control men.[52] Without a strong participatory element, large-scale representative government would not be all that different from life under a good king. Jefferson's solution was ward democracy. He proposed dividing the nation's counties into self-governing wards based on the New England township model. "These little republics would be the main strength of the great one."[53] Every resident of an area would be part of the local ward.

Following his presidency, Jefferson wrote that he had "two great measures at heart"—that of general education to enable every man to "judge for himself" and to "divide every county into hundreds."[54] Besides supporting a school, residents of each ward would take care of their poor, their roads, police, elections, and the choice of jurors, among other things. "Making every citizen an acting member of the government, and in the offices nearest and most interesting to him, will attach him by his strongest feelings to the independence of his country and its republican constitution."[55] Jefferson believed the psychological and political benefits of incorporating the town-hall meeting into the Constitution would enable the United States to make good on its goal of being the world's leading democracy: "Where every man is a sharer in the direction of his ward-republic, or of some of the higher ones, and feels he is a participator in the government of affairs, not merely at an election one day in the year."[56] The ward-republics constituted the essence of democracy for Jefferson because "government is more or less republican, in proportion as it has its composition more or less of this ingredient of the direct action of the citizens."[57]

Jefferson's perfect republic combines his ward-republics with Madison's federal constitution. A democratic revolution is really a two-stage affair. There is liberation from tyranny and then affirmation of political freedom. Put differently, democracy is more than the protection of individual rights; it means the exercise of political voice as well. Watching the French Revolution spin out of control, Jefferson learned the importance of putting freedom to positive uses. In his eyes, the ward system would ensure that every citizen had access to the political life. Jefferson "expected the wards to permit the citizens to continue to do what they had been able to do during the years of the revolution, namely," writes Arendt, "to act on their own and thus participate in public business as it was being transacted from day to day."[58] This direct participation in local political life would build bonds between neighbors, develop affection for the local community, and help prevent people from retreating into cocoons of self and family.

Madison's idea of a national political community sharing a common purpose combined with a decentralized scheme of political power and administration lies at the heart of the Constitution. Although we may disagree with his elite scheme of representation, his idea of government remains our ideal. In addition to inventing our system of federalism, Madison, like Jefferson, sought to modernize the civic republicanism tradition. He was committed to many republican principles: government by discussion, the existence of a public good, and a modern understanding of civic virtue based on openness to other opinions and a search for the truth. Due to his individualistic premises and defense of the propertied minority, Madison is often portrayed as a prototypical Lockean liberal. This stereotype is flawed. Madison's political thought—like Jefferson's—combines both liberal and republican themes. Yes, Madison was a liberal, but he was a liberal republican who continually sought the common good. He had republican goals, even if his method cut against the grain of traditional republican thinking; like most revolutionary leaders he continued to hold out for the possibility of a virtuous politics. Madison and the Federalists desperately wanted to foster leaders who were animated by civic virtue and a concern for the public good, even as much of the public focused on individualistic needs and commercial pursuits.

Benjamin Franklin once quipped, "It's a republic, if you can keep it." Recognizing our great population and the impossibility of direct participation of every citizen in government, it is worth reconsidering Jefferson's ward scheme—with a representative twist. Today, the Constitution gives all power to the citizens in terms of final sovereignty "without giving them the opportunity of *being* republicans and *acting* as citizens."[59] It is time to shift our republican understanding from Harrington to Machiavelli. By extending Madison's representative scheme downward and amending Jefferson's ward-republics in a representative direction, we can join two famed founders in a powerful synthesis.

THE REPUBLICAN TURN

Building on the founders involves more than just revisiting and extending Madison and Jefferson's arguments. It also necessitates articulating republican ideas that were submerged beneath liberalism for two centuries following the Constitution. That began to change during the past thirty years when historians rediscovered the republican tradition, and political theorists began to see the value of republican ideas for contemporary debates about democracy and deliberation. Republican thinkers such as Machiavelli and Harrington are among the intellectual founders of the United States. The institutional reform I propose and develop in Chapter 4 is designed to amplify and put into practice the idea of republican liberty as developed by Machiavelli and given sophistication and energy by a number of contemporary writers, including Sunstein, Michael Sandel, Quentin Skinner, Philip Pettit, Maurizio Viroli, and John McCormick.[60]

I argue for a version of republicanism that is focused on republican liberty understood as nondomination and favors an institutional mix of popular participation and popular representation.[61] Contemporary republicans have been accused of advancing a "hazy doctrine" with regard to the content of critical terms such as *civic virtue* and *the common good* as well as the specific mechanisms of public deliberation and participation they seek.[62] The challenge is: "How does a contemporary republicanism distinguish itself sufficiently from its traditional counterpart so as to succeed where its counterpart failed?"[63] Here I make clear how I understand republicanism as a political theory, and in the following chapter I turn my attention to institutions and practices.

Political freedom is the 'big idea' that distinguishes republicans from other schools of thought.[64] Republicans have an understanding of freedom that is neither exclusively Aristotelian nor liberal. In contrast to Isaiah Berlin's well-known distinction between negative and positive liberty, republicans argue for a third, and arguably superior, way of thinking about freedom that is "more radical and consistent than classical liberalism."[65] In an important sense, the republicanism commitment to liberty goes beyond the liberalism of John Rawls on the left and Milton Friedman on the right.

Rawls is heavily committed to individual liberty and designs his theory of justice so that individual rights trump utilitarian considerations. Likewise, Friedman articulates and defends the libertarian position of negative liberty with concrete examples of how state power interferes with individual freedom of action.[66] Sociologically grounded in historical experience, republicans are very conscious of the fragility of life and the instability and changeability of politics. Machiavelli and the American Founders were political realists who understood that people with political power sometimes do terrible things. If we are truly concerned with individual freedom, then it is imperative for us to (1) establish a democratic polity where people have the power to elect their leaders, (2) develop habits and institutions that encourage the public to "pay attention" to the political world, and (3) design a constitutional structure in which power is divided and no individual or group has singular control of the government.

Republican liberty is based on the idea that individual liberty is not safe unless a vigilant population makes sure their leaders do the right thing. If nothing else, the twentieth century drove home the lesson that monstrous deeds happen when evil individuals gain control of government. Yes, constitutional safeguards and an independent judiciary are crucial for freedom but, as Tocqueville observed in a chapter entitled "The Laws Contribute More to the Maintenance of the Democratic Republic of the United States Than Do the Physical Circumstances of the Country, and the Mores Do More Than the Laws," constitutions are mere pieces of paper without democratic norms and active engaged citizens.[67]

In his mechanistic understanding of politics, Thomas Hobbes defined freedom as the absence of interference with motion. For Hobbes and most modern liberals, the laws formulated by government necessarily reduce the freedom that people naturally possess. This negative understanding of freedom received its modern incarnation in Berlin's essay "Two Concepts of Liberty" (1958), an essay—similar to Schumpeter's revision of democratic theory—that was, in part, an ideological argument spawned by the Cold War. According to Berlin, negative liberty involves the absence of interference, where interference is intentional as in the case of physical coercion or a plausible threat. I am negatively free "to the degree to which no human being interferes with my activity," writes Berlin.[68] Thus freedom exists when a person enjoys unimpeded movement and uncoerced choice. Following Hobbes, Berlin says that there is no necessary connection between democracy and individual liberty.[69] As we will see, republicans strongly disagree.

Berlin's positive liberty is more ambitious and, he argues, dangerous in its totalitarian implications. This understanding of freedom requires the person to take an active role in gaining "self-mastery." But the instruction and training required can become tyrannical and repressive. Ringing in the background of positive liberty is Rousseau's dictum, "forced to be free." Thinkers who support the development of positive freedom include Rousseau, Hegel, and Marx, in addition to various religious sects and modern totalitarians. In contrast, Berlin finds negative freedom supported by Hobbes, Bentham, J. S. Mill, Montesquieu, Constant, Tocqueville, Jefferson, and Paine, and this is the approach he recommends.

Although negative liberty is a good thing, in some respects it is limited. The Hobbes/Berlin formulation is problematic for two reasons. First, the conception of freedom as the absence of interference is relatively indifferent to issues of power and domination. Thus liberalism is "tolerant of relationships in the home, the workplace, the electorate and elsewhere," that republicans view as "paradigms of domination and unfreedom."[70] Republicans contend that a definition of liberty focused on noninterference does not go far enough to actually protect a person's autonomy. For civic republicans, liberty consists not only of the absence of interference from other individuals or institutions, but also the absence of domination or dependence. A person cannot be free if he lives in fear of the arbitrary actions of another. Harrington made this argument against Hobbes, pointing out that "the most privileged subject of a king or sultan retains his life only as long as it suits the ruler."[71]

To illustrate the difference between interference and domination, we can imagine a woman who can be abused by her boyfriend without being able to resist; workers who can be exploited and abused by their supervisors; prep school students under the gaze of prefects; army recruits at basic training saluting their drill sergeants; junior faculty who realize that advancement depends more on personal relations with senior faculty than on scholarship; and a person living in a country where she can be thrown in jail on a judge's arbitrary whim. All of these situations are examples where there is no actual interference. According to negative liberty, these people are free. But are they? To differing degrees, each is subject to the arbitrary will of another and thus lives in a condition of dependence and subservience.[72] In the world of negative liberty, we might say "free to choose" has more than one meaning. Republican liberty differs from its liberal cousin in that it identifies the absence of liberty not merely in being obstructed by others, but in "the *constant possibility* of interference due to the presence of arbitrary powers."[73]

The Hobbes/Berlin idea of negative liberty is problematic for a second reason. Our liberty—both as noninterference and nondomination—is dependent on the social surroundings we inhabit. The best way to ensure our individual freedom is to unite with others to construct and maintain a political order where our rights and liberties are respected. Some believe that we have "natural rights," but in practice such belief means little. Republicans hold that a self-governing republic is the best guarantee that citizens will enjoy individual liberty. Skinner states the republican position succinctly when he writes, "If we wish to maximize our own individual liberty, we must cease to put our trust in princes, and instead take charge of the political arena ourselves."[74] To protect our political liberty, we need to live in a "free state" where the people band together to frame laws that govern all. In a republic, all are subject to law, but being subject to law is quite different from being subject to another's arbitrary will. Laws can and do interfere, but in contrast to domination by another person, this is not incompatible with freedom. Individual freedom is most possible in a republic because, as Harrington famously wrote, it is "an empire of laws and not men."[75] In sum, republicans understand, contrary to liberal mythology, that freedom is not a natural possession of individuals. It is a social construct, the achievement of a well-ordered state.[76]

The idea of political liberty goes back to Roman law where the status of free persons was defined as not being subject to the arbitrary will of another person. We enjoy political liberty when we live in a self-governing polity where the people participate in discussions about the major issues of the day and approve or reject the rules governing the life of the community. A nation is free when it lives under its own laws, just as the individual is free when she exercises her legal and political rights.[77] Although some liberals contend there is no direct connection between liberty and democracy, republicans disagree and argue that the two are joined at the hip. To try to separate one from the other is like trying to separate Siamese twins—very difficult and often fatal to both.

Political liberty is equal measures Arendt's fear of totalitarianism and Tocqueville's admiration of Jacksonian democracy. In Arendt's *The Origins of Totalitarianism*s we gain an understanding of social dynamics that regimes use to destroy public space and isolate individuals. When good citizens are inattentive or worn down, the political situation can spin out of control as it did in towns across Germany in the early 1930s. As communists and Nazi gangs engaged in street fights, moderates withdrew from the political arena and Hitler "won" the 1933 national election with 43.9 percent of the vote.[78] Conversely, Tocqueville's opus *Democracy in America* strives to make sense of the new, almost utopian, world created after the American Revolution.[79] His conclusion: the success of the American experiment with self-rule was based, in large part, on its republican ethos revealed in the public happiness of New England town meetings and the mores of self-interest properly understood.

HARRINGTON OR MACHIAVELLI?

Freedom depends on well-designed institutions and on citizens exercising civic spiritedness or civic virtue. It is endangered both by external threats and internal decay. In a world dominated by change, the indifference of citizens can lead to corruption and occasionally democratic breakdown. Identifying the conditions under which a nation can maintain free institutions despite the continual threat of corruption is the central republican dilemma. Understood as a "failure of rationality," corruption is the inability to recognize that our own liberty depends on a critical mass of citizens committed to a life of civic virtue and public service.[80]

Republican freedom as nondomination began as the ideology of male, property-owning citizens of independent city states. In the United States, we expanded the size of the republic to continental scale and, after the suffrage and civil rights struggles of the twentieth century, today include all adults in the demos. The battle over how to interpret political freedom remains active and is, in part, ideological. Like many political words, freedom's meaning is contested and, like the flag, it is a symbol to which politicians love to lay rhetoric claim. Describing Pettit's historical argument, Timothy O'Hagan writes, "The French and American Revolutions made it possible to extend political freedom more widely, ultimately to all adults, male and female, propertied and propertyless. At that moment, reactionaries returned to Hobbes's idea of negative freedom to replace what was by now the dangerous ideology of republican freedom. Alarmed by the egalitarian implications of non-domination, elitist liberals found non-interference to be a safer goal than non-domination."[81]

Traditionally, republicans have relied on virtuous citizens sacrificing self-interest to pursue the common good. Although these are noble sentiments, can we realistically think these norms will soon dominate American politics? The answer is clearly no. After all, as Wood explains in *The Creation of the American Republic, 1776-1787,* the founders adopted the liberal institutions of the Constitution, in large part, because of problems with received republican ideas. The result was the Federalist approach to constitutional government and Jefferson's refashioning of the republican toolbox. Today, we face the opposite dilemma, as it is liberal norms that are under fire for being inadequate expressions of political reality. The neutral procedural republic described by Sandel is a major source of contemporary discontent.[82] Machiavelli's republican paradigm, with its stress on civic virtue, appeals to MacIntyre and others because of its "notion of a public good which is prior to and characterisable independently of the summing of individual desires and interests."[83]

Still, because America is both Locke and Machiavelli, it would be a mistake to understand contemporary republicanism as an alternative to liberalism. Modern liberalism is constitutive of much that we are in modern America. Understanding two basic truths about human society, liberalism defends the irreversible cosmopolitan nature of the modern world and accepts that politics can only encompass a portion of human aspiration and fulfillment. The dominant ideology of ancient Greece and Rome, republicanism became a supporting cast member within the larger liberal project after the triumph of commerce, capitalism, and large-state democracy in the seventeenth and eighteenth centuries.[84] But, make no mistake, republican ideas remain critical because while liberalism aspires to a public sphere where all adults are included "as full and equal citizens rather than as political subjects or social subordinates," republican principles explain what must be done for this to be so.[85] Both the Marxist and republican critiques inform liberalism as to what it must do to make citizenship in the public sphere a reality and not a sham. As Karl Marx famously wrote, "Where the political state has attained to its full development, man leads, not only in thought, in consciousness, but in *reality,* in *life,* a double existence— celestial and terrestrial. He lives in the *political community,* where he regards himself as a *communal being,* and in *civil society* where he acts simply as a *private individual.*"[86]

The republicanism I am arguing for—more a cousin of liberalism than its opponent—departs from the classic republican worldview in a number of respects. Before discussing key concepts, it is important to recognize that the republican tradition is multifaceted and includes many contributors. Just as there is no single liberalism, there is no single republicanism. To simplify, we can say there are two main traditions in the republican history of ideas. Both can be seen in Cicero, the most influential writer of the Roman Republic. One emphasizes rhetoric and popular participation, the other emphasizes reason and elite deliberation.[87] In his writing, Machiavelli champions the first; Harrington's presentation of republican ideas after the English Revolution emphasizes the second. For my part, I side with Machiavelli. His republicanism of the *Discourses* is the more participatory, more egalitarian, and more democratic strand of republicanism. Harrington's republican utopia, *The Commonwealth of Oceana* [1656], is long on institutional design, yet strangely devoid of political life.[88]

Opposing monarchy, Harrington finds inspiration in the oligarchic republic of Venice, with its reputation for stability and reasoned discourse among the elite. He maintains an allegiance to the idea that the well-born should decide for everyone else, and although the people can vote on proposals presented to them, they are not allowed to discuss or debate. In Harrington's republic, the masses are to be seen, not heard.[89] Harrington's aristocratic understanding influenced both Hume and *The Federalist* authors. Madison's argument that the new Constitution should provide for the "total exclusion of the people, in their collective capacity" echoes Harrington's elitist stance.[90] Although Harrington's focus on deliberation is to be admired, he overemphasizes reason and is afraid of rhetoric, persuasion, and the wide-ranging, often emotionally charged, debate that is the essence of democratic politics. For example, Harrington disparages the political tumult of the Roman Republic. By contrast, Machiavelli views the competition between the elite and the masses and energy engendered by their passionate politics as the key to Rome's success.

The two different views of republicanism generate different approaches to the structure of government and the role that citizens play. One of the central themes of the *Discourses* is Machiavelli's argument that the people at large constitute the best safeguard of political liberty as well as the most dependable and trustworthy basis of decision making about the public good.[91] Harrington, even though he is severely restricted in his endorsement of popular participation, agrees. But as Gary Nederman points out, Harrington's passive assembly is "a far cry from Machiavelli's free people, who must be convinced of the goodness of a course of public action and who are deemed competent to discern between competing points of view." Starting with the premise that reason and rationality are a special attribute of an elite few, Harrington excludes public discussion and debate from his well-ordered constitutional order.[92] And while Machiavelli stresses the need for both a well-designed constitution and virtuous citizens, arguing that neither can do the job alone, Harrington insists that laws are enough. He has no need of good men.

For Harrington, participation and civic virtue are no longer central. Instead, because people are self-interested, the key is to devise institutions where even corrupt men act as if they are good. Although few contemporary Americans have heard of Harrington, he remains important because Hume, Madison and Hamilton in the *Federalist Papers,* and, thus, the Constitution follow his lead. As a result, the American political system is both liberal and republican, but the republican element emphasizes Harrington far more than Machiavelli. This choice is a mistake. One way to deal with the corruption of the large republic is to *re-inject Machiavellian* principles into our constitutional mix. The institutional reform I introduce in the next chapter blends Harrington's focus on deliberation with Machiavelli's central insight that popular participation is the key to a republic's long-term health.

MODERN, REALISTIC PRINCIPLES

If civic republican principles are to be part of the solution, they must be shown to be modern and realistic.[93] Can this be said about civic virtue, the common good, and participation—central republican concepts some-times criticized as being ill-suited for an era of economic globalism and postmodern sensibilities?[94]

The central republican virtue is captured in the idea of an active, en-gaged citizen who loves his or her country and is committed to protecting and promoting political freedom and encouraging the norms and practices that make democracy possible in a complex, diverse, commercially vital twenty-first-century society. Republican thought—from Machiavelli, to Tocqueville, to today—is characterized by the worry that too many people take their freedom for granted and that without a vigilant press and a watchful, engaged citizen body, it is easy—given human nature—for politi-cal institutions to be taken over by individuals and groups whose goals are private and selfish. For republicans, civic virtue and corruption—"a term of art the republican theorists habitually use to denote our natural tendency to ignore the claims of our community as soon as they seem to conflict with the pursuit of our own immediate advantage"—are inextricably linked.[95]

Civic virtues are those qualities essential to the continuation of the re-public. These include honesty; civility; an ability to understand and partici-pate in political argument; empathy for other people's positions and life stories; a commitment to the procedures necessary for a democratic politi-cal order including free and fair elections, freedom of association, a free press, and legal protections for the opposition; respect for the constitution and the law; and an appreciation of the importance of argument and dis-sent. In reviewing Pettit's republicanism, John Ferejohn makes a recom-mendation about the importance of virtue with which I am in agreement. He writes, "A useable republicanism today cannot, I think, make much common cause with communitarians. The extent and depth of social dis-agreement and conflict is too large to paper over. Having said that, I think Pettit underestimates the potential for virtue, morality, or common-interest seeking among the electorate and their representatives."[96]

Next, is the public good an impossible ideal, a chimera as Schumpeter and some social choice theorists believe?[97] Discussions of the common good often get colored by Rousseau's search for the general will, which ad-mittedly is a rare thing and attainable only if Rousseau's stringent condi-tions are met. But asking people to think about the common good as well as their own individual interests when making political judgments is a reasonable proposition. The republican position depends on the ability to feel empathy for others and seeing the world from a larger perspective than one's own shoes. Robert Goodin addresses just this issue when he describes how people create internal dialogues and deliberate within themselves.[98] Obviously, this is a challenge for egocentric human beings, but it fits with our understanding of psychological health and higher levels of moral and ethical development. Modern republicans do not expect constant self sacrifice. In fact, the historic stress on subordinating self-interest to the wider public good was aimed primarily at the aristocratic elite whose private interests were at odds with the nation as a whole and the masses who lacked a powerful voice in decision making. Today, the self-interest of the average citizen is not that different from the common good of the whole.[99]

A number of writers agree with Shelley Burtt who writes, "the good citizen need not jettison his selfish attachments, only place them properly in perspective. The key is to create the circumstances under which individuals come to define themselves as citizens."[100] Viroli offers these words on how we should understand the common good. Contemporary republicans, he writes, "do not foster the notion of an organic community where individuals work toward the common good, nor do they waste time fantasizing about republics where laws aspiring to the common good are approved unanimously by virtuous citizens." Instead, the common good is neither the "good (or interest) of everyone nor a good (or interest) that transcends private interests; rather, it is the good of citizens who wish to live free and independent and as such is opposed to the good of those who wish to dominate."[101]

Modern republicanism seeks to reclaim the classical tradition but without the baggage of the Aristotelian understanding of civic participation and without the elitism of a guardian class of decision makers knowing what is best for the rest of us.[102] For modern republicans, political life is not the highest realization of human nature; instead we recognize that living in freedom makes possible the realization of other ends, in other words, the rest of a good life. Likewise, modern republicans are as committed as liberals to the value of equality. Liberty as nondomination speaks to the importance of equality in both public and private spheres and thus meets the criticism of feminists who point out that earlier republicans (such as Milton) often sanctioned the subordination, while celebrating the freedom.[103]

Modern republicans do not ask everyone to participate all the time. That is why representative democracy exists, and representative government fits easily with the republican philosophy. But in those periods of life when they can, citizens should tune into the world of public affairs and join the discussion. Obviously, life in a modern democracy makes multiple demands on individuals. There are only so many hours in the day, and demands of family and work and the pleasures of friends, hobbies, entertainment, and recreation mean there is not much time left for civic duties. But participation is to be encouraged, and the stronger participatory ethos a republic has the better. A participatory political culture in which norms of civility and passion are equally distributed and where citizens feel they can make a difference is to be admired, not feared.

I differ from some republicans who see participation as having primarily an instrumental value—important because participation is essential to securing political freedom. Participation should be encouraged and valued, not only because it is good for the polity as a whole, but also because it contributes to a sense of wholeness for individuals. Although not essential to individual development, civic participation is one of the goods of a full life. Not all will choose to be active and involved, but a critical mass of citizens is needed. Participation in republican politics is compatible with a heterogeneous society and a fairly high level of political conflict. In fact, conflict is a good thing, a sign of a healthy polity where means and ends are continually contested. Pettit, for example, argues for introducing "systematic possibilities for ordinary people to contest the doings of government" because this is a much better basis for democracy than mere consent. [104]

In sum, the republican ideas remain powerful tools by which to analyze and think about democratic politics. The republican theory is no longer aristocratic and does not chase the dream of community or consensus. Instead, it is a workable, practical philosophy. It fits easily with liberalism and goes beyond liberalism in its commitment to political liberty and democratic participation. Republicans do not reject a politics of individual rights and consent, but, instead, argue that neither the liberalism of Locke nor Rawls is wholly satisfactory when it comes to democracy. All republics must stress participation, debate, and involvement in public life.

For the Federalists at the founding and elitist democrats today, what matters is getting able representatives into office. They see extensive republics as being superior to city-states not only because they escape deadly factionalism and provide national security but also because great size increases the pool of talent on which to draw.[105] Moreover, some believe that "as long as elections are popular the essence of republicanism is preserved, for it is not size or immediacy that counts, but the ultimate source of authority, which remains the people."[106]

As should be clear, popular elections do not, in themselves, constitute the essence of republicanism. Instead, the republican position remains that the few need the many to save them from corruption and that mere consent to the governed does not provide for this. For, as Machiavelli stressed, the elite have "a great desire to dominate," while the people "have only the wish not to be dominated."[107] This the Anti-Federalists understood. What is necessary is an institutional arrangement that allows citizens to display critical judgment on the major questions of the day. This is the idea that lies behind and informs Madison's goal of civic-minded majorities. The question is: How can republican self-government be implemented in a society as large and complex as the modern United States?

4.

A Virtual National Assembly

Representative government, as currently practiced, gives no institutional role to the assembled citizens. That this does not strike us as odd says a great deal about the success of representative government taking on the cloak of democracy while leaving behind a substantial part of its core meaning. Manin writes, "Conceived in explicit opposition to democracy, today [representative government] is seen as one of its forms . . . Representative government has undeniably a democratic dimension. No less deniably, however, is its oligarchic dimension."[1] Champions of participatory democracy recognize this and, beginning in the 1960s have mounted a challenge to the minimalist democracy offered by Schumpeter and the early pluralists. Although their critique of Schumpeter has been on the mark, their solution—direct democracy at the local level and in the workplace—dodges the problem of scale and our need for a more energetic and engaged democracy at the state and national levels.[2] In addition, the solution proposed by the Progressive reformers—direct mass democracy—has reached its logical limit. The inadequacy of the initiative and the primary are evident for all to see.

It is time for a new strategy. Among political theorists, there has been a burst of writing not only about republican ideas but also around the concept of deliberative democracy.[3] Both schools are moving in an institutional direction, but shifting from theory to practice is difficult. It is an especially long leap if the writer is Jürgen Habermas imagining a pure speech situation or Arendt describing an idealized Athens. The goal here is to connect the theoretical with practical reality. The authors of *The Federalist Papers* were able to do this, and so can we. In the previous chapter, I explained how Harrington and Machiavelli provide the building blocks for modern republicanism.[4] Our goal is to correct the elitism of Madison by institutionalizing greater popular voice and participation.

Obviously, political and economic elites are necessary in a modern nation-state. To think otherwise is fantasy. Still, we need to narrow the gap between politically aware citizens and the political class specializing in politics and government. Instead of rejecting representation and trying to craft direct democracy, we must embrace representative government and give it a healthy dose of Machiavelli and Jefferson's faith in the people to reduce its oligarchic tendencies.[5] Building on the synthesis of Madison and Jefferson suggested in Chapter 3, we are now ready to discuss a concrete, practical reform that has the potential to re-energize American democracy.

Four decades ago, the idea of participatory democracy inspired a generation. Today, it is possible to combine the traditional town hall and the Internet to fashion a new understanding of representative government that empowers citizens while rejecting the mass plebiscite of the initiative system. The Assembly reform offers a radical, yet practical, plan to give voters a true voice in national affairs and, potentially, a vote in Congress. In each of the nation's 435 congressional districts, there would be a local assembly of 100 citizens, selected by lot, who would meet to discuss the major domestic and international issues. In the first stage of deliberative reform, the Assembly, delegates would study and debate pressing issues—national health care and a second war with Iraq, for example—then offer their opinions. Their views would constitute a second, more sophisticated, more informed measure of public opinion than traditional opinion polls. In the second stage of reform, the People's House, delegates would gain formal power to initiate and amend bills as well as to vote yea or nay on major legislation that has passed the House of Representatives or the Senate.

At the end of Chapter 1, a diagram of democracy showed Rousseau and direct democracy at one pole and Madison and standard representative government at the other. The challenge: to invent a new institution in the middle of the continuum. Instead of starting from Rousseau, begin with Madison. We can combine Madison's ideas about extending the scope of representation with Jefferson's ideas about ward government and, with the help of the Internet, create an innovative twenty-first-century institution. In brief, the assembly reform would "reinvent" representative government by adding, first, an advisory citizen assembly to Congress, and then later, an empowered citizens' house to the national legislature.

Madison sought to extend the scope of representation horizontally across the continent. In a nation of nearly 300 million individuals, we could *extend representation downward* by adding 100-person assemblies beneath each member of the House of Representatives, with each delegate being selected by lot from a single ward (1 delegate to 6,500 constituents). This synthesis of Madison and Jefferson would solve the problem of scale and revitalize American democracy. Combining face-to-face town-hall meetings with modern communication links to form a decentralized national Assembly, this strategy would yield a new system of deliberative democracy and intelligent participation. Table 2 shows how the national Assembly reaches a middle ground between direct democracy and standard representative government. *Representative democracy on a small scale* would be an antidote to corruption and a powerful counterbalance to the current consultant-driven politics.[6] With an ethos very different from direct democracy on a grand scale it offers Americans the option of an intelligent assertive populism.

Table 2

Schema No. 2

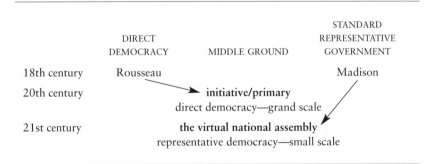

	DIRECT DEMOCRACY	MIDDLE GROUND	STANDARD REPRESENTATIVE GOVERNMENT
18th century	Rousseau		Madison
20th century		initiative/primary direct democracy—grand scale	
21st century		the virtual national assembly representative democracy—small scale	

STAGE ONE: THE ASSEMBLY

The Internet facilitates a creative union between representative government and participatory democracy. Imagine a magic wand passing over the American political system: The triad structure of government remains; we have become neither a parliamentary democracy nor a multiparty republic. Instead, beneath each member of Congress we add a local citizen assembly. Linked together electronically, these local assemblies would form a virtual national town hall to assist Congress and the president find solutions to the thorniest public problems. These citizen assemblies would not have formal political power, yet their votes would count in the political calculations of Congress and the president. On the most critical issues, these panels of 100 people per district would help us arrive at a public judgment both intelligent and powerful. Polling the 43,500 members of the Assembly would constitute a second, more considered, measure of public opinion on the critical issues of the day.

Although the votes of the 435 citizen assemblies would not be binding, their voice would be powerful because the political elite, the media, and the broader public would be interested in what an intelligent cross section of the public thought after study and debate. Delegate selection would be by lot. All adult citizens would automatically be part of the lottery pool, but people who wanted to opt out could. Allowing people to opt out, instead of opting in, would help ensure a large pool of potential delegates. Those selected would serve a single two-year term. At the end of the two-year term, each assembly would nominate one delegate for the national steering committee, which would consist of 100 people drawn by lot from the 435 nominated. This steering committee would set the agenda of the national Assembly and perform administrative and coordinating functions.[7]

Similar to the initiative process, the Assembly would ask the public to participate in policy making, but with a dramatic difference. Instead of millions of voters marking a ballot about which they know little, the assembly delegate would be one of 43,500 citizens nationally who were given the time and resources to study an issue and make an informed judgment. Over the course of two years, the delegates might be called to examine a foreign-policy dilemma, a budget proposal, and legislation to reform the mental health care system. Likewise, the delegates would be minipoliticians, but with a key difference: they would not be taking money and would speak with less calculation. And by encouraging the formation of the broad-based civic majorities central to Madison's founding vision, the assemblies would help check the power of single-interest groups. Those chosen to represent the community would be expected to take their responsibility seriously. Citizens would understand that when they serve in the local assembly their duty and demeanor are similar to that of a jury in the judicial system. As civic volunteers, it would be their moment of glory when they would stand for their neighbors and their country.[8]

The local assemblies would meet face-to-face two to three times a month. By virtue of their participation in the Assembly, delegates would get a crash course as to the complexity and tradeoffs involved in making decisions about public policy. Some of the delegates would be part of the politically aware public. Others would begin their two-year term as a delegate with more limited political knowledge, but because they had chosen to be part of the delegate lottery, they indicated their interest in participating and their willingness to learn about the issues at hand and to contribute, in albeit a small but important way, to the national dialogue.[9] As a concession both to their amateur status and to the economy of time, Assembly delegates would leave the committee work of legislation to the professional politicians and policy wonks of Capitol Hill. The Assembly's job would be to discuss issues in a way that both assists the legislative process and enlightens the general public and then, after listening to the debate and doing their best to educate themselves on the issues at hand, to make an informed choice.

The Assembly poll could be done one of two ways. Each delegate could vote within his or her assembly, with the decision being made by majority rule (50 percent plus 1), and then each local assembly would cast a single vote nationally. The votes of the 435 local assemblies in congressional districts across the nation would be tallied, and the magic number of 218 (50 percent plus 1) would signify the victor in the Assembly as a whole—just as it does in the House of Representatives. This approach has appeal because it would mirror voting in the House of Representatives. However, it would be better to tally the votes of the Assembly as a whole. Under this second method, all 43,500 delegates in national Assembly would be polled on specific questions much in the same way that opinion surveys are conducted today. Victory would go to the majority of individual votes cast, regardless of the congressional district in which they were cast. The second approach is better because if each district assembly has a single vote, then the Assembly would fall prey to the same problem as the Electoral College: a mismatch between aggregate preferences and the outcome. Suppose alternative A narrowly wins 51 percent of the assemblies while alternative B overwhelmingly wins the remaining 49 percent. In such a case, the preference of a majority of the Assembly's members would lose. This is not the case when we count all the votes at once.

Imagine Sam Giovoti, an accountant with a good grasp of politics and finance, serving on the local assembly in St. Louis. After the president has presented his budget to Congress, Giovoti is one of four speakers chosen to address the national Assembly. Chosen by lot from those local assembly members bold enough to want to address the national audience, two speakers have been selected who support the president's plan and two to argue against it. When it comes his turn, Giovoti makes an intelligent, focused speech criticizing the president's plan. As his address is discussed in local assemblies across the nation, other delegates begin to rally around Giovoti's view of budget sums and priorities.

What if Giovoti's bold challenge, in fact, showed that the president's budget had no clothes and that public opinion, first in the deliberative sphere of the Assembly and then in the broader public, came to agree with his version of the facts? Using his chance to address both the delegates and the wider public, Giovoti helped shape the budget debate. In addition, by speaking truth to power, Giovoti would change how he, his neighborhood, his city, and the nation at large understand citizen participation. Giving ordinary citizens the chance to argue, debate, and deliberate in the individual local assemblies and, occasionally speak to a national audience, could issue in a fundamental reorientation of people's views of democracy in America. Obviously, this is a rhetorical example. But on many important issues, where interest groups dominate debate and the public is kept largely in the dark, an ongoing national town-hall meeting would generate healthy discussion and inject common sense into political debate.

REAL-WORLD PREDECESSORS

My proposal of a national Assembly builds on James Fishkin's experiments with deliberative polling, the National Issues Forums conducted by the Kettering Foundation, and extends real-world legislative efforts in Congress and in the California Legislature. Fishkin champions the idea of deliberative opinion polls in which statistically representative samples of the population make recommendations on specific policy issues. Instead of just asking people questions via telephone, Fishkin brings them to a central location to allow them to study an issue, listen to experts, and discuss the pros and cons before letting them make a decision.[10] "A deliberative opinion poll models what the public *would* think, if it had a more adequate chance to think about the questions at issue." [11] To wit:

> A deliberative opinion poll gives a microcosm of the entire nation the opportunities for thoughtful interaction and opinion formation that are normally restricted to small-group democracy. It brings the face-to-face democracy of the Athenian Assembly or the New England town meeting to the large-scale nation-state. Most important, it offers a face-to-face democracy not of elected members of a legislature, but of ordinary citizens who can participate on the same basis of political equality as that offered by the assembly or town meeting. It provides a statistical model of what the electorate *would* think if, hypothetically, all voters had the same opportunities that are offered to the sample in the deliberative opinion poll . . . Its results have prescriptive force because they are the voice of the people under special circumstances where the people have had a chance to think about the issues and hence should have a voice worth listening to."[12]

The goal is for randomly selected lay groups, with no special interest in the outcome, coming together to "invest the time and energy necessary to make informed decisions."[13]

The Kettering Foundation runs a series of National Issues Forums premised on just these principles. Such an approach widens the circle of participation beyond interest group lobbyists, policy experts, and elected officials to include the public's point of view.[14] Having a subset of the broad public participate recognizes the principle of economy—not everyone wants to or needs to participate in the making of public policy—as well as the need for those who do participate to gain enough knowledge to be better informed than the average voter. If postwar political science has proven nothing else, it has shown conclusively that political knowledge among the mass electorate is thin.[15] We want the people who make up a policy jury to be able to make a sound judgment based on the merits of the arguments presented. As Shapiro writes, "The possibilities offered by deliberative polls are worth exploring because they provide a potential way out of Sirianni's paradox: they combine citizen control with the possibility of sophisticated decision-making in a complex world, and they do it in a way that takes account of the economy of time."[16]

The Assembly also has a close connection with the recently enacted health care reform plan introduced by Senators Ron Wyden (D-Oregon) and Orrin Hatch (R-Utah) aimed at launching a national dialogue on comprehensive health care reform.[17] The "Health Care That Works for All Americans" Act, which became law as an amendment to the 2003 Medicare reform bill, provides for a series of open, public meetings across the nation in which Americans would discuss what they want from a health care system, how much they are willing to pay, and what is realistically achievable.[18] Wyden says, "We need to zero in on health care that is essential, effective and affordable. We need to lay out for people the alternatives and proceed from there."[19] The national conversation would focus on the trade-offs citizens feel prepared to make to get the services people need at a price the nation can afford.

The idea is to frame the debate from the grassroots up. What Wyden and Hatch want to do is to break the pattern where a politician writes a bill in Washington, DC, the interest groups attack what they do not like, the scare tactics frighten the public, and nothing happens. In the case of President Clinton's failed health care reform effort, despite a great deal of public attention, the plan died a procedural death with never a single vote on substance. As originally drafted, Wyden-Hatch reads: "A bill to establish a Citizens Health Care Working Group to facilitate public debate about how to improve the health care system for Americans and to provide for a vote by Congress on the recommendations that are derived from this debate." Wyden says when he tested his idea "in labor halls and chambers of commerce lunches, the idea of being able to force a vote had tremendous appeal."[20] The Citizens Working Group would synthesize what it had learned from the national dialogue, make recommendations to Congress, and if Congress did not act in six months, any member could bring a bill to the floor reflecting the Working Group's recommendations and be guaranteed a vote on it. Unfortunately, the vote requirement was watered down in the final version of Wyden-Hatch to hearings in each congressional committee of jurisdiction within 90 days of the Working Group's report to Congress. Still, Wyden-Hatch is an important step toward improving public discussion and institutionalizing deliberative democracy.[21] The Assembly reform expands on the Wyden-Hatch approach and proposes creating an enduring civic discussion infrastructure crisscrossing the nation's congressional districts.

Finally, in California two Assembly members, one Republican and one Democrat, have teamed up to introduce legislation for a constitutional amendment — to be approved by the voters — to reform the state's election system. Introduced at the beginning of 2006, modeled after similar legislation in British Columbia, ACA 28 would enact the Citizens Assembly on Electoral Reform Act of 2006. It would establish a Citizens Assembly to evaluate potential reforms of the laws governing the electoral and campaign process for the Legislature and statewide elected executive officers. One man and one woman from each of the eighty Assembly districts would be randomly selected to serve in the Citizens Assembly and would meet two to three times a month.[22]

NEAR-TERM POSSIBILITY

The Assembly reform builds on these real-life examples, which indicate a ground swell of interest in reforming American democracy in a direction that is both deliberative and participatory. A decentralized national system of deliberative democracy is within our reach. The goal of the Assembly is nothing less than to create new civic habits and expectations. It would tap into the idealism and frustration that has led millions of citizens to flock to the reform messages of former Governor Howard Dean, Senator John McCain, Ralph Nader, Ross Perot, and others in recent elections. Across the nation many institutions could enlist in the effort, from nonprofit foundations to secretaries of state to civic organizations such as the League of Women Voters and the Coro Foundation.

The purpose of the Assembly is not simply to increase participation; the more fundamental reason is to improve public decisions. It would do so by creating a two-tier system of public opinion. We would have mass opinion surveys *and* the Assembly poll. The media, the political class, and the mass public would closely observe the second, and elites would sometimes side with the Assembly when a serious discrepancy arose between mass opinion and deliberative democracy. Similar to a judicial jury, these individuals would look at the evidence, hear the major arguments, and weigh the different options before deciding. These political discussions would be lively and passionate, but they would be conducted at a higher level than what now passes for political debate on talk radio. Think of the British Parliament writ large. Because people from across the nation would participate, because of a bias toward reasoned debate and informed argument, the opinions of these 43,500 Americans would matter a great deal.

The Assembly would enable Jane and John Q. Public to be players in the national debate. Of course, only a few people could serve on the local assembly. But the opportunity to participate in the lottery selection process would be open to all. In addition and just as important, even though the number of people who actually participate as delegates is small, the degree of separation felt from the federal government would be radically reduced. The chances of average citizens meeting or knowing their congressmen and congresswomen are slim when districts are 650,000-constituents large. But in a 6,500-person ward, the chances increase exponentially for you, your family, and friends to actually know the local assembly delegate. This simple dynamic would stimulate interest and conversation about the great issues of the day.

The Assembly has the virtue of being a reform with near-term possibilities. It could be institutionalized by a vote of Congress and is the sort of motherhood-and-apple pie reform that is difficult for politicians to oppose. "Senator Jones, why are you against the idea of American citizens having the chance to participate in a deliberative and thoughtful discussion about the great issues of the day?" Of course, entrenched interests happy with the current corrupt system would oppose such a reform. But, because the Assembly consciously builds on the framers and is an argument for improving representative—not direct—democracy, straightforward opposition would be difficult. Michael Lind argues in favor of proportional representation (PR) and says it would be relatively easy to institute such a system because changing to a PR system of voting does not require a constitutional change, only a vote of Congress.[23] So too with the Assembly. However, the Assembly would have an easier time getting congressional approval because a system of electronic town halls does not jeopardize the power of the two major parties.

STAGE TWO: THE PEOPLE'S HOUSE

Discussing the proper scale of congressional representation in *Federalist* No. 58, Madison states: "With each successive term of 10 years a census of inhabitants is to be repeated. The unequivocal objects of these regulations are, first, to readjust, from time to time, the apportionment of representatives to the number of inhabitants, under the single exception that each State shall have one representative at least; secondly, to augment the number of representatives at the same periods, under *the sole limitation that the whole number shall not exceed one for every thirty thousand inhabitants.*"[24] Of course, contemporary congressional districts of 1: 30,000 would give us a House of Representatives of 9,380 members. A more realistic alternative would be to triple or quadruple the size of the now 435-member House. But, as previously noted, the trouble with this remedy is that a House of Representatives with more than 1,300 members would be extremely cumbersome to run. Leaving the House at 435 members and creating a representative assembly beneath each member of Congress is a decidedly better solution.

The Assembly would go a long way to bridge democracy's great divide between political elites and common citizens. However, the power of the Assembly is limited because its members would only advise, give their opinion, but not vote. For argument's sake, let's say the Assembly was a rousing success. Would there be a way to give deliberative democracy more power? What if we gave the local assemblies formal voting authority? What would be the benefits of doing so? Enter Stage Two of deliberative democracy with a representative twist.

Adding formal power to the equation, the People's House is the Assembly with a vote. In the People's House, the number of American citizens having an actual vote on federal legislation would expand from a tiny 535 (100 senators and 435 House members) to a larger cross section of nearly 45,000 (44,035 to be exact). In our new multicameral legislature, the face-to-face interaction taking place in the People's House, the House of Representatives, and the Senate would combine with the Internet to create a unique form of face-to-face and digital democracy. In the new legislative branch, the Senate continues to consist of 100 members, two from each state, regardless of population; the House of Representatives would remain at 435 members meeting physically in Washington, DC, and the People's House, made up of the 43,500 delegates, would meet physically in each of the 435 congressional districts and virtually on the Internet.

While each member of the House of Representatives would continue to represent the entire congressional district of 650,000, delegates to the People's House would each represent 6,500 people. One hundred persons per congressional district would be a large enough number to require significant participation from the community, yet still allow face-to-face debate and discussion among delegates. It would be large enough to split into smaller groups focused on specific tasks. For example, in 2005, local assemblies might have formed working groups on the war in Iraq, the president's proposal for Social Security reform, the legality of detaining terror suspects, and America's economic strategy vis-à-vis China and India, to name four hot topics. As with the local assembly, delegates to the local people's house would meet two or three times a month. Each local delegation would be connected electronically to the People's House as a whole—as well as to the House of Representatives and Senate.

Delegates to the People's House would be our representatives—just like the current members of the House and Senate—but these people would be our neighbors. Who would participate in a lottery for the chance of becoming a delegate to the local assembly and thus to represent the local community in the national People's House? People with knowledge and ideas who never thought they would have their voices heard in national government. A cross section of America: small business owners and elementary school teachers, scientists and architects, white-collar managers and factory workers, janitors and sales clerks, police chiefs and financial planners, attorneys and high-tech engineers, secretaries and auto repair servicemen. As a national network of electronic town halls formally connected to Congress, the People's House would act as a way station between average citizens and the political elite.

Pollster Yankelovich says an institution occupying the middle ground between elite insider knowledge and mass ignorance is precisely what the American political system needs, but currently lacks.[25] Living in a nation awash with college-educated talent and blue-collar common sense, both the Assembly and the People's House would tap that resource. Together they would enlist the energy and talent of those interested enough in public affairs to participate in the selection lottery and ask these individuals to represent us in a twenty-first-century town hall. In addition to the knowledge and political judgment gained by those who serve as delegates, there would be a ripple effect through the general population.[26]

SPECIFIC, LIMITED POWER

The key to the People's House reform is giving these elected delegates specific, limited power. Although the People's House would have greater power than the Assembly, there is no need to duplicate the full powers of the House of Representatives and Senate.

First, delegates to the People's House would have the power to deliberate and vote yea or nay on the most important bills that have passed the House of Representatives or the Senate. This veto power would allow members of the People's House to send bills back to the House and the Senate for reconsideration. Either of these houses could override the People's House veto with a three-fifths (60 percent) vote.

Second, in addition to having the power to approve or reject laws, the People's House would have positive powers to help set the legislative agenda. These would include the authority to initiate a limited number of bills in either the House or the Senate, the power to offer amendments to bills under consideration on the floor of the House or the Senate, the ability to pass formal instructions to individual representatives, and the right to draft at-large resolutions addressed to the House of Representatives or Senate as a whole. To avoid undue complexity, the People's House would not be involved in committee deliberations about bills.

Third, the People's House could have a "gate-opening" power to assist in breaking legislative gridlock. A major problem with the American system of government is that so many people have the right to say "no" at so many points along the legislative path. The gate-opening power would help us say "yes." Acting in concert, the local assemblies would be able to force floor votes on vital measures bottled up in committee. This "gate-opening" authority would increase the responsiveness of Congress and act as an important counterbalance to the power wielded by interest groups. Sometimes popular legislation supported by a strong majority of the public never comes to a floor vote. Why? Because committee chairs exercise a power not granted by the Constitution, but developed by Congress during the twentieth century.

Being a delegate to the People's House would be similar to serving on a busy city council. Delegates would keep their full-time jobs; the assembly position would be paid a modest per diem similar to that of other local government bodies. The assembly would formally meet two or three times a month, and the meetings would rotate between four or five locations in the congressional district.[27] Each local assembly would pick a moderator and a secretary to run the meetings, and the main items for discussion would be selected by a national steering committee made up of assembly delegates selected by their colleagues.[28]

The Kettering Foundation and the National Issues Forum (NIF) provide one model for how the discussion process could be structured. In the NIF process, before coming together as a group, each participant is given a briefing booklet on a particular subject—national energy policy, the practice of jailing terrorism suspects, the estate tax. These briefing materials present three or four perspectives on the issue, not always on a left-right party line basis, to give the participants basic information on the subject and get participants thinking about the policy choices involved and the tradeoffs and values that need to be discussed in order to make an informed decision. In addition, depending on the issue, it would be possible for the two major parties to prepare video presentations for the assemblies and for the national steering committee to put together a panel of experts to debate the issue and provide a live video conference for the national audience. It is easy to imagine CSPAN, PBS, or CNN hosting such a debate and televising it for both the assembly delegates and the general public. The steering committee could prepare lists of articles, books, documentaries, and websites for interested delegates to consult. The idea is not for Assembly members to become policy wonks. Rather it is for delegates to get a primer so that they debate from a base of knowledge and not just sound bites.

Each local assembly would elect a president of the assembly who would be similar to the foreman of a jury. The president would be responsible for running the meeting and maintaining order. The person selected would act as a moderator during debate and refrain from interjecting her or his views. Another option would be to invite an outsider—a nonprofit leader, a lawyer, a judge, or a professor—to play the moderator role. The moderator would be responsible for keeping the discussion focused, giving various delegates the chance to speak and determining when enough debate has taken place for a vote to be taken. How would 100 people interact and talk with one another? Again the NIF process is instructive. The moderator would introduce the topic and ask if one or two people want to speak at the beginning of the session. Then the group would break into four smaller groups, and here individuals would talk about their views on the topic, argue and debate their differences, and see if they could reach a consensus on some points. Joining the main group, each small group would present the results of their discussion, and then the group as a whole would discuss and see if there was consensus on some of the issues raised.

Another option is the Athenian model where the topic is known in advance and, when the moderator for that session asks who would like to speak, several of the best orators would present the arguments pro or con. Other members of the assembly would be able to participate in the dialogue, but at least two delegates would make prepared speeches focused on winning the audience. If the Athenians could make this work in an assembly of 6,000, it is certainly possible in an assembly of 100.[29] New Englanders have practiced town-meeting democracy with good results since before the Revolution. Frank Bryan, the author of *Real Democracy: The New England Town Meeting and How it Works,* writes "Town meetings are not public hearings . . . They are legislatures—places for speaking and making law. In effect every citizen of a town is a legislator."[30]

HOW WOULD THE NATIONAL SYSTEM FUNCTION?

A key question facing the People's House as a whole is how to deal with complexity and the sheer number of bills churned out by modern legislative bodies. One answer would be to establish a steering committee to coordinate the work of the 435 local delegations across the nation and link them to Washington, DC. The steering committee would have a function similar to the Council of 500 in ancient Athens that prepared the agenda for the Athenian Assembly and carried out its decisions.[31] Theoretically, the People's House could vote on every bill that passes the House of Representatives. But busy adults with careers and families would not want to waste hours debating trivia. The steering committee, selected from the local delegations, would reduce the workload to a manageable level by focusing attention on the most important bills and issues that affect the nation as a whole.

This fifty-member panel, made up of a cross section of representatives from each region of the United States, would be the administrative brains of the national Assembly and would be used for both the Assembly and the People's House. Its structure and function would be similar to the Democratic and Republican steering and policy committees in the House of Representatives. Where the legislation is trivial, industry specific, or uncontroversial, the steering committee of the People's House would forward those bills to the House of Representatives or the Senate without interference. After a bill has passed the House of Representatives or the Senate, the steering committee would decide to (1) let the bill go directly ahead to the upper or lower house, or (2) send the bill to the full People's House for review, debate, and a vote. When considering a bill passed by the Senate or the House or Representatives, the People's House would work under a time limit to avoid legislative delay.

In addition to selecting which congressional bills to debate, the steering committee would monitor the legislative calendar and coordinate meeting schedules, direct research efforts, and generally set the direction and pace of the agenda for the People's House as a whole. Members of the steering committee would be well-versed on the legislative process and public policy. People who demonstrate leadership in the local assemblies would be natural candidates for the steering committee position. The job would require significantly more energy, attention, and performance than that of a regular delegate to the People's House.[32]

Because the steering committee could conceivably abuse its authority, it is important to give the body power without giving it too much. Care would be taken in the selection of its members. After a year of service, delegates in each local assembly would nominate by secret ballot one individual to take part in a national lottery that would then select the steering committee. Twenty-five people would be selected one year and twenty-five the next year; together they would make up the fifty-person steering committee. Once on the steering committee members would serve a two-year term, with those in their second year having executive power and those in their first year helping with administration, research, and running the Assembly system. Such a seniority system would ensure that those running the national Assembly system and charged with the important responsibility of setting the agenda would come to the job with experience. Individuals could serve only one two-year term as a steering committee member. A selection process such as this would limit the danger of an abuse of power by the people charged with directing the national system.

Apart from the steering committee, how would the 100 people from the congressional district interact with the other 43,500 delegates to the national Assembly? How, exactly, can 43,500 people talk with each other about anything in a coherent way? These are critical questions, and my answer also addresses another concern—how to ensure that discussion gets beyond the parochial biases and concerns of each local jurisdiction.

Just as a single assembly of 100 people can be broken into smaller groups for discussion, so the national system made up of 435 assemblies would be broken into smaller units to make communication and discussion possible. We would break the national assemblies into six groups (Pacific Coast, Rocky Mountains, Midwest, Deep South, Mid-Atlantic, Northeast) and randomly match each local assembly with five groups from other parts of the nation. Similar to the two-party system, this technique would help people understand the great diversity that is America. It is much easier to imagine techniques for constructive dialogue between 600 individuals than 43,500. One way to structure the national dialogue would be for at least one of the monthly meetings to be a session in which the six matched local assemblies join together for discussion of an issue. In a group of 600, oratory skills would become important, and video conferencing would put speakers on display for all to see. It would be difficult to have a single national roundtable of nearly 45,000 people unless, as in the case of Sam Giovoti addressing the Assembly as a whole, we follow the

Athenian model where talented speakers were chosen or self-selected to present one side of the argument. This type of approach would certainly be possible on the great issues of the day.

Structuring the national discussion so that each assembly is forced to confront the diversity and moral pluralism that is modern America would prevent local assemblies from becoming echo chambers of homogeneity.[33] Every delegate in the national Assembly would come from a particular congressional district and thus would see a world colored by personal experience and geography. But national issues and discussions with far-flung assemblies from five other regions would contribute to a gradual education of cosmopolitan sensibilities. Assembly delegates would begin to think far past the local concerns that occupy officeholders on the city council, water board, and board of education. This aspect of the national Assembly would make it quite unlike local government service.

On a day-to-day basis, e-mail chains, chat rooms, and telephone conversations would tie people together across the Assembly network. People would be friends with delegates from the next congressional district and across the country. In addition to conversations online and on the telephone with delegates from different regions, delegates would begin to have internal dialogues with themselves—what Goodin calls "democratic deliberation within"—about the great issues of the day and what can be done about them. Building on models of everyday conversational dynamics, Goodin suggests that people can imagine themselves in the position of other people they have met or talked to or heard about and can ask, "What would they say about this proposal?"[34] The experience of serving on the national Assembly could not help but force people to expand their horizons and see problems from multiple perspectives.

On this point, and on the positive educational impact of the Assembly in general, consider these observations by John Stuart Mill. In *Considerations on Representative Government,* Mill wrote:

> It is not sufficiently considered how little there is in most men's ordinary lives to give any largeness either to their conceptions or to their sentiments . . . in most cases the individual has no access to any person of cultivation much superior to his own. Giving him something to do for the public, supplies, in a measure, all these

deficiencies. If circumstances allow the amount of public duty assigned to him to be considerable, it makes him an educated man. Notwithstanding the defects of the social system and moral ideals of antiquity, the practice of the *dicastery* [judges] and the *ecclesia* [Assembly] raised the intellectual standard of an average Athenian citizen far beyond anything of which there is yet an example in any other mass of men, ancient or modern . . . he is called upon, while so engaged, to weigh interests not his own; to be guided, in case of conflicting claims by another rule than his private partialities; to apply, at every turn, principles and maxims which have for their reason of existence the general good: and he usually finds associated with him in the same work minds more familiarized than his own with these ideas and operations, whose study it will be to supply reasons to this understanding, and stimulation to this feeling for the general good . . . Where this school of public spirit does not exist, scarcely any sense is entertained that private persons . . . owe any duties to society except to obey the laws and submit to the government.[35]

SELECTION OF DELEGATES

National Assembly delegates could be selected by election, by random sample, or by lot. Election by ward (neighborhoods and cities within the congressional district), instead of at-large across the entire congressional district, would keep campaign costs low, nurture a sense of community, and keep representatives close to the voters. Small districts would encourage campaigns based on precinct walking, lawn signs, and coffee chats and enable low-budget candidates to compete effectively. Shoe leather and persistence often beats slick mailers and money in small wards. Campaigns would be conducted at the same time as regular congressional elections; piggybacking would allow voters to focus on the House of Representatives and the People's House at the same time while holding down costs for the Registrar of Voters. Thus, in addition to voting for their representative to the House of Representatives, every citizen would vote for one candidate to represent their small 6,500-person ward in the local assembly or the local people's house. That would be one vote for a representative in the House, one vote for a delegate in the national Assembly or the People's House.

While elections are the standard way of selecting officials in American politics, there are distinct drawbacks to this approach. First, there are already so many local elections that voters may pay little attention to yet another contest. Although we can hope that constituents will take the time to learn about the candidates running for local assembly, in races beneath the U.S. senate and governor most voters know little about the candidates other than party affiliation. In most congressional districts, races for Assembly delegate would piggyback on the congressional race and turn into conventional elections featuring parties, advertisements, campaign financing, ideological interest groups, and the rest. Although the small size of the districts would allow for a personal touch, small size is not an ironclad protection given the politics of city wards in U.S. history. On balance, the Assembly would work best apart from the general political machine. If our current system were not so corrupt, then ward elections might make sense. But, as it stands, money and party machines would too easily dominate. The modern technique of a random sample or the ancient device of a lottery is a better option.

A second way to select delegates would be by stratified random sample. A selection task force would choose from a stratified random sample of 500 men and 500 women in each congressional district. Each eligible person whose name is drawn would be given the opportunity to indicate their interest in becoming an Assembly delegate. Local selection meetings would be held in each congressional district to inform interested individuals about the scope, duties, and responsibilities of the citizen Assembly. From this pool, 50 men and 50 women would be randomly selected to serve in the local assembly for that congressional district.[36]

A final alternative is selection by lot. In each congressional district, every competent adult would have his or her name placed in a lottery pool. The resulting delegate pool would provide a wide cross section of the community—rich and poor, young and old, representation by ethnicity and race. The mentally ill, noncitizens, and ex-felons would be excluded.[37] Delegate selection by lot, with individuals automatically included in the lottery unless they request to be excluded, would result in a large delegate pool roughly matching the demographic mix of the district.

Most social scientists would argue for selection by random sample because a great deal hinges on the statistical representativeness of the delegates selected. Otherwise, why would any such system be regarded as legitimate? Viewed as an imperative, having a statistically representative sample could raise the need for compulsory service. But before we automatically endorse the modern random sample as the obvious tool by which to select delegates, we should recall how often we accept as legitimate situations that are not perfect statistical representations. Three examples suffice.

Was the Athenian Assembly a perfect statistical sample of the 50,000 to 60,000 citizens who made up the demos? No. The roughly 6,000 male citizens who gathered at the Pnyx, a hillside near the Acropolis, were, on balance, older and more urban than the population of citizens taken as a whole. Farmers, for example, had a more difficult time attending than did those who lived in Athens itself. And the composition of 6,000 in attendance changed with each session so that the quorum that decided one issue was not the audience that decided the next. And what about the famed U.S. Constitutional Convention of 1787? Were the 55 well-to-do white males who attended the secret sessions that drafted the Constitution a perfect representative sample of the population at large? Hardly. Yet few today view the Constitution as illegitimate. Quite the contrary, it is the holy grail of American politics. What about contemporary politics? We rely on random sample techniques when doing national polls, but the dirty little secret in the polling community is that many people have unlisted phone numbers, and many more decline to participate when contacted. Both the stratified random sample and lottery are acceptable methods of delegate selection. Both would ensure that a wide cross section of the population is represented in the Assembly. Although the case for a random sample is well-known, the beauty of a lottery is less understood. Drawing on the experience of ancient Athens, I develop the following argument.

Although the delegate lottery pool would not be an exact statistical representation of the congressional district, it would be a rough approximation. As important as this rough approximation is, it is equally important that the 100 people chosen at random as delegates indeed want to serve. The goal is for those selected to take the responsibility seriously. In Athens, the jurors and the Council of 500 selected by lot knew their neighbors, and the general community would be observing their conduct. The same would be true of our modern assemblies.

About Athens, Manin writes, "Those who did not feel up to filling a post successfully could easily avoid being selected." The arrangement had the "effect of giving every citizen who *deemed himself* fit for office an opportunity of acceding to the magistracies."[38] Say we placed 500,000 adults from a congressional district into a lottery pool and 30 percent opted out. We would still have a large pool. We may wish it were otherwise, but it is clear that we live in a political culture in which many people choose not to participate. Although the Assembly and the People's House would not change this situation in any dramatic fashion, they would offer individual citizens the chance to participate in a powerful, significant, and consequential manner. As this fact is better understood, lottery participation would increase. Today, voter participation in local elections often hovers around 20 percent. If, say, 70 percent of the public decided to participate in the lottery, it would be a much more equitable method of choosing representatives.

The lottery is a good selection method for several practical reasons. First, selection by lot would help counter fears of local assemblies being overrun by passionate well-organized factions (Christian evangelicals, environmentalists, ethnic groups, the Chamber of Commerce, for example) or local assembly candidates being given secret donations by key interest groups. Second, people lead busy lives and running for office—even a minor office—is a major undertaking. Many people who would be outstanding assembly delegates would be unwilling to submit themselves and their families to a campaign, knowing that the expense, time, and sometimes public embarrassment are often spent in a losing effort. For most adults, running for office is not a rational choice. Selection by lot makes these people eligible for office holding.

Third, delegates chosen by lot would be able to focus on doing the job required without having to think and act like a candidate. Although there is an electoral connection between elected representatives and their constituencies, there also would be a connection between an assembly delegate, selected by lot, and the particular ward of the congressional district where that delegate lives. We could divide the congressional district into 100 equal 6,500-person wards (echoes of Jefferson), drawing the lines to follow neighborhood and city boundaries as much as possible, and then hold a lottery drawing of the adult citizens in that ward. Here we would have the most basic democratic connection—you are one of us, stand for us, and in helping to make the laws of the community, do your best to speak for what we believe and think (echoes of the Anti-Federalists). In the Assembly system, a person selected as a representative would not have to change his or her personality to become a candidate. Instead, assembly delegates can remain the persons they always were.

A fourth practical advantage is familiarity. Americans have a high regard for selection by lot because it is how juries are chosen in the United States. The American jury system is one of the most respected and highly regarded governmental institutions. It is admired at home and abroad because of the sense of fairness, seriousness of purpose, and probity that jurors bring to their task. Compared to elections, the lot is closely connected in people's minds with the ideal of virtuous public service. However much we grouse when we are called for jury duty, we respect the institution and believe that people serving on juries strive to be upright and fair in deciding cases.

As a civic institution, the jury has undergone a transformation from traditional republicanism to modern republicanism. Until recently, jurors were chosen by a "key man" system in which a local selectman had the discretion to pick jurors of "exemplary moderation and wisdom." In practice, however, the search for jurors with these qualities led to a systematic underrepresentation of minorities, the poor, the young, and women. In a 1975 case, *Taylor v. Louisiana,* the U.S. Supreme Court struck down Louisiana's exclusion of women jurors and ruled that a jury should represent "a fair cross section of the community."[39] To implement this ruling, much of the United States has adopted a lottery system for jury selection. Here again, we see the shift from a classic republicanism, with its elite bias, to an egalitarian republican vision, where everyone has an equal chance to be selected and serve.

Given that the jury works well in the justice system, it makes sense to extend the idea to the political world. We do this to a certain extent with grand juries and citizen commissions. For example, Dahl recommends the establishment of a system of policy juries to study complex issues. He says a thousand persons could for a year study a single complex issue—national, state, or local. The group would meet regularly, investigate the issue, hold hearings, and issue a report. Standing for the public, this mini-populus "would reflect public opinion at a higher level of competence." Dahl says a central task of these policy juries would be to "assess risks, uncertainties, and trade-offs."[40] Both the policy jury and the Assembly fit what Dahl calls the "Strong Principle of Equality. The Strong Principle holds that a "substantial portion of adults are adequately qualified to govern themselves" and this is based, in part, on the assumption that "no person is more likely than yourself to be a better judge of your own good or interest or to act to bring it about."[41]

ELECTION BY LOT AT ATHENS

The philosophical reasons supporting selection by lot go deeper than the practical and familiar. When we understand these we begin to see why lot is a powerful and valuable democratic tool. I begin with a brief description of how the lot was used in ancient Athens and then consider the value of lot in terms of representation and equality while meeting the objection concerning talent. Athens of the fifth and fourth centuries B.C. was a direct democracy, and every male citizen was automatically eligible to attend the Assembly (*ekklēsia*), which met at least forty times during the year. An outdoor gathering that consisted of the first 6,000 men to arrive at the Pnyx, the composition of the Assembly varied at each meeting. The leading economic, intellectual, and cultural center of Greece, the Athens of Pericles' time struggled with issues of wealth and class conflict. It was not a tiny polity where everyone met face-to-face and harmony reigned.[42] In Athenian democracy, although the assembled citizens were the fulcrum of power, never did the approximately 40,000 to 60,000 Athenian citizens come together in a single body.[43]

At the Assembly, every citizen had the right to speak and address his peers. To Greeks, the universal right to speak (*isēgoria*) was synonymous with democracy. When individuals arrived at the Pnyx, they knew that each meeting of the Assembly was complete in itself. It was its own dramatic play with star players and a beginning, a middle, and an end. "The normal procedure was for a proposal to be introduced, debated and either passed (with or without amendments) or rejected in a single session."[44] Every speech, every argument aimed at persuasion. Decisions were made by a simple majority vote—a raising of hands—of those who attended.

In addition to the Assembly, Athenian democracy relied on other governmental institutions and here selection was accomplished by lot, except in a few cases such as the election of generals. The administrative functions of government, the magistracies, the Council of 500, and the courts, were all positions filled by lot. In his classic *Election by Lot at Athens,* James Headlam writes, "It is scarcely too much to say that the whole administration of the state was in the hands of men appointed by lot: the serious work of the law courts, of the execution of the laws, of police, of public finance, in short of every department (with the exception of the actual commands in the army) was done by officials so chosen."[45]

The Athenians were well aware that lot appoints people indiscriminately, yet they used the system successfully for 200 years. Why? First, lot exemplifies the principle of equality and gave every citizen a reasonable chance of exercising a public function. The Athenians were deeply committed to the principle of rotation and believed that if people had experience in both the roles of ruler and ruled this would lead to a just and successful polity. In *The Politics,* Aristotle writes, "One principle of liberty is for all to rule and be ruled in turn."[46] The experience of being an average citizen who also occasionally took on a position of authority meant "they were able to visualize how their orders would affect the governed, because they knew, having experienced it themselves, what it felt like to be governed and to have to obey."[47]

Second, the Athenians understood that elections have an aristocratic bias in which people with money, a family name, or exceptional talent stand out from the rest. By contrast, they identified lot with democracy. "For example," wrote Aristotle, "the appointment of magistrates by lot is thought to be democratic, and the election of them oligarchical; democratic again when there is no property qualification, oligarchical when there is."[48] Today, running for Congress requires a de facto property qualification. If a candidate lacks access to wealthy contributors—which is most easily had if one is in a lucrative profession or rich—being able to run a serious and competitive race is rare.[49] Aristotle continues, "We should rather say that democracy is the form of government in which the free are rulers, and oligarchy in which the rich; it is only an accident that the free are the many and the rich are the few."[50]

Using lot to select those in administration meant there was less likelihood that the Council of 500 would challenge the authority of the Assembly. In fact, the Socratic criticism of Athenian democracy for lacking a captain at the helm misses the point.[51] The Athenians used elections to select their generals and sometimes their finance ministers. But they were purposefully cautious about turning authority over to elites and experts. The point of selection by lot was to prevent those with talent and expertise from taking power away from the Assembly. In modern electoral systems in the period following the vote, the people lack direct control over the fate of the nation. By contrast, in a pure democracy, the people rule themselves as a king does a monarchy. They make all the decisions and, to keep authority in their hands, they must not create powerful officials. As Aristotle knew, the demos, like the tyrant, "must prevent any individuals or institutions from acquiring too much power."[52] Choosing the Athenian administration by lot accomplished this aim and ensured the primacy of the Assembly.

Thus, in ancient Athens, lot protected the sovereign authority of the Assembly. In modern America, lot would add a pure democratic element to an otherwise elitist representative government. Selection by lot to the national Assembly would provide "the People" a modicum of pure democratic power to counter the inevitable corruption of a large republic. Elections are inegalitarian because they do not provide every individual seeking office an equal chance of success. They are aristocratic because they favor prominent individuals. True, the people en masse have the ultimate authority to choose whom they wish as their leaders. But representative democracy has an undeniable oligarchic dimension that is amplified in large republics. The question becomes one of balance.[53] The American system has plenty of elites and experts. What we need is a check on the oligarchy of money, power, and meritocracy. Using lot as a selection method for the local assemblies would help counter the advantages that wealth and privilege grant in the modern political economy.

Using lot to select members of the Assembly would add an Anti-Federalist understanding of representation to our constitutional mix.[54] The Anti-Federalists, Manin says, "formulated with great clarity, a plausible, consistent and powerful conception of representation."[55] Their understanding was fundamentally at odds with that of the Federalists, and the difference between the two helps explain the gulf that separated the Founders. The *Federalist* authors sought representatives who stood out because they were part of a region's elite and therefore different from and superior to their constituents.[56] By contrast, the Anti-Federalists insisted that, if representative government were to be genuinely popular as opposed to elitist, "representatives should be as close to their constituents as possible: living with them and sharing their circumstances."[57] The People's House understands representation in just this way.[58] For Madison and Hamilton, power was to be exercised by men having the most wisdom and most virtue and, of course, this meant those of talent in the upper class with wealth and property. The Anti-Federalists diverged with the Federalists not on the need for elections but in defending a popular and non-elite form of representation.

The Constitution of 1789 institutionalized the Federalist understanding of representation. The People's House would add the Anti-Federalist understanding to the Constitutional framework. Yet how much of an effect would lot and a "resemblance" conception of representation have when we are talking about 43,500 delegates out of a population of nearly 300 million? Obviously, we cannot hope to have Athenian style democracy in the modern world. That time has passed and is not our goal. Instead we aim to reinvent representative democracy and reduce the gap between citizens and their representatives. The size of our democracy is far too great for the direct democracy the Athenians enjoyed. But, as a second best option, we can give every American citizen an equal right to participate in government.

Today we have an equal right to consent to the power of our rulers. We have an equal right to participate in politics but not in government itself. In the People's House only a few would be picked, but everyone would have an equal probability of being chosen. The People's House grants the most important democratic right—a right that Americans do not now enjoy—an equal right to participate in government and, if chosen as an Assembly delegate, an equal right to speak (*isēgoria*) in the national Assembly, the People's House. By adding a lot-selected national Assembly to our representative menu, regular people would take their turn at ruling and having a voice in the government. In sum, the Assembly is about power and participation from the inside.

5.
Three Benefits

Writing about democracy ancient and modern, M. I. Finley observed, "Public apathy and political ignorance are a fundamental fact today, beyond any possible dispute; decisions are made by political leaders, not by popular vote, which at best has only occasional veto power after the fact. The issue is whether this state of affairs is, under modern conditions, a necessary and desirable one, *or whether new forms of popular participation . . . need to be invented.*"[1] A new form of participation, the national Assembly would be a representative cross section of the people as a whole whose existence would fundamentally alter American politics. Currently, citizens vote for a candidate or a platform and then the power flows to the political leaders chosen. It is the president and 535 members of Congress who make the decisions on whether to go to war, whether to prepare for natural disasters, whether to increase the deficit, and so forth. Giving the People's House a vote on legislation redirects the flow, restores an element of popular power to the equation, and institutionalizes the popular energy that Jefferson saw as the soul of the republic.

Paradoxically, we are not talking about massive change. The Assembly is a modest and practical proposal; the People's House is more ambitious. The technological challenge is minimal, and only a small fraction of the total population would be able to participate in any one year. Still, every adult would have an equal chance of selection in the Assembly lottery and that would affect their outlook on—and possibly their engagement with— the political system.[2] The rest of the political system would remain unchanged. However, this modest change would have a profound effect on how the system works and political culture. A national Assembly chosen by lot would allow a true cross section of Americans to have a voice in debating the nation's priorities.[3]

The payoff of the Assembly is the promotion of civic majorities and a new understanding of representative government. The Assembly is designed to make civic majorities possible. When public deliberations are entrusted to a national assembly representing the entire citizenry, it is more likely that the debates will affirm the general good, rather than the specific interests of a powerful lobbying group or cronies of powerful politicians. It would therefore protect the citizens at large from both the danger of domination and the hazard of paying taxes to a government benefiting private interest more than the public's greater welfare.[4] The goal of the Assembly is to get beyond the interest group pluralist model with its focus on groups competing for limited resources but few of the competing groups thinking about priorities or trade-offs. Our representatives in the House and Senate are supposed to act as judges of the competing interests, and to some extent they do, but because today's legislators are so dependent on a constant supply of campaign cash they are hardly neutral when it comes time to evaluate who gets what.

A republic—especially on a large scale—must combine elements of both oligarchy and democracy. In Schumpeter's minimalist theory, elites rule but are chosen by the people in elections. The current system is biased toward oligarchy because elites have a great deal of freedom of action between ballot days. To amplify the democratic aspect and gain more control over the elites, Machiavelli recommends creating "an unambiguously popularly dominated republic."[5] The Assembly, based on extending representation downward in the system and recovering the Anti-Federalist passion for participation and less-distant representation, would push the American system in an *intelligent* populist direction.[6]

Institutions and social systems are heavily dependent on norms. As capitalism depends on social norms for the invisible hand to work properly, so polyarchy (the rule of many) depends on republican norms of citizenship for the procedural forms to function correctly. Connected to power and knowledge, delegates would have a reason to exercise republican citizenship and an arena in which to do it. They would have the ability to form the civic majorities that Madison saw as the key to democracy's future success. Instead of Mr. Smith going to Washington, the Assembly reform would bring Washington to thousands of Mr. and Ms. Smiths across the nation and give a small, but critical, dose of power back to the people in their own communities. During the 1960s, radicals railed against the system but never figured out how to combine participatory democracy with representative government. In the twenty-first century, the People's House puts the puzzle together.

A virtual national Assembly would strengthen American politics in three specific, critical ways. No other reform on the horizon offers as many benefits while staying true to Madison's vision of large-scale democracy: First, it would give the public back its voice by creating opportunities for intelligent participation. Glendon writes: "Self-government not only requires certain civic skills (deliberation, compromise, consensus-building, civility, reason-giving), but *theaters* in which those arts can be meaningfully exercised."[7] Second, it would curb the excessive influence of special interests that have gained strength in an era of consultants and weak local parties. We desperately need a reform that will counteract the tendency of proliferating interest groups to clog the arteries of government and prevent sane solutions to pressing problems.[8] Because of its Madisonian focus on promoting civic majorities aimed at the broad common good, this reform is one of the few on the horizon with the potential to counter special-interest muscle. Third, it provides the public with a mechanism to break legislative gridlock. For decades, committee chairs have held life-and-death power over legislation. This power is not in the Constitution; it evolved as the Speaker and the Senate Majority leader were forced to share power with other legislators at the start of the twentieth century. It is time to add a gate-opening power to give the public the option of forcing a floor vote on popular bills locked in committee.

The Assembly and the People's House are designed to boost both participation *and* efficiency. Let us examine these benefits in more detail. Although a greater voice for citizens and curbing special interest power apply equally to both the Assembly and the People's House, the argument about breaking legislative gridlock via a committee gate-opening power applies only to the People's House.

GIVING THE PUBLIC BACK ITS VOICE

In the modern world, power is both local and distant. A national town hall would give us a way of touching distant centers of power and promoting deliberative discussion. Traditionally, average citizens have participated in "self-rule" through city councils and school boards. Yet this mode of civic participation is, by itself, no longer adequate for the modern world. Many local issues have their origins or remedies across the nation or around the world. Local unemployment can depend on state and national policy decisions. Environmental hazards often are generated by corporations with headquarters far removed, and their cleanup depends on state and federal budgetary priorities. Traffic problems on local streets head toward gridlock depending on regional and national transportation plans. The list goes on. Modern Americans must live with the reality of centralization, hierarchy, and national elites, but we need not capitulate to forces that currently rob us of our democratic sovereignty.

In the current system, very few people can hope to be elected to Congress. Adding a national town hall to the system would give many more Americans the opportunity to serve. For a few years during busy lives, people would bring their energy, attention, creativity, and energy to bear on public affairs. In this era of politics by consultant and checkbook, many people with education, ideas, and interest are given very little to do. Imagine, at a young age, realizing that you might one day be chosen to serve as an Assembly delegate. With the Assembly lottery taking place every two years, people would have many chances of being chosen over the course of their adult lives. Gradually, Americans would begin to know friends, neighbors, and relatives both close to home and across the nation who were serving as delegates in the national Assembly. For youngsters this would be a strong signal that there was value to becoming involved, competent citizens. We could reverse our present predicament, eloquently stated by Christopher Lasch:

> In the "age of information" the American people are notoriously ill informed. The explanation for this paradox is obvious, though seldom offered: Having been effectively excluded from public debate on the grounds of their incompetence, most Americans no longer have any use of the information inflicted on them in such large amounts . . . it is debate itself, and debate alone, that gives rise to the desire for usable information. In the absence of democratic exchange, most people have no incentive to master the knowledge that would make them capable citizens.[9]

Grafting deliberative democracy with a representative dimension on to the present system would open up "new public spaces where citizens meet, argue, decide and meet again." It would be a busy, assertive democracy of neighborhood gatherings with a most unusual twist—national influence.[10] Ordinary people would be transformed into active, attentive citizens who read newspapers; understand the major issues; and can find Brazil, China, and Iraq on the map. After several months of Assembly service all would gain a basic understanding of American government; some would develop a sophisticated grasp.

A national Assembly would dramatically increase opportunities for citizens to do their civic duty by serving their country. Yet it would be a mistake to confuse the Assembly with traditional notions of participatory democracy.[11] Instead, it builds on Lippmann's insight that asking the average citizen to be well-informed on numerous policy issues is an impossible ideal in our complex modern world.[12] We would ask a representative cross section of the community to think and act for us. These people would not be omnicompetent citizens, but they quickly would become more informed than the average person.

In addition, the Assembly also would help the public at large appreciate the laws that govern society. Early in his political career, Lincoln gave a speech to the Young Men's Lyceum of Springfield, Illinois, in which he spoke of the importance of teaching citizens "reverence for the laws," saying this was the surest way to maintain a peaceful and fair society even in the face of difficult economic and social problems.[13] For democracy to work well, we must not only be equal under the law, we must also be able to understand ourselves as the authors of the laws that bind us.[14] Given enormous scale, it is difficult for people to do this under the current constitutional structure; the leap from the average citizen to the floor of the state legislature and the House of Representatives is too great a distance. A national Assembly would help citizens embrace the nation's laws as their own.

The small face-to-face scale of the local assembly would make it likely that a person would have a friend or an acquaintance who knew the assembly delegate. Delegates would talk to their friends and work colleagues and, like ripples in a lake, political conversations would spread out in ever-enlarging circles, engaging more people. This circle of conversation follows from the Assembly having a "talking" function more like the British Parliament or the traditional town meeting than the House and Senate with their committee focus.

The insights of Yankelovich and congressional scholar Nelson Polsby help explain the important niche that the Assembly would fill in our political life. Our current system has no mechanism by which to cultivate the more elevated, more considered, opinion Yankelovich calls public judgment.[15] For public opinion to actually mean something on complex issues, we need the constructive, informed dialogue that the Assembly reform is designed to foster. In addition, the Assembly would provide a healthy balance to the "law-centered" approach to government that characterizes American legislatures. Open debate in a public forum is the principal method for conducting business in classical British parliamentary and New England town meetings. Polsby refers to this as "arena" style democracy because legislators or citizens face each other and give reasons for their positions. [16]

American national government retreats from the arena debate in two directions. In the first, individual citizens are given the vote and have the option of joining the interest group of their choice to promote a cause dear to their heart. We write letters to our elected officials and individual checks to the National Rifle Association or the Sierra Club to assuage our guilt at not knowing how else to participate. In the opposite direction, American legislatures have lawmaking powers not found in parliamentary systems. Congress is special precisely because it has the power to make laws—with or without the executive branch's consent. In contrast to the British Parliament, most of the "action" in the American Congress takes place in committee meetings where laws are drafted. As a young scholar, Woodrow Wilson sat dumbfounded in the visitors' gallery, staring at the empty Senate floor. There was no one there; they were locked away in committee.[17] The Assembly would unlock the door and encourage the public to join the debate.

Finally, the local assemblies would help foster a sense of community in cities and towns across the nation. Designed to occupy the vacant civic space once held by local political parties and town meeting government, the local assembly would weave a web of personal relationships complementing other associations at the local level. Students of modern society insist it works best if market economies and democratic governments are combined with a robust associational life among citizens. Civic volunteer groups, neighborhoods, PTAs, religious groups, schools, unions, and youth sports organizations all fill the space between the solitary individual and the megastructures of market and the state.[18] The local assembly would provide another place where people could come together to discuss their common future.

CURBING SPECIAL INTERESTS

Next, the deliberative assemblies would curb the excessive influence of special interest groups while promoting decisions made in the broad public welfare. The Assembly reform counters the power of narrow factions by encouraging the development of just those civic majorities that lie at the heart of Madison's political vision. Extending the sphere of legislation beyond the House and the Senate to a national network of local assemblies would make it more difficult for business lobbyists, PACs, and special interests to dominate legislation. Although it easy to bash special interests, organized groups are a time-tested and effective method by which people lobby a democratic government. Since 1960, they have taken on increasing importance as traditional parties and mass mobilization for elections have faded. Steven J. Rosenstone and John Mark Hansen report,

> at precisely the same time that participation in elections was sliding, Americans were becoming increasingly likely to take part in other kinds of political activities. Whereas only 5 percent of the adult population wrote a letter to a representative or senator in 1961, 16 percent did so in 1983. Over the same period political organizations of all kinds—interest groups, community organizations, and political

action committees—swelled in numbers at both the local and national levels.[19]

As candidates now speak directly to voters through direct mail and television ads, so interest groups use the new campaign technologies to pinpoint members, raise money and lobby legislators. Although American voting rates are lower than in Europe, the United States has "some of the world's most numerous, most active and most powerful interest groups."[20]

Do all Americans participate equally in interest group politics? No. As with voting, there is a heavy bias toward those who are affluent and well educated. "People who have better educations, better incomes, more experience, and greater senses of political competence are better able to meet the costs of political involvement."[21] In addition, people with a direct interest in a particular governmental policy are more likely to get involved and lobby for the action they want the government to take. In a way that was not as true when parties were stronger, politics today is dominated by the most advantaged. In terms of political parties and interest groups, the clout of the middle class, the working class, and the poor lags far behind that of the affluent. Part of the reason is that successful interest groups often depend on institutional or personal patrons.[22]

The Assembly and the People's House would help rebalance our political equilibrium. First, the Assembly would be a demographic slice of America economically and socially from top to bottom and across ethnic and racial lines from white to brown to black to all the shades in between. The composition of the Assembly would be a representation of the United States as a whole and, in terms of the voting-age population, would not be biased toward any one particular group or interest. Second, because no particular group would dominate the outlook of the Assembly, all views would get a hearing, but in contrast to the House and the Senate, the advantages that particular groups have in gaining access to legislators (especially big business and wealthy contributors and to a certain extent unions, environmental groups, and other well organized groups) would be less of a factor. Unlike interest groups, the Assembly would be tasked with looking at the big picture, whether in energy policy or health care or transportation policy. The Assembly would debate priorities and trade-offs and focus on the enlightened pursuit of broad public good. In their public roles, people take on the norms and point of view required to do the job asked of them.[23] There is substantial research showing that voters and public officials internalize "public spirited conceptions" of their particular responsibilities. In the Assembly, delegates would be asked to think about the issues and to make decisions in the spirit of Madison's civic majorities.

Finally, by extending the sphere of representation downward, thus enlarging the sphere of discussion, we would counterbalance the power of special interest groups by following E. E. Schattschneider's ideas on political power.[24] Increasing the number of people involved in decision making changes its dynamics. Schematically, think of a circle divided unevenly between two parties. If X and Y are in conflict and X has 75 percent of the support, then Y loses. That is, unless Y can increase the number of people involved in the discussion. Drawing a larger circle around the first circle expands the "scope of conflict" by giving more people a voice in the decision. If the newcomers are more persuaded by the arguments of Y than of X, Y wins. In the Assembly system, instead of focusing on making campaign contributions to a few key legislators in Washington, DC (or the state capital), lobbyists for corporations, environmental groups, and unions would all be forced to make their cases to a broad cross section of the informed public—the 43,500 members of the Assembly. The Assembly would expand the scope of discussion and debate beyond the Washington beltway.

Madison argued that extending the geographic scale of politics would make it more difficult for small factional groups "to discover their own strength and to act in unison with each other."[25] Yet, it is clear that the problem of faction continues to exist, assisted by modern technology. Today, computer-generated letters, e-mail, and faxes connect people with similar interests. Fitting Madison's definition of faction, many of these groups have goals averse to the interests of the whole. By his logic, to accomplish their goals, these groups should be obligated to form coalitions with other groups and become less extreme in their views. When groups are trying to promote change, they often end up taking this path. But many special interest groups, the National Rifle Association for example, spend the bulk of their energy blocking legislation. To block change, they do not have to reach out and broaden their views. This is a serious flaw in Madison's scheme. Adding the Assembly network to our political structure would change the calculus of decision. True, the best organized and funded interest groups would still have an advantage in communicating their message to Assembly delegates, just as they do today to members of Congress and the mass public. But, and this is critical, Assembly delegates would be far more informed than the mass public while being far less susceptible than current legislators to lobbying pressure and campaign contributions.[26]

Dahl and others argue against the idea of a power elite.[27] Neither an elite nor the majority rule on matters of specific policy. Instead, specific policies are selected by a process of "minorities rule"—by those interest groups, politicians, and administrators most concerned with that issue—be it education or transportation or taxes.[28] Policy is made primarily by the interest groups, policy elites, and issue networks working in a particular area. In each field—banking, defense, education, health, transportation—people who are specialists dominate the debate. For pluralists, government is a neutral umpire that sets the rules for the political struggle and assures access to the most effectively organized groups.

In *The End of Liberalism* (1969), Theodore Lowi offered a biting critique of interest group liberalism: "Parceling out policy-making power to the most interested parties tends strongly to destroy political responsibility. A program split off with special imperium to govern itself is not merely an administrative unit. It is a structure of power with impressive capacities to resist central political control."[29] For example, in the iron triangle that is agriculture policy, legislators develop favorable policies for financial and electoral support; farmers and agribusiness exchange votes for programs, and bureaucrats administer programs that the industry and representatives want.[30] Issue networks made up of technical specialists, journalists, administrators, and policy entrepreneurs dominate different policy arenas.[31]

In government by interest group, those most interested in and most affected by the policy are most heavily involved in crafting legislation. Given human nature and a need for a division of labor, this is to be expected. The problem, as Lowi pointed out, is that a wider perspective, one that the Assembly would help supply, is required as well. When the government primarily reacts to the pressure of interest groups, other important priorities and needs are overlooked, underfunded, and ignored.

When political parties ensure public involvement and a wide perspective on society's goals, "minorities rule" can work. But when parties are primarily vehicles for fund-raisers and mercenary consultants, "minorities rule" becomes a recipe for "hogs feeding at the trough," to use David Stockman's phrase. Each group grabs as much as it can, and the result is a gradual paralysis of the government.[32] Over the past quarter century, both Democrats and Republicans have transformed the pluralist conception of interest-group politics from minorities rule to a Gucci Gulch system of influence peddling.[33] The Abramoff scandal reveals lobbying influence pushed to the extreme. Corporate welfare is not just a catch phrase; it is a K Street reality. Today proliferating interest groups demand programs that benefit the few and clog the arteries of government. A bloated, ossified government with no ability to respond to new challenges helps only those already hooked up to the spigot.[34] In *Government's End,* Jonathan Rauch writes, "the American government probably has evolved into about what it will remain: a sprawling, largely self-organized structure that is 10 percent to 20 percent under the control of the politicians and voters and 80 percent to 90 percent under the control of the countless thousands of client groups."[35] Rauch delves into the paradox that "the rise of government activism has immobilized activist government" because although Washington can create programs it is very difficult to change or kill them. The result is a lack of dexterity and a growing incapacity to confront and deal with new problems in a creative fashion. Flexibility, not size, not money, is the key to effective government, says Rauch.[36]

The problem for politicians who want to make government an active, creative agent of change and good works is that most legislators recognize that they "operate in a political system in which any serious attempts at change produce instant, well-organized opposition from the small minority who are hurt by the change . . . this is the heart of America's dilemma today."[37] The factional problem that Madison thought he solved is alive and well in Washington, DC, and the state capitals. Narrowly focused interest groups work hard to dominate the agenda.

Rauch's perceptive diagnosis demonstrates why the health of the political system depends on finding a way to create and nurture civic majorities.[38] The Assembly is one of the few reforms with the potential of curbing interest-group pluralism gone haywire. Pork-barrel spending will always be a part of politics. But a national town hall would help set priorities, occasionally put a brake on wasteful projects, and generally assist focusing attention and funds on the problems of the present and future, instead of on the past. The Assembly might also help us recognize the difference between consumption and investment spending. As Dionne writes, "The current deficit argument is a dead end because it treats all government spending as the same, much as if an individual treated the purchase of expensive restaurant meals and investments in a home or a business as being equivalent uses of money."[39]

COUNTERING GRIDLOCK

A third major benefit of the virtual national Assembly is an improvement in governmental efficiency. Most reformers insist on choosing either increased participation or governance. It need not be a zero-sum choice. In contrast to parliamentary systems, passing important legislation often takes decades in the American system, not only because of the separation of powers, but also because of the gridlock power of committee chairs who can stonewall or accelerate legislation. The power of committee chairs is a relatively new phenomenon; the U.S. Constitution is silent on how the legislature should be organized. In the nineteenth century, legislative leaders were all-powerful and the committee chairs relatively weak.

A dramatic change came in 1910 when House members rebelled against Speaker Joe Cannon's autocratic methods and shifted legislative power to committee chairs who earned their position via seniority. In the mid-twentieth century, committees served as the gatekeepers of legislation. In the early 1970s, the seniority system in the House of Representatives was modified and the speaker made more powerful, and today, under the GOP, party leaders direct the flow of legislation. Still, particularly in the Senate, the power of committee chairs remains potent. Chairpersons by themselves or with the support of the leadership often delay or kill bills that the majority of the public supports. The power of a stubborn committee chair was well demonstrated during the Clinton administration when Senator Jesse Helms refused to hear testimony on the proposed nomination of Governor William Weld as U.S. Ambassador to Mexico, thus dooming the appointment.

Many more bills are proposed than are passed and many die in committee. Often this is how it should be. However, there are instances when a well-drafted bill on an important issue is favored by both a majority of the legislature and a majority of the public, yet remains stuck in committee.[40] In cases like these, the American system could use a push in a civic-majority direction. The People's House would provide the public with a mechanism to break legislative gridlock via a committee gate-opening power. Gate-opening power would allow the public, via their People's House delegates, to insist on a floor vote on vital measures. The gate-opening power, a potent check and balance against intransigent committee chairs and excessive special-interest leverage, would go into effect if 50 percent of the local assemblies across the nation vote in favor of an at-large resolution regarding a particular bill. When the People's House votes this way, a bill that was previously stalled in committee would be reported to the floor of the House of Representatives or the Senate for debate and a roll call vote.

There is a democratic logic behind the gate-opening power. We are simply asking the question: If you are winning in a small arena, where campaign donations have maximum leverage, can you win in the larger sphere, too? Following Madison and Schattschneider, gate-opening is another example of encouraging civic majority decisions by widening the sphere of discussion. When we force the matter out of the committee to the floor, we spark debate. The crux of democracy is articulate reason as opposed to brute force. Committee chairs and special interests would whine about the People's House and its gate-opening power, but publicity forces those with narrow, selfish interests to adjust their aims to benefit a wider public. Debating the measure in the wider arena does not seal its fate in either direction. In fact, the minority who want to defeat the measure still have multiple chances to kill the legislation on the floor, in the other house, by executive veto, or by a judicial challenge.

DELIBERATION *AND* AGGREGATION

In addition to these three specific benefits, the Assembly should be attractive to those who yearn for a more accurate and fair aggregation of interests and preferences than the current system affords.[41] In addressing the problem of special interests, plutocracy, and gridlock, the People's House would help bring—through proper aggregation of popular preferences—national policy closer to what people actually want. Even if political discourse were to remain at the same level and republican aspirations for civic majorities were unrealized, the Assembly and the People's House would enable the public to help shape public policy in a way that is now not possible and to do so in a manner that would be consistent with the public's expressed preferences as communicated by Assembly delegates.

Aggregation and deliberation are often viewed as being in opposition to one another. Aggregation totals up preexisting preferences; deliberation is about changing preferences and arriving at consensus. Aggregation is about individuals knowing what they want; deliberation is about people sharing ideas and converging. However, some writers recognize that the two approaches actually complement each other. In fact, deliberation is the key to making aggregation more coherent, more rational. As the social choice literature explains, the problem with counting votes is that there is "no way to determine which voting method most accurately represents the popular or collective will."[42] As a result, the idea of a coherent popular will is viewed by many as impossible and this, in turns, lends support to the minimalist idea of democracy in which elections only serve to cycle elites. But further research shows that endemic cycling identified by Kenneth Arrow and Duncan Black occurs when political disagreement ranges over more than one dimension. When people agree about what is at issue, when they have a common view of the political situation and focus on a single dimension, this situation increases the possibility that individuals will have what social choice theorists call "single peaked" preferences. Thus, deliberation can help people agree on what is "at stake in a particular political conflict," with the result being that decision by majority rule can show a true winner.[43]

The Assembly and People's House would furnish us with an institutional setting in which deliberative democracy could help generate coherent social choices.[44] In sum, the often-used dichotomy between aggregation and deliberation is too simple.[45] "Majority rule," as Dewey wrote, "is as foolish as its critics charge it with being. But it is never *merely* majority rule." This is because the "counting of heads compels prior recourse to methods of discussion, consultation and persuasion."[46] And structured deliberation followed by aggregation can lead to more informed, more thoughtful decisions. Although it is certainly possible to aggregate voting preferences alone, it is also possible to deliberate first and aggregate later.

OTHER DELIBERATIVE REFORMS

Chapter 4 briefly discussed Dahl's idea of policy juries and Fishkin's experiments with deliberative opinion polls. A widespread use of policy juries and deliberative public opinion polls would allow people to discuss, debate, and advise their government on the most critical domestic and foreign policy issues of the day. The fundamental goal is to pursue the democratic ideal as sketched by Dewey and Habermas: "To cultivate the habit of suspended judgment, of skepticism, of desire for evidence, or appeal to observation rather than sentiment, discussion rather than bias, inquiry rather than conventional idealizations."[47] However, as Bok points out:

> For all their attractions, however, citizen panels have definite limitations. A few days [or a single day] will afford too little time for a group of lay persons to arrive at thoroughly informed, considered judgments on many of the most complex issues confronting the nation [*Fishkin's model*]. In considering a single subject in isolation, participants may not fully appreciate the budgetary limits under which the legislature must function and the tradeoffs that have to be made in deliberating over an entire legislative program [*Dahl's model*]. As a practical matter, moreover, once panels have completed their work, why should members of Congress prefer the panel's recommendations to the wishes of their own constituents?[48]

The proposals of Dahl and Fishkin are admirable but the Assembly proposal is superior in several respects.[49] I approve of Dahl's basic thrust, but see no reason why some modes of democratic deliberation should not be ongoing. Fishkin's approach of focusing on deliberative polling helps get deliberative democracy jumpstarted, yet bringing together a small statistical sample is both cumbersome and artificial. Most busy citizens are not going to want to pack their bags for a three or four day deliberative convention in a far-off city with complete strangers to discuss the great issues of the day.

In addition to the practical difficulty, there is the question as to whether convening randomly selected citizens is the best method to follow in fostering deliberative discussion as a normal part of public business. Walzer, for one, thinks the idea of situating deliberative participation in local communities is superior to Fishkin's approach of transporting citizens to another location where they deliberate. Althaus writes, "Given the importance of these interpersonal networks, the process of removing people from their usual social settings, sitting them down in a laboratory and encouraging them to read position papers—as was done in Fishkin's National Issues Convention—seems a very artificial way of informing them."[50]

In the national Assembly, by expanding the deliberative exercise to include a much broader swath of the population, we largely eliminate the need for the random sample technique. And organizing deliberative participation in the same organic communities that elect the House of Representatives is a better participatory solution. Compared to the proposals made by Dahl and Fishkin, the Assembly reform has the major benefit of encouraging and facilitating ongoing civic life.

Continuing to focus on single deliberative events, Fishkin teamed with Bruce Ackerman of Yale Law School to propose a national civic holiday for deliberation and discussion to be held just before a presidential election. In *Deliberation Day*, Ackerman and Fishkin unveil a plan for a two-day national holiday for structured debate of the presidential contest. Every registered voter in the nation would be invited (and paid $150) to gather in local schools and community centers to "discuss the central issues raised by the campaign."[51] Building on Fishkin's decade-long work conducting small-scale deliberative polls in the United States and Great Britain, the authors propose asking the entire voting population of the United States to participate in one of thousands upon thousands of simultaneous mini-deliberative polling exercises across the nation. A massive undertaking, "deliberation day" would require participation by tens of millions of citizens and require that the two major parties provide "more than thirty thousand well-informed spokespersons!"[52] The event would have a direct cost, at minimum, of $3 billion every four years and would have to be scheduled over two days because police, fire, hospital, and transportation workers all could not take the same day off. The economic costs to the economy of a two-day civic holiday would be considerable, "tens of billions of dollars might be lost for every day of civic discussion" say the authors, but this would be lessened if Ackerman and Fishkin's idea of moving President's Day to October to coincide with Deliberation Day met with approval.[53]

The basic conundrum of Deliberation Day lies in the cost/benefit ratio. As a single event just before a presidential election, Deliberation Day would coincide with the period in the political calendar when people are already the most engaged with the political world. People would emerge more informed and possibly more civic minded, but the event would only occur once every four years and would come so late in the presidential cycle that it would not affect the agenda or candidate choice. As one critic writes, "it is hard to see what benefit would result from so vast an expenditure of funds once the candidates had been selected, platforms chosen, interest groups deployed, and campaign funds expended."[54]

As Ackerman and Fishkin rightly point out, it is important to provide a social context and physical setting for deliberation and discussion to take place.[55] Yet it is also important to think about how this might be done in an ongoing manner, instead of as a stand-alone event whose effects would quickly fade. As the proposal stands, Deliberation Day is another example of the Progressive impulse to push ahead with direct mass democracy. Fishkin and Ackerman argue that such a holiday is a feasible reform. Possibly, but such a holiday would only marginally change how we experience politics—and it is worth pondering how many people would join in deliberation versus going shopping or driving to the lake. In addition, such a holiday would not do much to diminish the gap between the political class and the public at large.

Asking every American to participate in deliberative discussion one day every four years is one approach. Asking a representative cross section of the American public to participate in deliberative discussion on an ongoing basis and giving these super citizens the means by which to actually influence and help shape public policy is another. In contrast to Deliberation Day, the Assembly and the People's House make use of an economy of scale and would require the active participation of far fewer Americans in order to bring a direct and ongoing deliberative benefit to the polity. Asking 43,500 Americans to participate intensively and to represent the rest of us is, on balance, a better approach than asking tens of millions of Americans to participate in limited debate under constrained circumstances defined in large part by political campaigns hyper-focused on winning the White House. Consultants in the mode of Karl Rove and James Carville would not be interested in creating an honest deliberative debate; they would look for ways to bias the proceeding to their strategic advantage. In terms of human effort, financial cost, and potential positive results for democracy in America, a national town hall is the better choice as a deliberative institution. The Assembly would do a better job deliberating the major issues facing the nation and is better suited to fight corruption and defend liberty. This is not to say that we shouldn't have a deliberation day before our national elections. If the civic holiday already existed, it would be a wonderful tradition to continue. But in choosing where to invest the limited resources of time, money, and people's political attention, the Assembly reform is a better bet than Deliberation Day.

HERE TO THERE

It would not be easy for something as innovative as the Assembly reform to become a regular part of the political process. Yet a constituency certainly exists for a reform of this nature that would give people a greater sense of felt power about their sovereign selves. Witness the success of Howard Dean and Ralph Nader in mobilizing millions of people on the liberal side of the spectrum in 2004, the large group of independents and moderates Dionne calls the "anxious middle" who powered Ross Perot's 1992 presidential bid and the moderate Republicans and independents who flocked to Senator McCain in the 2000 presidential contest. Taken together, these three groups represent a sizable chunk of the American electorate unhappy with politics as usual; they are eager for positive change. In addition, millions of disaffected former voters would be receptive to a reform that is rooted in our common history and would bring us closer to realizing America's democratic promise.

It would take time and a series of civic experiments to educate the public to the advantages of institutionalizing deliberative democracy. A grassroots organization pushing for the Assembly would be crucial for success. Endorsement of the Assembly idea from innovative governors would be important as well. The Progressive era reforms were championed by reformist governors such as Hiram Johnson in California and Robert La Follette in Wisconsin. Initially, it would make sense to test the reform in small- or medium-sized states, such as New Hampshire or Wisconsin, with strong civic traditions. States with a history of progressive reform would probably be more open to the experiment than more traditional states. In addition, states that have recently experimented with term-limit reform also would be good targets for reform. Here the old legislative power brokers have been forced from office and the new crop of legislative leaders may be open to reform, especially if the public clamors for change. Success in one or two states would excite interest and encourage others to push the reform.

The Assembly could come into being via the legislative process or by the initiative. Left to their own devices, most state and federal legislators would not fight for the Assembly for a very simple reason. It would be a body of informed and noisy citizens in their backyard. Given the uncertainty of politics as a profession, legislators have a strong self-interest to keep politics on their home turf as simple—and controlled—as possible. Some legislators would recognize the benefits of the Assembly for the political system, but others, skittish about giving activists a forum, would magnify imagined negatives. Of course, given the low level of trust the public has for elected officials, having some politicians speaking out against the Assembly might accelerate its eventuality. Advocates for the reform would remind legislators that, in contrast to the initiative process, the local assemblies would not strip them of power and authority. In addition, on politically sensitive issues—such as immigration, bilingual education, welfare reform—elected legislators could use the judgment of the local assemblies as a shield against an angry mass public.

The Progressive reformers recognized problems, figured out solutions, and acted. They invented the initiative and referendum, cleaned up urban corruption, and ended child labor practices. They also amended the U.S. Constitution to elect senators directly and to extend suffrage to women. Gazing into the future at the beginning of the twentieth century, with industrial plutocrats in full control and populist forces demoralized, who would have guessed that the Progressives would remake American society? But they did.

One of the great advantages of the federal system is that the states can be used as political laboratories. It is common for policy experimentation to take place in the states before being tried at the national level. The same should be true of the Assembly and the People's House. But if states as varied as Arizona, California, Connecticut, Florida, Iowa, Kentucky, Wisconsin, and Vermont, for example, instituted first the Assembly and then the

People's House, and the experiment flourished, implementation of a national Assembly at the federal level could be accomplished by a vote of Congress. However, moving to the stronger reform, the People's House, would require a constitutional amendment. We all know that constitutional amendments are very difficult to achieve. Most attempts fail.[56] Why try?

Many Americans assume the Constitution is sacred and untouchable. But Dahl suggests that a more realistic attitude is to see the founders as our political Wright brothers. Madison, Hamilton, and the other framers did a spectacular job in creating the basic institutional structure of American politics. Yet the edifice is not perfect. Dahl writes: "Considered in the context of its present difficulties, we are entitled to wonder whether the constitutional system that has evolved from their design is, two centuries later, adequate for governing a modern country."[57] Dahl points out that although formal constitutional change is difficult to achieve, it is striking that a majority of the amendments to the Constitution since the Bill of Rights in 1791 have further democratized it. Eleven of sixteen amendments in the past 200 years have expanded democracy in one way or another. The amendments have democratized the Constitution by reducing or eliminating exclusions from the full rights of citizenship (slavery, suffrage), limits on popular sovereignty (direct election of senators), and limits on majority rule (income tax by Congress).[58]

The People's House would be a small but important change in our constitutional structure. It would radically improve American democracy. It may seem presumptuous and dangerous to tamper with a system of government that has served us so well. Yet, both the framers and the Progressives understood that institutional change was sometimes necessary. We can remain more closely connected to them by recognizing the need for reform today than by blindly adhering to the framers' exact design.

The Assembly confronts the problems bedeviling the American polity. The national town hall deals seriously with the enormous size of representative districts by restoring earlier ratios of representation when average citizens knew their elected legislators. Those chosen as delegates of the Assembly or the People's House would continue to live and work in the community—instead of moving to far-off Washington, DC, or the state capital. The virtual town hall is a healthy antidote to our current style of politics by consultants and interest groups because citizen-delegates would be able to counterbalance the influence of big-money lobbyists and single-interest fanatics. Anchored in their respective communities, delegates to the Assembly and the People's House would have a broader vision of the public good than interest-group lobbyists, would be less vulnerable to the influence of large campaign contributions than regular politicians, and thus, would have a freer hand with which to seek the public good. By encouraging participation and giving people an outlet where they can influence the major issues of the day, the virtual national Assembly cultivates the civic virtues extolled by the republican tradition. The deliberative Assembly, in short, creates opportunities for intelligent participation and provides a space for citizens to practice their political skills. Although the local assemblies would not bring about the "participatory society" that some dreamed of in the 1960s, they would provide a way for a small representative portion of the public to participate in a powerful and constructive fashion.

The House and Senate would remain the primary movers and shapers of legislation because the power of the local assemblies would be carefully limited. Still, on major issues as important as intervention in the Middle East, fixing Social Security, or improving health-care coverage, the virtual town hall would ensure that a representative segment of the public not only understood the merits of the various proposals but also had a voice (the Assembly) and possibly a vote (the People's House).[59]

LOOKING BACKWARD 2025-2004

Imagine the Year 2004

At the end of 2003, in a fit of civic zeal, Congress passed the Citizen Assembly Act putting into place a system of town halls in congressional districts across the nation. Both Republicans and Democrats rallied around the idea of improving democracy in America at the same time as the United States attempted to foster democracy in Iraq.

What did the Assembly accomplish in its first year of operation? Following the deterioration of the war in Iraq during the spring and summer, poll results from America's electronic town hall put pressure on Democrats and Republicans to do what neither wanted to do in an election year—increase the number of troops in Iraq by 50,000 to fight a growing insurgency and institute a quicker rotation of reserve units. After strongly supporting the 9/11 Commission's requests for full and timely cooperation from all branches of the federal government, the local assemblies were instrumental in pushing the Congress and the president to implement the Commission's forty-one recommendations, in particular the creation of a national intelligence director—with the authority and budgetary power to assume full responsibility for national intelligence. Initially, President Bush said he agreed that a national intelligence director was needed, yet balked at giving the position power and budget authority. Polling of Assembly members was instrumental in rallying broader public opinion and bringing pressure on the president and key legislators to change their minds.[60]

On the trade front, the national network of local assemblies insisted that congressional leaders remove special interest favors such as tax breaks for NASCAR racetracks, makers of sonar fish finders, and a $10 billion buyout of tobacco farm quotas from a bill needed to stop the European Union from imposing punishing tariffs on selected U.S. exports. Domestically, the Assembly pushed Congress to quickly pass a bipartisan bill to repair the nation's electrical grid in the wake of the northeast blackout. Initially, congressional leaders wanted to combine this legislation with a comprehensive energy strategy that was mired in controversy. Senator Charles Schumer of New York (D) said, "The fact that Assembly members were paying attention when most of the public was asleep made all the difference in passing this critical legislation." Similarly, the informed opinion of the Assembly helped Congress, the president, construction, and environmental lobbyists arrive at a compromise on the highway bill, which had state and local officials exasperated over congressional delay in approving $300 billion worth of construction projects. With the president saying the bill was too expensive, a compromise of $225 billion was reached. Journalists covering the issue said that without the intervention of the Assembly the highway bill would have been delayed until 2005 or 2006.[61]

Imagine the Year 2012

After a quick dinner, Henry Rodriguez says goodbye to his wife and two sons and leaves his bungalow-style home in Pasadena, California, for a People's House meeting downtown. The San Gabriel Mountains glow with the last rays of the sun as Henry heads down Lake Avenue and turns right at Colorado Boulevard. Henry picks up local architect John Wagner at Volmer's Bookstore, and they drive west toward the civic center. Turning right at Garfield Avenue, they pass the Spanish-style city hall and see the Pasadena Public Library straight ahead. In the parking lot, they are joined by Evelyn Wilson, a secretary who lives in northwest Pasadena—a working-class African American and Latino neighborhood and the childhood home of baseball great Jackie Robinson. Entering the library's main hall, Joan Rifkin calls them aside. Joan lives in the fashionable neighborhood near Caltech where Pasadena merges with San Marino—one of Los Angeles' wealthiest suburbs.

The four friends—an architect, secretary, high school science teacher, and nonprofit executive—join ninety-six colleagues from Pasadena and nearby cities of Glendale, La Canada, and South Pasadena. People take their seats as Stephanie Wu, the administrator of a prominent Los Angeles law firm, calls the meeting to order.

Back in Washington, DC, House of Representatives Speaker John Astor (R-Tenn.) has been holding up consideration of President Brian Moore's controversial energy plan. An alarming report by the Petroleum Institute and statements from CEOs of the major oil companies regarding a dramatic drop in worldwide petroleum reserves has prompted the president to propose an increase in the federal tax on gasoline.[62] While no one likes to pay more for fuel, Moore says the United States needs to institute a tax that fixes the pump price at a certain level—no matter whether world oil prices rise or fall. The president says the tax, while economically painful, is necessary to accelerate the shift to a more fuel-efficient economy.[63] Addressing the nation, Moore says, "If we want the United States to remain competitive for the long term we must lead the transition to a less oil-dependent world." In addition, he says we should use the revenue raised to jumpstart reforming the rickety Social Security system. The president wants to change the system to a pay-as-you-go insurance program in which payroll taxes collected would be invested and earn interest for workers instead of contributing to today's retirement coffers. He says such a system would put the Social Security program on solid footing and prevent a recurrence of our current imbalance between a large cohort (the

Baby Boom generation) retiring and a small cohort (Generation X) being asked to pay for the Baby Boomers' retirement.

House Republicans are opposed to a tax increase on principle and intend to let the bill die in committee even though public opinion polls show 59 percent of the public supports a gasoline tax if fixing Social Security is part of the deal. Powerful special interests oppose the plan. Automotive and tire companies fear the tax will reduce driving, and the insurance industry sees a revitalized Social Security system as a threat to their hope for a privatized retirement system.

In Pasadena, Debra Mills, a sales representative and PTA president from Glendale, is the first to speak. "In our meeting two weeks ago, we discussed in some depth the pros and cons of the president's plan. Whatever your views on the issue this is a matter of grave national importance and it certainly deserves to be debated on the floor of the House. Speaker Astor needs to release this legislation from the Commerce Committee."

Seth Mehta, an engineer at Parson Construction, replies. "While I respect Ms. Mills, the legislation deserves to die in committee. We do not need more taxes. A tax reduction for companies involved in energy research and conservation is more in order."

Retired insurance agent Bob Farmer chimes, "Compared to Europe and Japan our pump prices encourage waste."

"I am not in favor of higher gas prices," says Evelyn Wilson. "Too many working poor families will suffer. Still, I am offended that the leaders of the House of Representatives have bottled HR 211 in committee when this issue cries out for national attention and debate."

Truck driver Isaac Thomas interjects, "The Republicans are the majority in the House because the American people voted for the Republican agenda even as they elected a Democratic president. This bill has been handled fairly in committee."

Henry Rodriguez rises to speak to the local gathering; a hush falls over the hall, for his views are widely respected.

"My fellow delegates, Mr. Thomas is certainly correct about who holds the majority in the House. However, we should remember that the Democrats control the White House and the Senate and though the Republicans are the majority in the House this issue was not before the country when the 112th Congress was elected. On issues of such importance, partisan advantage and the majority party's ability to control the agenda to a much greater degree in the House than in the U.S. Senate should yield to the public's desire for the president's plan to be considered and debated by the full House. This is a case where committee intransigence goes against the best interests of the nation. This is a case where the assemblies of the People's House should make use of the gate-opening power granted to them. We must require the House Commerce committee to report HR 211 out of committee to the floor for debate and a vote by the full House. Ms. Wu, I ask that we take a vote on the at-large resolution requiring such an action."

Bob Farmer seconds the motion and Stephanie Wu calls for a vote on the at-large resolution. The vote in California's thirty-third congressional district's local assembly is 72-28. On this same evening, similar debates and votes are taking place in every congressional district in the nation. When the votes are tallied in public libraries, high school auditoriums, union halls, and civic centers from California to New Hampshire, from Louisiana to Minnesota, the measure passes the People's House with 28,126 voting yes and 15,374 voting no. HR 211 will now be debated on the floor of the House of Representatives.

In the spring of 2012, the people have spoken, and popular sovereignty is enjoying a remarkable renaissance in the United States of America.

Imagine the Year 2025

In the afternoon, e-mails fly across the People's House Intranet as delegates talk to friends and allies locally and across the nation in preparation for this evening's meetings when delegates will congregate in meeting halls from Atlanta to Boston, from Des Moines to Cleveland, from Portland to San Diego.

The Issue: Territorial Rights on Mars.[64] The question facing the Congress and the People's House is whether the United States should subordinate its territorial rights on Mars to the "Earth Community" as proposed by the new, revamped United Nations Committee on Extraterrestrial Policy.

The background: Since the first manned mission to Mars in 2014, the United States has established six bases in the southern hemisphere of the red planet and has begun construction of huge oxygen generators needed to transform the planet's atmosphere and terraform the planet. Mineral exploration has reached an advanced stage with promising commercial possibilities. When the European Union (EU) arrived on Mars in 2015, the United States rendered assistance and entered into agreements for co-operative mining operations.

Disagreement emerged with the discovery of large deposits of Zodium in the region controlled by the United States. The United States rejected the co-ownership claims of the EU and established territorial "colonial boundaries" to define mineral rights. The EU retaliated by claiming the rest of planet for itself. Finally, the issue became more complicated when the new, more powerful Chinese Space Program established its own exploration base in the northern hemisphere and claimed a large portion of the territory for mining and colonization. Tensions on Mars and Earth reached a dangerous pitch in 2023 after armed conflict arose between the Chinese and Americans over ownership of a region near the Martian equator.

Here is a foreign policy issue of profound significance. Although the Senate is the only branch of the national legislature with the power to make treaties, the local assemblies of the People's House play a key role in the national discussion unfolding about what course of action the president and the Senate should take.

6.

Institutional Impact

Adding a national network of citizen assemblies and creating a third legislative house would be an important change to the American system. A key question is whether adding another element to our complex system would cause more harm than good. Why should we add an additional component to "the most intricate lawmaking system in the world"?[1] Would not doing so increase the chances of gridlock at a time when complaints about the difficulty of passing major legislation occasionally rise to crescendo level? Is the People's House a reform that would improve deliberation and participation at the cost of government efficiency? If so, many people will rightly say, "No thanks."

In terms of legislative reform, we have three choices. The first impulse is to simplify. If we have a complex system, why not streamline? But unitary parliamentary governments, while faster and more nimble than the American system, with its separation of powers, federalism, and bicameral legislature, are not necessarily better. In Chapter 8, I discuss the drawbacks of parliamentary systems. Here I only want to point out the obvious. Proposals to simplify the system are unlikely to bear fruit because Americans are not going to junk the Madisonian system. The second option is to add direct mass democracy to the formula. Early in the twentieth century, the Progressive reform effort left the core of the system alone and attempted an end run. The initiative and presidential primary system are the results, and to push further in the direction of direct mass democracy would be a mistake. Third, we can take the basic dynamics of the Madisonian system and work to improve them. The Assembly reform, with its focus on fostering civic majorities, follows this path. In defending this third approach, I begin by discussing gridlock, the advantages of bicameralism, and then focus on the filibuster in the U.S. Senate as the key source of gridlock in American politics.

GRIDLOCK

"Gridlock represents a lack of policy consensus regarding the difficult decisions we ask our representatives to make," say David Brady and Craig Volden, a political science duo who have studied congressional politics from Jimmy Carter to George W. Bush. They see gridlock as the result of both complex policy issues and supermajority institutions—especially the filibuster rule in the U.S. Senate. Changing the status quo is difficult in the American system, not only because our institutions are designed to make change difficult, but also because the public rarely gives politicians clear signals about what they want done. "The budget should be balanced while taxes are slashed and programs increased" is the classic example of the mixed messages that politicians receive. Or, if they do have clear signals from constituents at home, this runs up against building broad-based coalitions. "The harsh reality that new members discover is that developing supermajority coalitions around complex issues is difficult. Policy gridlock is the result of not being able to build such coalitions without violating the trust of the folks back home."[2]

For many years, divided government was blamed for gridlock in Washington, DC. Journalists and political scientists assumed that it was easier for the American system to produce significant legislation when the presidency and Congress are controlled by the same party. Then David Mayhew took a careful look at the postwar data and found—surprise—that divided government was not a factor in gridlock. "Controlling for other variables, unified and divided governments are essentially indistinguishable from one another in terms of their propensities for gridlock or, conversely, for producing important legislative enactments."[3] More recently George Tsebelis examined gridlock and "policy stability" in a comparative context. Any political system can be described in terms of the institutions and political players whose agreement is necessary in order to change the status quo. Dissatisfied with the traditional typologies in comparative politics examining democratic versus authoritarian, presidential versus parliamentary, unicameral versus bicameral, Tsebelis focuses on "veto players."[4] These are individuals or collective actors whose agreement is required for a change in the status quo.[5] Italy and the United States are nations with multiple veto players, for example, while Greece and the United Kingdom have only one.

Are having multiple veto players bad? Tsebelis takes an agnostic position. "It is reasonable to assume that those who dislike the status quo will prefer a political system with the capacity to make changes quickly, while advocates of the status quo will prefer a system that produces policy stability."[6] His main finding fits casual observation: the more veto points in a system the more stable it is and the more difficult it is to change the status quo. Nations with few veto players produce significant laws and few nonsignificant ones while "countries with many veto players produce few significant laws and many nonsignificant ones."[7]

The key to gridlock in the American system is the filibuster rule in the Senate enacted in 1917.[8] In the American system, significant legislation cannot pass without clearing filibuster obstacles in the Senate, and most of the time the minority party controls the required forty seats. This means that gridlock is built into the American system, "not because of the requirement that all three veto players [president, Senate, and House of Representatives] agree on a particular change of the status quo, but because of the filibuster rule that essentially prevents partisan legislation from passing the Senate."[9] In his seminal 1998 study of the dynamics of U.S. lawmaking, Keith Krehbiel focuses on those legislators who are the pivot points for the passage of legislation. Because of the filibuster rule, the pivot vote in the Senate can often be far from the median voter. Krehbiel reports that gridlock, which he defines as the absence of movement to change the status quo even when there is majority support to do so, is a "common but not constant" in the American national legislature. When gridlock is broken, Krehbiel writes, "it is broken by large, bipartisan coalitions—not by minimal-majority or homogeneous majority-party coalitions."[10]

BICAMERALISM

If the Senate filibuster is the key reason for gridlock, or stability, in American politics, what about bicameralism? To better evaluate the effect of the People's House on the American system and see why it would be a plus to efficiency it is important to understand why bicameral legislatures are, on balance, better institutions than unicameral legislatures. Here we turn to the work of William Riker. Historically, bicameral legislatures, such as the House of Lords and House of Commons, were invented to protect the aristocracy from the masses. As can be seen in The *Federalist,* the arguments for the upper house were couched in the rhetoric of gentry having greater wisdom and capacity to withstand the passions of the moment. "The traditional liberal justification of bicameralism," Riker writes, "is that it slows down the legislative process, renders abrupt change difficult, forces myopic legislators to have second thoughts, and thereby minimizes arbitrariness and injustice."[11] Of course, the injustice that the gentry and bourgeoisie feared was the redistribution of wealth, not Pinkerton guards attacking striking workers.

Eighteenth-century Britain was a tricameral system divided between the king, the House of Lords, and the House of Commons. Today, all power lies with the House of Commons. Across Europe, as the justification for a legislative house dedicated to the upper class faded, many nations eliminated the upper house, as in the case of Denmark and Sweden, or rendered it a eunuch, as with the House of Lords. Although the old reason for bicameralism has vanished, there are sound social choice reasons to maintain a multicameral legislature. Today, the United States is a bicameral system, or nearly tricameral given the presidential veto. True, unicameral governments such as Great Britain can act with dispatch, but they suffer from the danger of majority tyranny and policy instability. Without the separation of powers, a simple majority of the parliament gives a party control of the government. The old justification for bicameralism was elite protection; the deeper reason is the protection from temporary legislative majorities moving too quickly to impose their vision on the society.

Riker recognizes the merits of bicameralism, which he interprets as "two or more legislative houses."[12] He notes that there are numerous ways to slow down legislation so as to allow more time for consideration. These include supermajorities, multicameralism, plural executives and judicial review. Among these, and especially against supermajorities, he argues bicameral is the superior solution. Why? First, majority rule is a fairer decision rule than supermajorities. As Dahl points out, under supermajority rules, a minority is granted extraordinary power that is hard to justify on democratic grounds.[13] Why should *this* minority have such power? In general, majority rule is an attractive decision rule because it gives every citizen an equal vote, "does not contain a bias toward any particular choice (such as remaining at the status quo), and is decisive in the sense that it takes only a bare majority to make a collective decision."[14] When a system has many veto points—as does the United States with its federalism, bicameralism, and separation of powers—a majority rule decision rule helps speed the process.

Second, under the condition of a one-dimensional spectrum on a policy—for example, social spending for the needy versus tax cuts for the wealthy—majority rule in a bicameral situation is less likely to fall victim to voting cycles, which occur when no single alternative beats all competitors in head-to-head competition for majority support. This is important because a single dimension accounts for approximately three-fourths of all voting decisions in Congress.[15] In a voting cycle, as Arrow and Black have shown, first option A wins, then option B, then option C.[16] The advantage of bicameral constitutional design is that it prevents majority tyranny while allowing for a Condorcet winner—the selection of an option that does indeed beat all the other competitors. Thus, Riker says, multicameralism "allows majority decision when an unequivocal majority choice exists. Thus it captures the advantages and avoids the disadvantages of the method of majority rule." Although supermajority rules can prevent majority tyranny, they cause more gridlock than bicameralism. It is very difficult for voters to find an equilibrium point that all can support when more than 50 percent plus one is needed for victory. Thus, no decision is reached. By contrast, Riker writes, "substitute a bicameral system operating by simple majority. Then the equilibrium is realizable in both (or three) houses. Hence the delay mechanism of supermajorities upsets the one-dimensional equilibrium of simple majority rule, while the delay mechanism of *multicameralism* does not."[17]

THE U.S. SENATE AND GRIDLOCK

The key to passing legislation is identifying the pivotal voter. On most issues, legislators can be assigned positions from the most liberal to the most conservative. Their comparative ideological leanings can be gauged from interest groups' rating and other measures of position taking. Passing legislation that changes policy depends on knowing the policy preferences of those members of Congress near the median (at or about the 218th member of the House and at or about the 50th member of the Senate, and on most major legislation, knowing the policy preferences of the 60th member of the Senate who could bring a cloture vote and thus stop a filibuster. David Brady and Craig Volden write, "Gridlock can be overcome only when the status quo is further from crucial members' preferences than are the alternative policies proposed by the President and others. In short, if current Social Security policy is agreeable to the 218th House voter or the 50th Senate voter, then attempts at dramatic change, such as partial privatization through person accounts, will fail" and the status quo remains.[18]

The Senate is known for its allowance for extended debate. Although House members are lucky if they get more than five minutes to speak, Senators regularly give windy addresses. When a senator or a group of senators use their right to speak to slow or stall the advancement of a bill, the tactic is known as a filibuster (extended debate). In 1917, the Senate adopted a parliamentary procedure known as cloture as the method by which to halt a filibuster and cause a vote on the motion at hand. To invoke cloture, sixty Senators must agree that an issue has been sufficiently discussed.

At one time the filibuster was reserved for grave national issues. Today, the threat of a filibuster is a normal part of Senate business and part of the calculus on major legislation. As a result, it is not the median voter in the Senate who is important. Instead, the pivotal voter is the member who may side with the minority and be the 41st vote to keep the filibuster alive. As Krehbiel wryly observes, the practical effect is to make "the off-center filibuster pivot a locus of—to put it benignly—accommodating activity . . . if the filibuster pivot [member] is not accommodated—more precisely, if she prefers the status quo, *q,* to the bill, *b,* that is offered—she and all colleagues with more extreme preferences can mount a filibuster and vote no

on cloture, thereby keeping the status quo intact."[19] The result is that filibuster pivot voters and their spatially nearby colleagues attract a great deal
of attention from congressional leaders attempting to put together coalitions either to move the legislation ahead or to stop it. Successful legislative
leaders learn to expend their time and resources on those legislators who
are both pivotal and largely indifferent. If a Senate colleague is strongly
committed on an issue or to an interest group, it is unlikely that he or she
will change position. But if the member is relatively indifferent between the
proposed legislation and the status quo, a legislative leader or president can
succeed with gentle persuasion or a vigorous twist of the arm.[20]

Scholars agree, the real veto problem in the American system is not bicameralism. It is the U.S. Senate, where the filibuster threat means bipartisan supermajorities are required for nearly all important legislation. Although bills can
pass the House of Representatives on a partisan basis, in the Senate major
bills need bipartisan support. On its face, this appears a good thing. When
Mr. Smith went to Washington, he filibustered to stop the bad interests, and
on major bills why wouldn't we want a bipartisan coalition?

There are two major problems with the Senate as it is. First, supermajorities and bicameralism both slow down legislation, but as I explained
above, bicameralism is much the better technique. Second, the Senate's
supermajority problem is compounded by the representative logic of the
Great Compromise during the Constitutional debates that grants each
state two Senators regardless of population. In "The Infernal Senate: The
Real Source of Gridlock," Thomas Geoghegan writes, "We have a
Louisiana Purchase of Rotten Boroughs." As he explains, the perverse effect of representation by state instead of population is that the forty senators from the twenty smallest states by population represent a population
base of only 10 percent. This means senators representing ninety percent
of the population are not enough by themselves to pass a bill. If we take
the fifty senators from the twenty-five smallest states, here the senators
representing slightly more than 16 percent of the population base can
block a bill. Conversely, Geoghegan writes, sixty senators from the thirty
smallest states representing only 24 percent of the nation's population can
pass whatever they want.[21]

Would the People's House make the gridlock caused by supermajority
voting in the Senate worse? No, because Madison, knowing that he was

giving up on majority vote in the Senate, thought that majority faction (that is, civic majorities) focused on the general welfare and the common good would counter the power of powerful narrowly focused factions.[22] The People's House is organized to help create these civic majorities. As a practical matter, while the filibuster rule means that the pivotal vote in the Senate is usually ten steps to the left or the right of the median, in the Assembly the pivotal vote will be the median delegate. Similar to the 50th vote in the Senate and the 218th vote in the House, the 21,750th vote in the People's House will represent the "sensible center" of American politics.

ADVANTAGES OF THE PEOPLE'S HOUSE

Although it does indeed add another veto point to the system, the People's House will not add to gridlock—unless maintaining the status quo is what a majority of delegates want to do after having investigated the policy options available. Why is this so? First, the People's House would have more than the power to say no. It would have the capacity to act either as a brake—or an accelerator. It could force a bill out of committee for a floor vote as well as reject a bill passed by the House or the Senate. There will be times when the median vote at 50 percent in the People's House added to the median vote at 50 percent in the House of Representatives will place pressure on the minority of 41 in the Senate to find common ground for compromise and thus break the deadlock.

Second, the voice of the People's House will have a certain moral authority because it will speak for the nation as a whole and not a particular state or region or industry (as when the senator from Washington State was referred to as the senator from Boeing). In the American system, as currently constituted, interests of all types—economic, social, ethnic— lobby Congress, and their views are factored into public policy. This is a good thing. However, it is sometimes difficult for members of Congress to speak for the national community and the wider public good. It is much easier for members to represent and speak for particular interests. Today, apart from the president, we do not have an institutional player looking out for national interests. This is because each member of Congress, both in the House and the Senate, is first geographically tied to a particular constituency and second to a cadre of interest groups and political donors who fund the campaign cycles. The People's House—because lot selects it and because the members are not beholden to local supporters or particular special interests—would have a perspective similar to the president and possibly broader. Unlike the president and the White House staff, delegates to the People's House would not be working 24/7 to build and maintain a dominant coalition to ensure him or her and their party's re-election. Thus, the People's House, to a greater extent than either house of Congress or the president, would be able to speak for a national constituency and focus on the "enlightened pursuit of broad public interests."[23]

There is a third reason why the Assembly would not cause gridlock. Veto powers are bargaining chips as well as votes. The possibility of a veto causes the other party to modify its strategy and take into account the concerns of the party with veto power. The possibility of a veto—whether by one extremely powerful individual, the president, or by a broad cross section of the public in the People's House—would encourage the legislative leaders of the House and the Senate to respect what the president and the People's House say about certain issues. In most instances, accommodation would be reached and the veto not used.

At bottom, the question is whether this particular veto point, the People's House, would increase system rigidity? The answer is no because the People's House is not your normal veto player. We would expect the People's House to act on civic majority motives more often than narrow special interest constituent motives. For example, if a budget bill is stuck in Congress, powerful members regularly ask for special favors for their constituencies as a condition for supporting the legislation. (The practice of earmarking—the designation of a specific amount of funds in an appropriation bill or a direct revenue source for a particular project or entity—has recently come under scrutiny.) By contrast, delegates to the People's House, looking at the larger picture and not obligated to any particular interest groups, would not focus on narrow constituencies. If the People's House simply added another narrow perspective to the vote calculus, then the occasional delay and frustration caused by an additional veto would not be worth it. But the People's House is different.

In sum, would the addition of the People's House make the passage of important legislation more difficult? Yes and no. Yes, because another step means another place on the legislative steeplechase where bills can trip and fall. No, because when a proposal is slightly better than the status quo we would expect bills to pass. No, because in our multicameral system important legislation only passes the Congress when a broad consensus emerges. It is rare that major legislation passes on its first try. Often when the bill comes back, it is redrafted to correct faults and meet objections; the virtual national Assembly would be part of this information loop, an important reality check. Currently, major legislation dies because interest groups build a coalition against it. The People's House is not another interest group, so it won't compound the problem in a linear fashion. Having a civic majority logic, the People's House will probably object to some bills that currently sail through Congress, while lobbying to help bills survive that narrow interest groups would like to kill.

The separation of powers, bicameralism, and the Senate's filibuster rule all make passage of new laws difficult. Conversely, when new laws are enacted, the same system protects "these achievements from subsequent reversal."[24] Thus, although the American system is slower than the British system, ours has a distinct advantage. A decision once made is difficult to reverse. Examples include the decision during the Second New Deal (1935-38) to establish a policy of economic regulation and the Civil Rights Act of 1964 that ended segregation and instituted civil rights for African Americans and other minority groups. By contrast, in Britain postwar economic policy has shifted dramatically depending on whether the left or the right is in power. "The nature of majority tyranny," Riker writes, "is that a statute is passed by one majority that is opposed by another majority. The losing majority knows its majority status and resents it, so at the next opportunity it repeals the statute."[25]

A VETO PLAYER AND SOMETHING MORE

The People's House is both a veto player and something more. In an insightful article, "Institutionalizing the Public Interest," Goodin explains why. One way of interpreting the separation of powers is to think of the result as a least-common-denominator definition of the public good. If each branch of government is independent of the others, represents a distinct partition of the population and has a veto over outcomes, then the enacted laws represent a "least common denominator" of what can be agreed upon among all branches of government.[26] But there is another way of approaching the problem. Instead of focusing upon interests "we *happen* to have in common," we may focus upon interests "we *must* have in common," Goodin writes. Looking at our public roles, we can say, the public interest is that interest which we all share as members of the public.[27]

This "highest common concern" model of the public interest requires something more than veto powers to work. Institutionalized vetoes send the wrong signals because they encourage people to think in terms of narrow personal and sectorial interests. A veto is a device to protect one particular interests; it is not a device (by itself) by which a group of people can collaborate to decide what they want to do. To go beyond veto power we need something like the People's House where the focus is on open communication, not strategic bargaining; where the goal is for people to think about shared concerns, not interest group claims. Institutions such as the Assembly, that reflect a nationwide constituency, are more able to "take an all-encompassing, highest-common-concern view of matters."[28]

In short, although we don't want major legislation to pass the U.S. Congress until there is strong majority support for the measure, the current veto structure does little to encourage cooperative discussion. The People's House, with its "highest-common-concern" approach to the public good, would help engineer the social consensus that must occur if significant legislation is to overcome the various political and institutional hurdles. A national Assembly would help the system go fast when needed and slow down when warranted. It would allow the public at large to have a hand in framing national debate too often controlled by "powerful players who make it their business to shape the terms of public debate through the financial contributions they make available to politicians and political campaigns."[29]

All institutions have bias. The Senate with 100 members, the House of Representative with 435 members, and the People's House with 43,500 delegates all have representative biases, and the tendencies of the People's House would help correct the problematic biases of our current bicameral legislature. At the Constitutional Convention, the "Connecticut Compromise" awarded each state two senators regardless of population. This gross inequality of representation is locked in the Constitution because of the phrase at the end of Article V: "No State, without its Consent, shall be deprived of its equal suffrage in the Senate."[30] The representation of states over people and the minority rule of the filibuster create a bias in the Senate favoring small, rural states at the expense of large urban ones. The fact that small state senators can, if they are talented politicians, create a bond between themselves and their constituencies that large state senators cannot match gives them an advantage in terms of re-election and, in turn, in longevity and the seniority that leads to chair positions and real legislative power.[31] The House of Representatives represents the nation's population in a much fairer manner. But representation in the House of Representatives is biased by its electoral method. Because American elections are based on a winner-take-all method of selection, the effect is to over represent the views of the majority in a district and under represent those on the losing edge of the ballot.[32]

In contrast to the current Congress, the 43,500 delegates of the People's House would represent the population of the nation as a whole. Because delegates would be selected at random by lot, people from many different minority groups would be represented in the People's House in a way that they are not visible in the House of Representatives. In a nation growing increasingly diverse in terms of ethnicity, race, religion, age, educational background, and occupation, this would be a valuable addition to the national legislative calculus. In a sense, the People's House would have a proportional representation effect without being a proportional representational (PR) system. If we want "representative government" to reflect twenty-first century America, then we had better start thinking of representation in the manner made possible by the Assembly and the People's House. If we do not, in our "new multiracial America, the big state minorities individually will have even less voting power than they do now . . . and the people-of-the-interior, the non-Hispanic whites in most of the small states will get more and more heavily weighted votes." This is not a place we want to go, says Geoghegan; it would be "past gridlock, and heading into something worse."[33]

Given that there is no realistic chance of changing the small state bias in the Senate, the People's House would give us a method by which to counter this flaw in the Constitution.[34] The Assembly (voice) and the People's House (a vote) would accentuate the decision rule of majority vote (as in the House of Representatives) and offer representation based on population (as in the House of Representatives) in a deliberative assembly that would function much like an intelligent referendum on the most pressing issues of the day—whether it be a foreign war, education policy, or preparing for disasters.

If we were to add the People's House to our national legislative branch, we would have the People's House *and* the House of Representatives taking votes based on majority rule and the Senate operating under the minority rule of the filibuster tradition. If we were truly concerned about gridlock, we would press the Senate to either eliminate the filibuster altogether or lower the supermajority needed for a cloture to a more modest fifty-five votes. A multicameral system of three houses, not to mention the judicial branch, would provide minorities with more than adequate protection against hasty majorities enacting unwise or harmful policies. If the Republicans or Democrats held slim but powerful majorities in the House and the Senate (as, for example, the GOP does under George W. Bush) major bills would still have to pass the reflective judgment of the People's House where delegates, chosen by lot, would represent the population at large and not the partisan extremes reflected in today's legislatures.[35]

THE PRESIDENT AND THE PEOPLE'S HOUSE

Outside of the legislative branch, there is an additional institutional benefit of the People's House. The role and importance of the presidency has increased dramatically since the New Deal and the origins of the Cold War. An imperial presidency is not something the founders anticipated, as Richard Neustadt made clear in *Presidential Power*.[36] In *The Personal President*, Theodore Lowi recounts the rise of the modern presidency and wonders loudly whether a plebiscitary-type presidency is a good idea.[37] The modern presidency puts enormous responsibility and pressure on a single individual and his or her senior staff. The media spotlight on the president and the West Wing makes the rest of us spectators, not players, in the national drama that is democracy. The addition of the People's House would help rebalance the constitutional system by placing some measure of power in the people's hands and asking a representative sample of the population to participate in governing the nation.

Obviously, the president, the 100 senators, and the 435 members of the House would remain the primary actors, but responsibility for direction of public policy would be shared with the delegates to the national Assembly. The president, in addition to being commander in chief, running the executive branch, and setting the agenda for Congress, is the only elected official in the national government whose constituency is truly national. A national Assembly anchored in each of the 435 congressional districts, would provide us with another institutional player responsible to the nation as a whole. Yes, People's House delegates would be drawn from particular congressional wards, but selection by lot means they would be free of the usual constituent-official bonds. Their job would be to reflect on what "people *want* to have in common, rather to things they just happen to have in common."[38] Their role would be to fulfill Madison's vision when he wrote, in *Federalist* No. 51: "In the extended republic of the United States, and among the great variety of interests, parties and sects which it embraces, a coalition of a majority of the whole society could seldom take place on any other principles than those of justice and the general good."[39]

Finally, the United States is not unique in facing difficult public policy choices. Although we often blame gridlock for why the government does not do a better job solving the problems we face as a nation, a good deal of the difficulty is not government structure but rather a plurality of views about what to do and the complexity of the problems faced. As Brody and Volden point out, many democratic governments face a similar predicament.

> Democratic countries from Japan and Korea in the Far East to Europe and Canada all face the same problems—corporate downsizing, high wages in the face of competition from the third world, exorbitant entitlements, electorates unhappy with high tax rates, aging populations, and questions about foreign policy in any unsafe world. Forms of government in these countries range from strong parliamentary systems to decentralized American-style governments. None has the answer.[40]

The Assembly is not a quick fix, one-stop reform that once installed will quickly solve "the problem," whatever that is. Instead of being a specific policy prescription or institutional fix, the Assembly is merely a method by which we can talk to one another about the choices we face in our common life together. Joshua Cohen writes,

> At the heart of the institutionalization of the deliberative procedure is the existence of arenas in which citizens can propose issues for the political agenda and participate in debate about those issues. The existence of such arenas is a public good, and ought to be supported with public money . . . public provision expresses the basic commitment of a democratic order to the resolution of political questions through free deliberation among equals. *The problem is to figure out how arenas might be organized to encourage such deliberation.*[41]

The goal of the Assembly and the People's House, deliberative democracy on a national scale, is to provide a social context and physical setting in which citizenship can take place.[42]

THE WISDOM OF CROWDS

Selection by random sample or lot inevitably brings up the question of the competence of people who are picked at random to represent their fellow citizens in the national legislature. Many observers, including such brilliant individuals as Hume, Jefferson, and John Stuart Mill, believe average people have a good deal of common sense and make rational judgments about choices presented to them. In *The Wisdom of Crowds,* James Surowiecki pursues this line of thought arguing that groups are remarkably intelligent, often more intelligent than the smartest people in the room. "When our imperfect judgments are aggregated in the right way, our collective intelligence is often excellence." Recent research shows, he writes, "if you put together a big enough and diverse enough group of people and ask them to make decisions affecting matters of the general interest, that group's decisions will, over time, be intellectually superior to the isolated individual, no matter how smart or well-informed he is."[43]

It requires the right conditions—which the Assembly meets—including diversity, members making independent judgments, and a decentralized structure. The best results occur when people come from a variety of backgrounds with different knowledge and information. Next, the members of the group talk to each other, but each person should make up his or her own mind. People in the group may agree on some points, but consensus is far from necessary. In fact, collective intelligence works best by aggregating diverse opinions.[44]

A decentralized structure is critical because it encourages local or tacit knowledge that is specific to a particular place, experience, or job. Google works, Surowiecki says, because it is able to aggregate local knowledge and private information for collective use. Applying this point to politics, Washington insiders are creatures of the beltway. Members of the House and the Senate know the folkways of Washington but are largely cut off from the "local" knowledge that comes from living the life of an ordinary citizen. As Surowiecki writes,

> Politics is ultimately about the impact of government on the everyday life of citizens. It seems strange, then, to think that the way to do politics well is to distance yourself as much as possible from citizens' everyday lives . . . a healthy democracy needs the constant flow of information it gets from people's votes—[and opinions.] This is information that experts [and elected members of Congress] cannot get because it is not part of the world that they live in.[45]

Living in an age when the ratio of electors to representatives has escalated dramatically, the result is a system of representation that is increasingly distant and separate from the "real world." Former President George H. W. Bush's amazement at seeing grocery store scanners for the first time stands out in this regard, but the point is more general and the effect pervasive, if subtle. Increasing the distance between the representative and the public is what the Madisonian system has done for more than 200 years. In Surowiecki's view,

> trusting an insulated . . . elite to make the right decisions is a foolish strategy . . . most political decisions are not simply decisions about how to do something. They are decisions about what to do, decisions that involve values, trade-offs, and choices about what kind of society people should live in. There is no reason to think that experts are better at making those decisions than the average voter.[46]

What we need is "local" knowledge to balance elite and expert opinion. Both the Assembly reform and deliberative polling foster local knowledge that is more informed than standard public opinion polls.

In general, groups are only wise if their members actually know something about the relevant question. For example, a group of farmers might be good at guessing the weight of a bull, but it is unlikely that they would know much about its DNA. Conversely, scientists might know about the bull's DNA but be clueless as to the animal's weight. By their service on the Assembly, delegates will soon surpass most of their contemporaries in their knowledge of politics and the major issues. On this point, the Condorcet Jury Theorem is a crucial consideration. Condorcet demonstrated mathematically that the probability of a correct majority vote in a group of moderately well-informed individuals increases dramatically as the size of the group grows. The basis of the theorem is that "groups are likely to do better than individuals, and large groups better than small ones, if majority rule is used and if each person is more likely than not to be correct." The last point is important because if each person is more likely to err, then the dynamics go the opposite direction, and the larger the group the less probable its members arrive at a correct answer. Thus, slightly better knowledge about the political world than the average person has, says Sunstein, is a fourth necessary condition if the Assembly is to make wise collective choices.[47]

Fortunately, as Fishkin and others have documented, participation in deliberative forums quickly raises the level of political knowledge.

> When ordinary people have the chance seriously to consider competing sides of an issue, they take the opportunity to become far more informed. Their considered judgments demonstrate higher levels of knowledge and greater consistency with their basic values and assumptions. These experiments demonstrate that the public has the capability to deal with complex public issues; the difficulty is that it normally lacks an institutional context that will effectively motivate it to do so."[48]

Finally, and importantly, the question of competence is also, in part, a philosophical question about guardianship and experts in a democracy. Essentially, I agree with Dahl that in a democracy we cannot have experts passing judgment on experts. Dahl argues that most issues, including the most complex and esoteric, have a moral dimension that makes it imperative for the public to be involved in the choices that are made.[49] If this is the case, and ordinary Americans need to pass judgment, having a second more deliberative public opinion to listen to (the Assembly) and to consider as a vote (the People's House) is certainly an improvement over the current system.

ISSUES AND CONCERNS

The Assembly proposal raises a host of issues beyond that of competence. Here I briefly consider some of these questions. First, would people pay attention? Given that voting rates in local elections are very low, often much lower than national elections, what evidence gives us reason to think that citizens will pay attention to the local assemblies and the discussions that take place there? Nobody much cares when the County Central Committee of the Republican Party meets. Why would the assembly meetings be any different? First, editors know that readers want to know what is going on in their local community. For the local press, the local assembly will become a regular news beat much like the city council and school board. Because of the parliamentary debate format, these civic forums will be more interesting and stimulating than the administrative detail that constitutes city council meetings. Second, the national media love polls, and the Assembly poll could quickly become a regularly quoted poll much like the ABC News or Gallup polls. We would expect that the leading national reporters would want to know the considered judgments of the Assembly on the pressing issues of the day.

What about the danger of group polarization? When like-minded people deliberate in isolation, the result can be alarming because their conclusions tend to go to the extremes. For example, if people who are moderately critical of the war in Iraq gather to discuss it, after the discussion they will most likely be more opposed than before. This social dynamic appears with statistical regularity and leads Sunstein to wonder: "If the effect of deliberation is to move people to a more extreme point in the direction of their original tendency, why is it anything to celebrate?"[50] But the problem is isolation, not deliberation. Group polarization is a problem when small like-minded groups are not exposed to competing ideas. The Assembly lottery, by contrast, draws a wide swath of society. In addition, in the unlikely event that one or two local assemblies were dominated by a like-minded cult, the resulting group polarization would not affect the rest of the Assembly network. According to Sunstein, it is "total or near-total self-insulation, rather than group deliberation as such, that carries with it the most serious dangers."[51] The key to avoid group polarization from biasing deliberative settings is making sure people have sustained exposure to competing views. In the Assembly and the People's House, competing views would be the norm. Polarization is avoided when deliberation occurs in a "large and heterogeneous public sphere"—an apt description of the national Assembly.[52]

Why such a focus on federal and state government? Why not start at the local level with city councils and county government? First, there are already plenty of opportunities to participate in politics and influence policy at the local level. Second, this reform is situated in local communities yet has a cosmopolitan outlook. This paradox is explained when we compare the Assembly and the People's House to municipal neighborhood councils. Neighborhood councils formally connected to city councils are increasingly common at the municipal level of government.[53] The neighborhood council has a parochial focus; the Assembly and the People's House do not. Although each local assembly is based in a particular neighborhood and congressional district, the Assembly has its focus on the nation as a whole. It would be rare for a local delegation to address a problem in its own backyard and, even if this were the case, votes in other local assemblies would overwhelm its local bias.

To date, no large American city has given formal powers to the neighborhood councils. However, the reluctance to empower neighborhood councils is specific to city issues.[54] There is the concern that giving neighborhood councils formal power over budget and zoning in their neighborhoods will fragment political authority and make it difficult to get things done. People reasonably ask: Do we want a new layer of city government with decision-making authority? The answer is no. Next, business interests argue correctly that neighborhood councils would strenuously oppose many development projects. What incentives do neighborhood councils have to think beyond the neighborhood and consider the good of the city as a whole? Very few. Protecting and enhancing the neighborhood is their prime motivation. Putting deliberative democracy into action has a different dynamic, in large part because it is focused on national legislation, not administration and municipal issues. Each local assembly is part of the legislative process, not the executive branch. A good argument can be made against giving neighborhood councils formal power; an excellent argument can be made for giving limited, yet potent, power to the national Assembly.

Would the Assembly add another layer of government? No, the national Assembly is an addition to the legislative branch, not another layer of administration. The Assembly and the People's House would add voices to the legislature, not programs to the bureaucracy. To say the reform would enlarge the government misses the point; it is about controlling and directing the government we have. The Assembly is about brainpower and giving civic majorities increased influence over public policy. Libertarian fantasy aside, "the government" is not going away. However, in a democracy, we can, if we choose, help run the show.

What about Madison's fears of factional infighting and communal discord? Factions and personal animosities would develop in particular delegations the same way they do in city councils, state legislatures, and the House of Representatives. Similarly, alliances and long-term friendships would emerge. Such is human nature. In the People's House as a whole, issues would count more than personality because delegates would not meet face-to-face except in the respective congressional districts. In the virtual national People's House, the dynamics of distance and impersonality would overwhelm petty personal passions, much as Madison predicted in *Federalist* No. 10.

Are there sufficient incentives to motivate people to participate in the delegate lottery? The flip side of a fear of chaos is apathy. Would there be enough interest for an Assembly system to work? Power has a way of drawing attention and interest. A push to implement the Assembly, and then the People's House, would educate the public and spark interest in serving as a delegate. Incentives include holding a position with a modest amount of power and prestige, a concern for the community's welfare and interesting subjects to debate. All this without having to run an exhausting, expensive campaign and leaving home to live in Washington, DC. The main incentive, of course, would be taking part in the governing of the country.

What would a People's House system cost to implement? The cost of implementing and running the Assembly or the People's House would be modest compared to many governmental expenditures. The delegates would be paid a modest per diem similar to what city council and school board members receive. Of course, with 43,500 delegates nationally at $100 per month it would be $4.3 million. Another cost would come from setting up a computer network, not difficult in an age of browsers and the Internet, and in paying salaries for the 50-member national steering committee. Could the computer system and software be donated by business? This is an ethical question with which proponents would have to wrestle. Annual cost to taxpayers for the 50-member steering committee at $75,000 each: $3.75 million. Add in an administrative and technical staff of 25 at an average of $60,000: $1.5 million. The annual cost for a national People's House system could range from $15 to $50 million or higher. (By comparison, the budget for a modest-sized suburban school district is approximately $175 million annually.)[55] When we don't even blink at spending billions on military aircraft, this amount seems a small price to protect freedom at home.

Could we trust people to act responsibly? To do otherwise in a democratic society is to sanction guardianship. In the words of Jefferson: "I know no safe depository of the ultimate powers of society but the people themselves; and if we think them not enlightened enough to exercise their control with a wholesome discretion, the remedy is not to take it from them, but to inform their discretion by education."[56] When people serve on a jury, they take the responsibility seriously. We can expect the same with the Assembly and the People's House.

Is the discussed proposal the only way to connect local assemblies to Congress and give them actual power? No. It is but a sketch of one possible approach. I don't claim to have perfect knowledge about exactly how local assemblies should be connected to national power. The important thing is for the public to start thinking about adding a national Assembly to the governing equation. Advances in technology allow for it; the imperatives of popular sovereignty demand it. The eventual design will be a product of many minds as well as trial and error at the state level—which is where the reform would first be tried. The goal is the creation of real-world institutions and practices that foster deliberation, participation, and the creation of civic majorities. In this way, the people can reclaim sovereignty over the political process and assist the Congress and the president in making public policy.

7.

Giving Publics Power

Modern democracy needs not just elections and interest groups, but "publics." Today, politics is the domain of administrators, elected officials, interest groups, policy wonks, and political consultants. The public sometimes engages in rational, critical debate about the issues, but its primary role has been reduced to that of a spectator. The idea that politics is just another specialized area of market society—similar to medicine, mortgage banking, or aerospace engineering—that should be left to experts is a central contention of Schumpeter's procedural theory. By contrast, the republican view argues that, as equal citizens, politics is the one area of life where we all must have some competence, some knowledge, and some interest. Otherwise, we might as well be living in an authoritarian regime where private lives thrive and capitalism powers the economy, but the rule of law is fragile and political decisions reserved for the oligarchy in power. Franco's Spain was a good example of such an arrangement. For many Spaniards it was not a bad life. Unlike Saddam's Iraq, people did not fear a knock on the door in the dead of night. But Franco's Spain was not a democracy.

Most of us would agree with the following thumbnail sketch of what democracy means and why people in the United States and in much of the world want to live by democratic rules:

Democrats are committed to rule by the people. They insist that no aristocrat, monarch, bureaucrat, expert, or religious leader has the right, in virtue of such status, to force people to accept a particular conception of the proper common life. People should decide for themselves, via appropriate procedures of collective decision, what their collective business should be. They may reasonably be required to consult and take account of one another, and of others affected by their actions, but beyond this no one may legitimately tell them what to do. *The people are sovereign; in all matters of collective life they rule over themselves.*[1]

The question, of course, is how to make this sovereign power an actuality. Single individuals can watch commercials and vote, but republican democracy exists only when people come together to talk about their goals for their community and country. When people engage in political discussions in small face-to-face groups or in public meetings they constitute a public. Publics are the heart and soul of democracy; they constitute the political community talking to itself. As ongoing fixtures of open democratic societies, publics constantly spring to life and dissolve from view, enlarging and shrinking as time and interest dictate. Within the roots and branches of democracy, these little cells of democratic talk support the institutional trunk of the government. Sitting high atop a national pyramid of discussion circles is Congress—the "archetype of the little circles of face-to-face citizens discussing their public business."[2]

Arendt saw totalitarianism's evil core as the ability of the modern state to destroy public life. Because the exchange of ideas is the seedbed of freedom, despots view any meeting of more than three people as suspect. At the other extreme of political life, Arendt viewed Athens and the American Revolution as embodying the democratic ideal: equal political citizens sharing the public stage and using voice, not violence, to shape their political future. Arendt, Dewey, and Jürgen Habermas, three of the most important political thinkers of the twentieth century, approached politics in strikingly different ways.[3] But they are unanimous in stressing the necessity of publics for robust and healthy democratic politics, especially in an age dominated by bureaucratic organizations and a global economy. For Habermas, the public sphere "designates a theater in modern society in which political participation is enacted through the medium of talk. It is the space in which citizens deliberate about their common affairs" and an arena conceptually distinct from the state. Its collective judgments are the locus of state power, but the discussions generated are often critical of the administration in power. It is also distinct from the economy. It operates by the logic of the forum, not the market.[4]

In *The Structural Transformation of the Public Sphere,* Habermas explains how modernity began when a restlessness with absolute monarchy, the emergence of the bourgeois economy, and the Protestant Reformation combined to encourage individuals to think for themselves.[5] As Kant observed in *"What is Enlightenment?"* individuals by themselves would have a hard time working their way out of tutelage.[6] This changes when people talk to one another and share ideas. As Habermas writes, "thinking for oneself seemed to coincide with thinking aloud and the use of reason with its public use."[7] To Habermas's regret, the robust public ethos of democratic revolutions subsequently gave way to the culture of consumption of the postwar era. Public discourse shifted from an emphasis on critical debate to negotiation and bargaining. As interest groups arose, the "exercise and equilibration of power" began to take place "directly between private bureaucracies, special interest associations, parties and public administration" with the public only occasionally included in the "circuit of power."[8] As the deliberative ideal deteriorated into interest-group squabbling less attention was given to thinking about the common good. The importance of publics waned, and the pluralist struggle for power came to the fore. It is against this backdrop that the participatory activism of the 1960s and the more recent republican and deliberative chorus must be seen.

A central insight of republican thought is that the formation of the will takes place during discussion—not prior. Political obligation may spring from individual wills, from choices arrived at by individuals, but these individuals make up their minds by listening to, and sometimes engaging in, political discussion and debate. Republican and deliberative theorists hold that a mechanical aggregation of particular individual wills by means of a vote is insufficient to confer legitimacy on a collective choice. The only way it could be so is if the vote were unanimous, but, as we know, this is extremely rare. As Manin writes, "The source of legitimacy is not the predetermined will of individuals, but rather the process of its formation, that is, deliberation itself."[9]

Deliberation can search for points of consensus, but unanimity is not to be expected. The aim is the broadening of the participants' knowledge and insight into the problems at hand. The goal for each citizen is to discover his or her own preferences after listening to a multiplicity of views. Manin argues, "it seems reasonable to seek, as an essential condition for legitimacy, the deliberation of *all* or, more precisely, the right of all to participate in deliberation.[10] The possibility of agreement is far less important than establishing conditions where as many people as possible partake in political discussion, argument, and debate. In contrast to Rousseau, a legitimate decision does not spring from the will of all (being the sum of already-formed opinion), but results from the deliberation of all. As a practical matter, the goal becomes one of constructing democratic institutions that approximate this test.

This ideal harkens back to the Athenian principle of *isēgoria*—the universal right to address the assembly. The republican position views participation and deliberation among citizens—not just between political elites, legislators, and interest group leaders—as being the sine qua non of the democratic experience. Modern theorists as diverse as Jon Elster, Habermas, and Rawls hold that, "political choice, to be legitimate, must be the outcome of deliberation about ends among free, equal and rational agents."[11]

It is certainly possible to use Schumpeter's conception of competitive election and Dahl's model of the basic freedoms necessary for polyarchy (the rule of many) as the minimal understanding of what democracy requires. Authoritarian societies making the transition to democracy must meet these hurdles to qualify as democracies. Yet, as Dahl points out, this is a rather meager understanding of democracy. Advanced industrial nations, especially ones such as the United States with long democratic traditions and strong constitutional norms, can aspire to higher stages of democratic development. The narrow procedural theory that gained prominence in the United States during the Cold War is incomplete and deficient precisely because it ignores the republican part of our civic nature. This empirical fact is demonstrated by the periods of democratic passion that periodically grip American citizens, causing them to search for better ways to participate in the governing of their nation. These tidal waves of civic energy retreat, yet return with regularity.[12]

DELIBERATION VERSUS ADVOCACY

One way to grasp the central place that deliberation and publics play in a republican conception of politics is to think of democracy as involving four stages of public discussion. Each stage involves the exchange of information, discussion, and dialogue, but each differs in important respects from the others. The stages are: (1) information gathering, (2) exploratory public discussion, (3) advocacy, and (4) decision making. Today, stages 1, 3, and 4 are well developed and identified with specific institutions: books, the Internet, libraries, magazines, newspapers, television (stage 1); interest groups, lobbyists, PACs, political parties, talk radio (stage 3); and the bureaucracy and the executive branch (stage 4). Congress is special in that its hearings and investigations (information), committee structure and floor debate (exploratory discussion *and* advocacy), and voting power (decision making) span the four stages.

Of these four stages, exploratory public discussion is underappreciated, amorphous, and considerably less institutionalized. Examples include friends talking over dinner, town halls, community meetings, and deliberative discussions in legislatures. Ideally, exploratory public discussion is characterized by a physical space where discussion takes place, a type of discussion that is open and evolving, and a sense of community based on mutual respect and political equality. When these three elements are present a fruitful discussion can take place and a common or "public" voice may emerge. Exploratory discussion (stage 2) differs in important respects from advocacy (stage 3). The harsh rebukes that often accompany the spirited debate of advocacy are not appropriate to the discussion stage. But when people grow up thinking about politics in terms of rigid ideological positions, it is easy to overlook the deliberative stage and to think of politics as moving straight from information gathering to advocacy. (Or more accurately, from ideological or partisan stance, determined by family background, to information gathering on a new issue, filtered by trusted sources such as friends, radio talk show hosts, and newspapers, to advocacy, and possibly organization.)

Procedural democrats, Schumpeter and the pluralists, tend to overlook the exploratory discussion stage because they think of democratic politics primarily as a mechanism for aggregating prepolitical interests. In this view, people come to the political arena with their political opinions already formed and unlikely to change during political debate. Thus, politics becomes the advocacy of entrenched positions and is largely a zero-sum game of winning or losing. By contrast, republicans understand that positions are constantly being modified and interests are partially formed through political debate.

In exploratory public discussion, where listening prevails over persuasion and positions are fluid instead of fixed, every participant must pay close attention to the discussion at hand and attempt to understand the values and beliefs that underlie various positions. Here, similar to the deliberations of a jury, each individual must work at understanding other people and wrestle with how divergent opinions might be bridged. As such, it is a stage of democracy that should not be skipped. Unfortunately, it often is. Dionne points out that "press and television may have produced livelier formats," such as *Crossfire* and *Hardball*, "without actually enlivening the public debate. The liveliness is, in some sense, artificial. It involves people tossing epithets and one-liners at one another as weapons." By contrast, Lasch writes, in genuine argument "we have to enter imaginatively into our opponents' arguments, if only for the purpose of refuting them, and we may end up being persuaded by those we sought to persuade." Thus, genuine open discussion is "risky and unpredictable and therefore educational."[13]

The analytical distinction between exploratory discussion and advocacy often blurs in practice. Yet, the distinction is important because democracy works best when citizens are skilled at both and are able to move back and forth between them. Although many people like the security of partisanship and feel vulnerable in exploratory discussion, stage 2 champions the benefits of uncertainty. Discussion asks citizens to open themselves to having their views modified; advocacy, by contrast, assumes that citizens have strong beliefs and ready arguments to answer the opposition.

The outlook required by deliberative democracy resembles that of a jury. While the lawyers are required to take an adversarial stance, the jury is required to listen and weigh the arguments and facts presented. The attorney's task is to present the best possible argument for one side in a dispute; the jury's mission is to be open to the evidence and search for the truth. At the same time, public discussion is more creative and less constrained than the judicial process, which limits the information that a jury can utilize in arriving at a verdict.

A public forum is an exercise in community thinking that is creative and projective. In contrast to dueling political professionals demeaning each other's well-known and oft-repeated arguments, deliberative assemblies strive to foster new ways of thinking about problems that are outside the normal ideological ruts. Instead of regurgitating standard positions, the goal of discussion is to promote new leaps of thinking. Dewey argued that real "thinking" happens precisely when we force ourselves to take mental leaps into the unknown. "Inference is always an invasion of the unknown, a leap." Acquiring knowledge is different from thinking, which is "a projection of considerations which have not been previously apprehended."[14] Because of this innovative quality, deliberation helps create new ground for consensus that did not previously exist. And where consensus cannot be reached, which is the case with nearly every question in public life, a fair hearing of the different positions can help an open-minded audience decide what is the right path to follow.

In exploratory discussion, every participant has a duty, a responsibility to think about the general good of the wider community. When individuals are capable of thinking beyond themselves, to imaginatively "see" how prospective public policies will affect others, then they have achieved a higher stage of moral and intellectual growth. This is a central goal of republican politics. Democracy takes advantage of many minds working on a problem and, in the free give-and-take of discussion, the narrowness and the one-sidedness of each person's view is amended, and a truer picture of reality emerges. Taken seriously, discussion is not only a way of registering consent, but a search for knowledge and truth. The sense of community that emerges as people begin to know one another through discussion assists in the search for consensus. This spirit of community is encouraged by the norm of friendship, which admonishes us to listen carefully to others even if we are strong advocates of a different position. Of course, it is easy to develop a connection with someone who agrees with you. But, legislators often feel a bond of friendship with an opponent they consistently disagree with politically but respect as a person. And even those troublesome individuals, who appear to take pleasure at rankling the nerves and the patience of others, will sometimes cooperate if they feel their views have been heard and considered.

Having a deeper appreciation of what publics are and how discussion differs from advocacy, we move forward to defend a "reasonable" idea of deliberation and consider the relationship between publics, power, and justice. In political society, a continuum of possibilities extends from brute force on one end to ideal deliberative democracy on the other. Violence is dramatic, attention grabbing, and sometimes deadly. It seeks to impose one view and obliterate all opposition. But violence, as Arendt understood, is also mute.[15] Democracy, by contrast, reaches its highest expression when citizens speak to each other as equals and open themselves to public reason. The principles of deliberative democracy define what sort of talk, under what conditions, should take place in publics. As publics define the "where," so deliberation is the "what."

What is the essence of democracy in ideal terms? In *Democracy and Its Critics,* Dahl sets forth five requirements necessary for a political society to be considered fully democratic. They are effective participation, voting equality at the decisive stage, enlightened understanding, control of the agenda, and full inclusion of all adult members (except for transients and those who are mentally defective).[16] Both the requirement for effective participation and enlightened understanding speak to the need for generous deliberative opportunities. Cohen, in an influential article, "Deliberation and Democratic Legitimacy," puts forth four ideal criteria by which to judge the degree to which structured deliberation may be said to generate the legitimate authority to make decisions and exercise power. For Cohen, ideal deliberation would be free, reasoned, equal, and consensual.[17] I agree on the first three criteria (free, reasoned, and equal) with minor modifications, substitute robust discussion in search of the truth as an alternative to consensual, and add two additional criteria: a concern for the common good and publicity.

What is critical is the journey, not the result. Public decisions should not be unduly influenced by money or external pressure. As Habermas writes, "What is important is whether it is deliberation—undistorted by private power—that gave rise to the outcome." In ideal deliberation, "no force except that of the better argument is exercised; and that, as a result, all motives except that of the cooperative search for truth are excluded."[18] When we deliberate as political equals, it is the reasons and arguments invoked that sway opinion, not the possibility of political contributions in the next election cycle. Deliberation is free from the threat of sanction or use of force and free in the sense of Pettit's idea of nondenomination.

Second, in ideal deliberation, participants have "equal standing at each stage of the deliberative process."[19] Each can place issues on the agenda and offer reasons in favor of a proposal or criticism. The distribution of resources outside the deliberative arena should not affect the equality between participants inside the deliberative sphere. Deliberative equality should not mean that each person has an equal effect on the outcome, rather, as Mansbridge says, the "force of the better argument should prevail." Equality also supports the idea of mutual respect between participants. This requires listening and, by imagination and empathy, putting oneself in the place of another.[20] Third, discussion should be "reasoned" in the sense that participants are required to put forth reasons for making arguments, supporting them or criticizing them. Power, or the lack thereof, should come in the form of logical argument that listeners can evaluate and judge. Yet the idea of reasoned argument holds a bias against displays of emotion, and a dichotomy between reason and emotion is artificial.[21] Passion is often the power behind reason. Thus, Mansbridge argues correctly that "considered" is a better label than "reasoned" for what we mean.[22]

Fourth, following in the footsteps of Rousseau's idea of the general will and Habermas's idea of a perfect speech situation, Cohen argues for an ideal of democratic consensus that is highly ambitious—and unnecessary. Cohen says deliberation aims to arrive at a "rationally motivated consensus—to find reasons that are persuasive to all who are committed to acting on the results of a free and reasoned assessment of the alternatives by equals."[23] I am in agreement with Cohen on his first three criteria, but not on consensus. There is no need to have a goal of consensus unless one is committed to Rousseau's radical idea of freedom—something that is utterly unrealistic in modern society. To view deliberative discussion leading to decisions by majority rule as being less than legitimate is a mistake.

What is important about deliberation, and I say more about this later, is that it is a method by which we can face each other as citizens and make political choices for the community at large in a fair and equal fashion. Most political decisions are based on power calculations having little to do with reasoned debate by free and equal citizens; they are based on arbitrary power, not public power. In addition, argument, conflict, and the contest of ideas are as essential to democracy as are well-mannered deliberation and a search for consensus. It is important to search for areas of accord, but not at the expense of papering over disagreement.[24] As a number of writers have pointed out, nondecisions and hegemonic definitions of the common good are ways that elites hide disharmony.[25] Deliberation sometimes reveals deep-seated conflict.[26] A focus on finding unanimity would make this a cause for concern. Instead, we need to recognize disagreement and conflict for what they are, a normal part of the human condition. Ideal deliberation seeks not consensus, but rather robust discussion and argument in a search for the truth.

Fifth, legislators, judges, and citizens should aspire to go beyond the simple aggregation of existing private preferences and think about the common good and the values we wish to promote when making public policy.[27] One crucial goal of democratic politics is to reflect on and sometimes change existing volitions, not simply to put them into practice. In a "republic of reason," to use Sunstein's phrase, preferences are not given, they evolve and are subject to revision. Flexibility and openness to rethinking one's positions is a desirable trait in democratic politics. "If you show him new information, he's willing to rethink his positions. That's one of his strengths."[28] The idea of intelligent discussion having an effect on how individuals view the world is related to Dewey's concept of taste.[29] People who become experts in a particular field continually refine their attitudes and understandings. Even people who know a tremendous amount about a certain subject, whether it is painting, managing a business, or hitting a baseball, constantly learn, adapt, and refine their knowledge. If this is true for experts, it is true to an even greater degree for laypersons involved in political discussion about the issues of the day.

Finally, publicity and open persuasion lie at the heart of deliberative democracy. In his book about how Congress should work, Bessette begins with this phrase from Madison in *Federalist* No. 42: "The mild voice of reason, pleading the cause of an enlarged and permanent interest, is but too often drowned, before public bodies as well as individuals, by the clamor of an impatient avidity for immediate and immoderate gain."[30]

Rawls makes this crucial point about persuasion and evidence. For deliberative democracy to work, he writes, "each of us must have, and be ready to explain, a criterion of what principles and guidelines we think other citizens (who are also free and equal) may reasonably be expected to endorse along with us." Put slightly differently, "what public reason asks is that citizens be able to explain their vote to one another in terms of a reasonable balance of public political values."[31]

The idea of publicity plays to our expectation that what is public must be open to scrutiny and debate. If a particular group's desires are so narrow and selfish that they cannot be expressed as goals that would benefit more than just themselves, then their aims do not meet the test of public justification. The glare of the media and the gaze of the public embarrass narrow, selfish interests and secret backroom deals. Sunstein writes: "Above all, the American constitution was designed to create a deliberative democracy." Under our system, legislators are "ultimately accountable to the people;" but they also "engage in a form of deliberation without domination through the influence of factions. A law based solely on the self-interest of private groups is the core violation of the deliberative ideal."[32] This, of course, speaks to the corrosive threat that wealthy and powerful interests pose to democratic politics.

In sum, the deliberative ideal "promotes a conception of reason over power in politics." Policies ought to be adopted not because the most powerful interests stack the deck, but because the citizens (or their representatives) propose solutions to public problems; discuss the merits of various policy options; and after hearing, testing, and critiquing the arguments, make a collective choice as to which is most worthy.[33] Deliberative democracy is not suitable for many political situations. It is not going to replace executive authority, congressional bargaining or bureaucratic gamesmanship. But deliberative debate is a particularly appropriate mode of action for the wider public represented in the Assembly and the People's House. A portion of the public, having a third party's intelligence informed by the media, interest groups, and their own research, would straddle the boundary between spectator and political insider. In this sense, delegates would have a perspective similar to that of an informed journalist. Able to share their informed opinions freely with each other, they would, by their deliberative opinions and votes, send signals to the Congress and the nation. In the case of the Assembly and the People's House, deliberative norms of "solicitous goodwill, creative intelligence, and a desire to get the right answer" are appropriate and not out of place.[34]

CASH VALUE

Dahl, Habermas, and Rawls all construct an abstract procedural account of democracy, in part, because they know a substantive description will be contested. This view is inevitable given the pluralism of values in the modern world. Rawls spells out the dilemma: "How is it possible that there may exist over time a stable and just society of free and equal citizens profoundly divided by reasonable religious, philosophical, and moral doctrines? . . . The work of abstraction, then, is not gratuitous: not abstraction for abstraction's sake. Rather it is a way of continuing public discussion when shared understandings of lesser generality have broken down."[35] Yet, while discussions of deliberative democracy at a high level of abstraction may be necessary, we also must descend from philosophic heights and think concretely about what deliberation and publics mean in actual fact.[36] Shapiro points out, "[E]very political theory rests on higher order assumptions, but it is also true that all such assumptions are controversial. Consequently, if we put off the questions of institutional design until the higher order questions are settled, we may get to them at the time of Godot's arrival."[37] What has been missing from debates over deliberative democracy is a discussion of political practice and institutional design. Once we have a grasp of what the democratic ideal can and should be, it is incumbent on us to re-examine our current practices and institutions with an eye on their possible improvement. If discussions about deliberative democracy are to have what William James termed "cash value," then, at some point, theory must meet practice.

Some argue that size and complexity make the ideals of deliberative democracy romantic and quaint. This might be true if all participatory theorists adopted Rousseau's position in opposition to representative government and if, as some believe, conceptions of deliberative democracy are oblivious to questions of power.[38] However, as the preceding discussion of the Assembly and the People's House shows, deliberative democracy need not be characterized in this way. The view of deliberation offered here is not the most demanding ideal; rather it is a reasonable, flexible, and practical approximation.[39]

Three basic facts need to be recognized. First, much of democracy is not deliberative. Walzer offers a sketch of organization, mobilization, demonstration, advocacy, bargaining, lobbying, campaigning, and voting as being critical to democracy, yet not being deliberative. He concludes by noting that although deliberation plays an important role in democratic politics, it does not have "an independent place—a place so to speak, of its own."[40] Maybe it should. If we want to protect deliberation from being squeezed out by other necessities of political life, then we should consider creating an independent place for publics to form and deliberation to take place. If deliberation—rational discussion between equal citizens—is the high point of democracy, we should do our best to actively promote it. Granted, deliberative publics are not all there is to democracy. Still, we don't want to marginalize them either—and that is precisely what current political practice does. Having a protected civic space where publics could investigate, probe, and deliberate about the public's problems would provide us with a more attentive, more deliberative set of public opinion to consult before deciding critical public policy questions.

Second, learning to deliberate in the United States may be "inseparable from indoctrination in familiar routines of hierarchy and deference," and a bias toward speech that is rational and moderate may implicitly exclude "public talk that is impassioned, extreme, and the product of particular interests."[41] True, deliberative discussion is a certain type of political talk. Compared to other speech, deliberative talk pays more attention to rational argument and to listening to other people's points of views. Iris Young says that we should expand the traditional elite understanding of "rational debate"—often viewed as unemotional, dispassionate, and disembodied—by adding three other styles of communication to our understanding of democratic dialogue: greeting, rhetoric, and storytelling. Greeting is explicit mutual recognition and caring for the other person; rhetorical devices such as humor recognize the needs of the audience; storytelling is helpful in situations of tension and conflict because narrative stories help ensure that the speaker and audience have at least some shared understanding and common ground.[42] It is certainly possible to widen our understanding of what deliberation can and should be to include multiple modes of discourse.

Finally, to be a useful tool, deliberative democracy must show that it can grapple with issues of power, hierarchy, and structural inequality. It is to the issue of power that we now turn.

PUBLICS, POWER, AND JUSTICE

The idea of deliberation between equal citizens is a powerful democratic ideal, but unless we can find a way to connect deliberation to power it will remain an ideal and nothing more. For some, democratic deliberation is idealistic chatter without consequence. It falls prey to Oscar Wilde's quip that socialism would be a good thing but would require too many evenings. What counts in the real world are power and interests; that is what Lyndon Johnson lived and Karl Marx observed. If deliberation and publics are going to make a difference in people's lives, then the deliberative approach must show how it can make a difference in the calculation and pursuit of power.

Deliberation alone will not suffice. Indeed, deliberation only becomes powerful if and when we (1) situate deliberation in publics and (2) strategically link certain designated publics to the political process. This is what the Assembly and People's House aim to do. Of course, we expect publics to spring up spontaneously and, to some extent, they do. Yet, in the early twenty-first century, discussion and debate, and the public spaces where these take place, cannot be assumed or taken for granted. A conception of democracy that places a high degree of importance on deliberation and publics is not a quixotic quest for direct democracy. When critics of participatory democracy argue that modern democracy has outgrown town hall discussions, they fall captive to the idea of assembling more and more people in one place.[43] But Tocqueville's America was not a city-state, nor could its citizens assemble in one place. If size was no bar then to so lively a democratic engagement, it need not be now.[44] The question is not one of size, but of motivation and institutional design.

Publics have a continuum of power. At one extreme are totalitarian and authoritarian regimes where publics are actively discouraged and public discussion can lead to imprisonment, or worse. At the other pole are gatherings where we begin to move toward the deliberative ideas expressed in Kant's ideal and Habermas' description of eighteenth-century London coffee houses. Here people meet regularly as political equals and take the time to discuss divergent views at length. Here there are "weak publics," those where discussion consists exclusively in expressing opinions and does not extend to making authoritative decisions, and "strong publics," those where people both exchange ideas and make decisions.[45] The Assembly is a weak public. The People's House is a strong public, as are state legislatures, Congress and Parliament. Strong publics have a high degree of power due to their ability to translate opinion into an authoritative decision.

In promoting a practical conception of deliberative democracy, it is critical to keep three points in mind. First, just having people talk to each other is not sufficient. We want to encourage and promote situations where the quality of discourse rises to a certain level. "Everyday talk is not necessarily aimed at any action other than talk itself; deliberation in assembly is, at least in theory, aimed at action."[46] Second, we want to include as many people as possible without diminishing the quality of discourse.[47] Third, it is necessary to consider the relationship between "weak" and "strong" publics and ponder whether that link might be strengthened.

In Dewey's work we find a definition of the public that can help us confront the dilemmas of power in modern society.[48] For Dewey, a public comes into existence not just when a group of people comes together, but when relations between two parties (be they individuals, groups, or companies) have ripple effects on third parties. In *The Public and Its Problems* (1927) he writes, "The public consists of all those who are affected by the indirect consequences of transactions to such an extent that it is deemed necessary to have those consequences systematically cared for."[49] These third parties are the public. They are observers of the action and feel the consequences of the action and thus should have a say in how the matter is resolved.

Dewey's problem-oriented definition builds off Charles Peirce's observation that all thinking starts from a problem. All of us have experienced the phenomenon of suddenly becoming interested in a certain subject—whether it is building a backyard deck or planning a vacation—and discovering a new world of information that had always existed but we had never noticed. Our new focus causes our minds to consider the issue at hand and to figure out the various connections and relations that need to be understood in order to make a good decision. In a public, this conversation aims at finding a solution and making a decision. As such, casual, personal conversations about most subjects do not come under its preview. It is discussions about *public problems*—issues that jump private boundaries and begin to affect third parties—that are its particular domain. When we move away from deliberation as an abstract ideal and think about deliberation in publics in the way Dewey suggests, we gain a framework that allows us to address the issue of power.

What is the connection between publics and power? Here we come to a question of definition. Often power is seen as something closely held and forced on others. One common definition holds that power is being exercised when A can get B to do something that B would rather not do.[50] Here the agent possessing power is most likely an individual or a small group. By contrast, Arendt argues that power "springs up between men when they act together and vanishes when they disperse." She writes that power belongs only to a group and not to an individual because it "corresponds to the human ability not just to act but to act in concert."[51] In making this distinction, Arendt aimed to turn the Orwellian tables on dictators and authoritarians. The quality they harness is not power, but the threat and use of violence. The violence of the few can be, and often is, greater than the power of the many. But in a democracy, the force exercised by a few is often suspect and must be justified as an exception to the rule of the many.[52]

Incorporating Arendt's insight, when thinking about power it is useful to distinguish between public power and arbitrary power. Arbitrary power is back-room politics, the muscle of special interest groups and corporate CEOs, such as Enron's Kenneth Lay, using generous political contributions to take control of the public agenda. Democratic power, on the other hand, fits with the understanding of deliberative democracy, civic majorities, and publics expounded here.

The core idea of public power is that third parties, with an eye on the common good, should help decide issues we have in common when the decisions made affect many. I am not arguing that deliberative politics is going to make arbitrary power disappear. Nor am I equating normal interest group bargaining, cajoling, and lobbying with arbitrary power. What we need is an appreciation of politics that does not dismiss the commitment to a deliberative politics as hopelessly naïve. Providing opportunity and space for deliberative politics will educate the public to the importance of coalition building and lobbying and the inevitable chaos and untidiness of democratic decision making. Participants might, in fact, gain "an appreciation for the ugliness of democracy."[53]

Historically, American political culture has attempted to institutionalize public power. At the founding, traditional civic republican doctrine held that the citizen gentry possessed the education and character necessary for civic virtue and thus were the best qualified to consider and ponder the general good. Later, this duty was assigned to the courts, and contemporary legal republicans such as Frank Michelman and Sunstein write about the judicial branch in this vein.[54] Public power also can be institutionalized if we expand the sphere of deliberative participation. This is the insight of Schattschneider: "All politics, all leadership and all organization involves the management of conflict . . . All forms of political organization have a bias in favor of the exploitation of some kinds of conflict and the suppression of others because organization is the mobilization of bias."[55] If Group A is winning a political struggle with Group B because Group A has 60 percent support within the small circle who are following issue X, it may well be in Group B's interest to expand the scope of conflict by inviting more people to participate in making the decision. By contrast, Group A controls the outcome if the boundaries of decision are respected.

The democratic question becomes, Is the power that Group A holds arbitrary or unjust? If third-party observers examine the situation and declare that the decision and resulting policy are unfair, perhaps blatantly, this would be an example of bad power. Public power gets the upper hand if the sphere is expanded, allowing more people to have a voice on the issue. Obviously, the initiative process and other techniques of mass direct democracy expand the sphere. However, the key to public power is the deliberative participation of an aware public making a choice based on informed, reasoned judgments. Impressions gleaned from thirty-second attack ads do not qualify.

Dewey's definition of the public has much in common with Madison's idea of deliberative democracy and civic majorities.[56] Madison had high hopes for his vision of deliberative discussion. In his view, widening the diversity of interests on which majorities are based would change the dynamics of discussion. The perspective of majority opinions would be elevated because of the transforming effect of deliberation on preferences to emphasize considerations beyond the immediate constituency, whether geographic or interest based. Understanding that majority rule in the exclusive interest of the majority is oppressive; Madison's goal with both civic majorities and bicameralism is to force any majority to widen its outlook. The expectation is clearly stated in *Federalist* No. 51: "In the extended republic of the United States, and among the great variety of interest, parties, and sects which it embraces, a coalition of a majority of the whole society could seldom take place on any other principles than those of justice and the general good."[57] As Beer observes, "The judgments of the extended republic will be more just because they are more general, and they will be more general because, perforce, they must include a greater variety of interests . . . Government would still be majoritarian, but the governing majorities would not be factious but civic majorities which uphold unbiased justice and express the public interest."[58] Like Dewey, Madison is speaking of the wider public as attentive third parties who can act as impartial jurors deciding the public's business.

Madison's system of representation based on civic majorities is designed to counter two common displays of arbitrary power. On one side, we have the phenomenon of modern mass society. Here we face the danger of unthinking (or at least simplistic) majority opinion—the sort of democratic tyranny feared by Madison, Tocqueville, and John Stuart Mill. Examples of this type of arbitrary power are ill-considered initiatives running rampant in some states and the danger of slick ideologues and hucksters dominating the airways. On the other side, we see special interest and money power driven by greed and a sense of entitlement, twisting public sector decisions in their favor. Here public power is needed to rebalance the system.

The idea of democratic power is ultimately linked to the question of democratic justice. Reflecting on Aristotle, Richard Kraut writes:

> Politics as practiced by modern liberal democracies is precisely the thing that Aristotle took political activity to be: free and public discussion among equals about matters of justice . . . Our rational and communal nature gives rise to expectations of fair treatment, and so we enter into debate with others who have different conceptions

of justice . . . The "problems of the political animal" are inherent in our rationality and sociability . . . We are natural equals who should enter into the political fray with the realistic expectation that at best we can achieve only partial agreement. Nor can we look to specialists in philosophy to resolve our disputes about justice, for the concept of justice is not sufficiently determinate to serve this purpose. What justice requires depends on what fair-minded individuals work out as they engage in the political process and seek workable accommodations.[59]

Obviously, politics has changed since Aristotle wrote, but when Americans get together to speak about their goals for their community, the subject matter is still justice. In *Power and Powerlessness*, John Gaventa discusses the realities of life in the coalfields of Appalachia. He discovered that power is both about institutional barriers and the "shaping of beliefs about an order's legitimacy or immutability."[60] Political scientists now think of power as involving three dimensions: the first being the bargaining and negotiating that everyone can see; the second being the "mobilization of bias" that refers to the ability of one party to keep certain issues off the agenda and set rules of the game to favor their side; and the third being the social construction of reality, in terms of language and shared understandings, such that people who have every right to be angry with the status quo passively accept continual defeat.[61] At the level of constitutional law, far removed from the coalfields of Appalachia and ghettos of the inner city, Sunstein speaks of passive acceptance of the status quo in Supreme Court decisions. In both of these arenas—and all those that lie in between—the power equation is defined by agenda setting and whether people decide to challenge what Sunstein terms "status quo neutrality."[62]

When deliberative discussion in publics lives up to its promise, citizens begin to think critically about the world around them. Argument and deliberation sometimes reveal "what the underlying interests at stake actually are."[63] The value of deliberation in the Assembly lies in delegates achieving a heightened awareness of the issues at hand and the dimensions of power involved. The goal is neither consensus nor deliberation for deliberation sake. Rather, the reason is to create a pool of super citizens who are assertive, engaged, and empowered in the sense of being unafraid to confront situations where power is being wielded arbitrarily and against public benefit. We will be asking the Assembly delegates to stand for and represent "us"—meaning average middle-class and working-class Americans.

Choosing delegates by lot, instead of election, means giving voice and standing to many of our fellow citizens who would not ordinarily be candidates for political office. In this way, we open the door to leadership by those previously left in the shadows. The elites and the wealthy will continue to have their spokespersons. The Assembly would counterbalance the power of the elite in American society by amplifying the voice of the broad public in the national conversation. The People's House (stage two) would have a powerful, sometimes decisive vote on national legislation, while the Assembly (stage one) would personify the public and provide national decision makers and administrators with a window on what the "sophisticated and informed" American public thought about issues X, Y, and Z.

The criticisms made of deliberative democracy can, at least partially, be met once we place deliberation within publics.[64] Among contemporary writers, Walzer sees an opposition between democratic struggle and deliberative publics.[65] He writes:

> Political history . . . is mostly the story of the slow creation or consolidation of hierarchies of wealth and power. People fight their way to the top of these hierarchies and then contrive as best they can to maintain their position . . . Popular organizations and mobilizations are the only ways to oppose this aim. Their effect is not—at least has never been—to level the hierarchies, but only to shake them up, bring new people in, and perhaps set limits . . . So democratic politics makes possible an amended version of political history: Now it is the story of the establishment *and partial disestablishment* of inequality. I don't see any way to avoid the endless repetition of this story, any way to replace the struggles it involves with a deliberative process.[66]

Walzer views deliberation as taking place in isolation and having few, if any, ramifications for those holding arbitrary power. Dewey, on the other hand, views deliberation in publics as the public coming to fuller consciousness and awareness of the political environment. These critically aware citizens would decide what is proper, what is fair, and what is just. Deliberation becomes a powerful and useful idea when we situate deliberation in publics and situate publics in the political process. The publics created by the Assembly and the People's House could help us confront and grapple with issues of power and inequality.

Any solution to the dilemma of democratic participation in the modern nation-state must take account of the problem of limited time and attention. Both of these realities push us to consider reinventing representation rather than expanding, yet again, direct modes of participation. To do this we need two components: new institutions and new habits. Both are possible. Dewey argued that average people have the ability to think about and weigh the issues of the day. "It is not necessary that the many should have the knowledge and skill to carry on the needed investigations; what is required is that they have the ability to judge of the bearing of the knowledge supplied by others upon common concerns."[67]

The problem for Dewey and for us today is how to help publics find and form themselves under modern conditions. "The prime difficulty," Dewey writes, "[remains] that of discovering the means by which a scattered, mobile and manifold public may so recognize itself as to define and express its interests."[68] This is what the Assembly and the People's House promise to do. It is critical that we find a way for the public to talk to itself. Schumpeter's system of competitive elites is, in essence, a system of competitive oligarchy. As Machiavelli understood, because the elite are infatuated by power and find it easy to dominate others, they often do. Liberty is in much safer hands with the people at large:

> I will say, that one should always confide any deposit to those who have least desire of violating it; and doubtless, if we consider the objects of nobles and of the people, we must see that the first have a great desire to dominate, whilst the latter have only the wish not to be dominated, and consequently a greater desire to live in the enjoyment of liberty; so that when the people are intrusted with the care of any privilege or liberty, being less disposed to encroach upon it, they will of necessity take better care of it; and being unable to take it away from themselves, will prevent others from doing so.[69]

8.

Constitutional Balance

Eight of ten Americans probably would agree that our political system needs reform. The question is, what is the right cure for our problems? Term limits and Ross Perot's idea of a national electronic town hall, two reforms highly touted during the 1990s, enjoy wide appeal. Term limits envisions citizen legislators striding up the steps of the Capitol to take charge; the electronic town hall imagines the nation as a single village on the Web. However, on close inspection, these advertised methods of empowering the public are misconceived. It would be a good thing if we could involve citizens in robust discussion on the issues of the day in a venue where their considered views could make a difference. Unfortunately, neither term limits nor electronic direct democracy does the job. Reforming American politics is a tricky business because the goal is a government that is both responsive and efficient. Americans may express frustration with the system, but they do not want Democracy Italian style, with governments as unstable as melting ice, or British-style majority rule, where the minority party automatically loses both the executive and the legislative branches. Reforms inspired by European experience face tough sledding on this side of the Atlantic because Americans show little enthusiasm for junking the Madisonian system—a creative blend of two contrary approaches to constitutional design.

Four major reforms discussed during the past two decades—electronic town hall, term limits, proportional representation, and parliamentary-style democracy—are fatally flawed. Two other proposed reforms, streamlining government bureaucracy and campaign finance reform, championed by the right and left, respectively, would help but are difficult to accomplish and alone do too little.

THE QUESTION OF CONSTITUTIONAL BALANCE

The Wright brothers of modern democracy, the founders led the first great democratic revolution and created our system of representative government. However, they are not the sole authorities on the design of modern democratic constitutions. In *Democracies,* Arend Lijphart, a leading scholar of the world's constitutions and their political implications, sets out two opposing schemes of democratic governments and explains how the American system is a hybrid.[1] He begins with this question: "Who will do the governing and to whose interests should the government be responsive when the people are in disagreement and have divergent preferences?" One answer is the majority of the people. The alternative answer is: as many people as possible. Both are equally valid ways to design a democratic constitution. British parliamentary democracy, the Westminster Model, is a pure example of majoritarian rule. However, less homogeneous nations—from Lebanon to Switzerland to the former Yugoslavia and post-Saddam Iraq—are sharply divided along religious, ethnic, ideological, linguistic, and racial lines and discover that simple majority-rule democracy leads to trouble. Lijphart argues that majoritarian democracy is especially appropriate and works best in homogenous societies; the second model, consensual democracy, is better suited to heterogeneous ones.

In British parliamentarian democracy, power is concentrated. The party that wins the most seats in the House of Commons forms the government. The leader of the winning party, say, Tony Blair, becomes the prime minister and chooses his cabinet from other senior Labor Party members in Parliament. There is no separation between the executive and legislative branches, and the courts do not have nearly the power and independence of the American judiciary. Majority rule is the name of the game in parliamentary democracy; exclusion is the problem.

In nations segregated into virtual subsocieties by ethnic and religious differences, majority rule can be undemocratic and dangerous. Straight-up majority rule in diverse societies means minorities are often excluded from power and their rights violated. Look at Lebanon and Northern Ireland, where groups continually denied access to power lost allegiance to the regime. Diverse societies need democracy based on consensus instead of opposition, inclusion instead of exclusion, and a style of government that maximizes the size of the ruling majority (via broad coalitions) instead of being satisfied with bare majority (50 percent plus 1) democracy. Lijphart points to Switzerland and Belgium as examples of "plural societies" that have created consensual democracy to cope with diversity and provide a democratic voice to all citizens. The characteristics of consensus democracy aim at restraining the power of the majority. This is done by requiring or encouraging the sharing of power (separation of powers or coalition governments), a fair distribution of power (proportional representation), a decentralizing of power (federalism), and a formal limit on power (a written constitution).

The United States, paradoxically and beneficially, combines a unique blend of the majoritarian and consensual perspectives. The American system borrows three key elements from the majoritarian (British) model. First, both the British and American systems give power to one chief executive. Second, both the British and American systems are dominated by two large political parties; third parties are only successful in times of crisis. Third, both the United States and Great Britain use a "first past the post," winner-take-all form of elections; the candidate with the most votes wins, and only one representative is elected per district. This plurality system of elections heavily favors the two leading parties. (In sharp contrast, most nations practice proportional representation in which each legislative district sends several members to the legislature. In proportional systems, second-, third-, and fourth-place parties get to send representatives to the national legislature as long as their party hits a minimum threshold.)

Accepting these three elements, the American system rejects four other principles of majoritarian democracy. The United States dispenses with fusion between the executive and legislature (the key feature of the parliamentary system), has two strong legislative houses instead of a weak House of Lords and a strong House of Commons, has a party system in which cultural issues are just as important as economic class and, finally, employs a system of federalism that fragments power between the national government and the states. In choosing these elements, Americans combine majority rule with minority protections.

Lijphart's typology shows *with precision* exactly how we are similar to the British system yet vastly different. The American system, traditionally, has the following *majoritarian* traits:

1. *Concentration of executive power.* All executive power is in the hands of the president.

2. *Two-party system.* Although a two-party system, the Democratic and Republican Parties are looser alliances of various interests than the disciplined, cohesive Labour and Conservative Parties in Great Britain.

3. *Heterogeneous political parties with similar programs.* American parties lack unity and cohesion in part because their social bases are very heterogeneous. But these differences are not translated into sharply divergent party programs. Both parties attempt to appeal to the broad middle of the electorate.

4. *Plurality system of elections.* The typical American electoral method remains the plurality single-member district. This is how we think about elections. However, in some presidential primaries, the delegates are amassed in a proportional manner.

At the same time, the American system has *consensual* elements as well:

1. *Separation of powers.* The United States has formal and strict separation of executive and legislative powers.

2. *Balanced bicameralism.* The House of Representatives and the Senate are examples of legislative chambers with virtually equal powers.

3. *Federalism.* The United States has a straightforward federal system based on territory.

4. *Written constitution and minority veto.* We have a written constitution that can only be amended by a cumbersome process, a tradition of judicial review that empowers the courts to speak for the Constitution and minority veto powers including the famed filibuster in the Senate.

In sum, the United States leads the world in demonstrating how the *majoritarian* and *consensual* approaches can be successfully combined. Just as American political thought is a synthesis of two distinct understandings of democracy (liberal and civic republican), so our constitutional structure is a mixture of two logically opposed models of democracy. As opposites attract in marriage, often making for successful couples and wonderful children, so a union of opposites in political design can produce not incoherence, but genius. In evaluating reform options, we must take care not to throw out of balance our hybrid constitutional system. A major advantage of the Assembly reform is that it maintains and improves our hybrid constitutional system. With Lijphart's constitutional primer in mind, we can now examine the major proposals to reform the American political system.

MINOR TUNE-UP

Incremental, bite-sized changes have the highest likelihood of being implemented. But unless they are part of an intelligent reform package, they will not change the system.[2] Of course, we could opt for a minor tune-up and hope it suffices. Two reforms in this mode are streamlining government bureaucracy and campaign finance reform.[3] The push to reinvent government agencies along the lines of the private sector has generated considerable interest. However, this approach can only go so far because private and public bureaucracies have different purposes, masters, and constraints. Reading conservative political scientist James Q. Wilson's *Bureaucracy* is a quick antidote to the panacea of reinventing government.[4] According to Wilson, the United States has bureaucratic rules precisely because our open style of democratic governance necessitates fairness and due process.

Money is a necessary evil. As size and scale have increased, politicians have been forced to raise greater sums of money in order to communicate with more and more constituents. Politicians hate to raise money, and average citizens resent how the process tilts toward the wealthy, who can write $2,000 checks without losing sleep. It would be a good thing if we could curb the pernicious effect of money on politics, but the reality is that politicians need massive amounts of cash to gain name recognition and get a message across to voters. Every successful politician must limit attention to citizens at large in order to build close ties with a second, more exclusive and well-heeled constituency—one carefully cultivated, cajoled, and flattered by professional fund-raisers. If candidates could gain free television time, especially if they could access television and radio time in chunks instead of thirty-second snippets, then political campaigns would cost less and political dialogue would be more informed. Reducing the power of money in American politics is most welcome, but very difficult to achieve.[5] It is nearly impossible for politicians themselves to reform campaign financing in a meaningful way because even the slightest change could be advantageous to one party or the other.

The McCain-Feingold campaign finance reform law focuses on curbing the proliferation of so-called soft money in the national political system. But by itself the Campaign Reform Act of 2002 will not reduce the importance of money in American politics. As Rauch correctly notes, "The one thing that no reform can do is eliminate private money from the political system."[6] Understanding this, Bruce Ackerman and Ian Ayres have proposed an ingenious approach to cut the Gordian knot of campaign finance. In *Voting with Dollars*, Ackerman and Ayres propose a "secret donation booth" similar to the secret ballot voting booth. Donors would be barred from giving directly to candidates; instead they would pass their checks through a blind trust. Candidates would have access to all the money deposited into their account, but would not know from whom the money came. "To be sure," write Ackerman and Ayres, "lots of people will come up to the candidate and say they have given vast sums of money, but none will be able to prove it." The reform, thus, undercuts the desire to receive quid pro quo from the candidate that spurs political giving from insurance companies, oil tycoons, trial lawyers, and all the other special interests. The beauty of voting with dollars is that it could be accomplished under *Buckley v. Valeo*, the 1976 Supreme Court decision that prohibits campaign spending caps.[7] The problem with the proposal is that it would be a tough plan to administer.

ELECTRONIC TOWN HALL

Today, the United States remains one of the few democracies in the world that has never had a national referendum. As such, one reform impulse is to push forward with direct democracy on a grand scale. Call this direct democracy—*writ large*. In the United States, representative government has traditionally been supplemented by populist direct democracy devices. The Progressive reforms of the initiative, referendum, and recall are used in many states and cities, and the presidential selection process is now based on primary contests. Political scientists recognize the major drift of institutional change in American politics as a "series of concessions to the advocates of more direct democracy."[8] Still, Americans remain ambivalent about direct democracy on a mass scale. Designed by the Progressives to be a vehicle by which average citizens could compete against organized interests, the initiative has been captured by those very same interests and their consultants. Today, initiatives and primaries are anemic forms of democracy. Current practice gives pause even to those who strongly support direct democracy in theory.[9] Large-state initiatives are normally qualified, not by gung-ho citizens, but by paid professional signature gatherers; voter knowledge in primary and initiative races is at least as shallow as in traditional races, and election outcomes depend on large amounts of money and polished media campaigns using poll-tested messages.[10]

Put simply, most citizens do not have the time, attention span, or background to decide complex policy issues.[11] Too often, initiative campaigns appeal to passions and prejudices, often exacerbating tensions and conflicts between groups in the community. The goal of political consultants is to win, so they have every incentive to manipulate voters with emotional images and incomplete portrayals of the facts.[12] Still, proponents of the national initiative have a strong Jeffersonian faith in the people. "I think the country would have been a hell of a lot better governed over the past 50 years if we had a national initiative," said George Gallup, the father of modern public opinion polling.[13] Gallup argues that the people are more likely to be right on the major issues than Congress. But the weaknesses of direct mass democracy that we see in the states would be magnified at the national level.[14]

Ross Perot gave the idea of direct mass democracy a major boost during his surprisingly strong presidential bid in 1992, when he received 19 percent of the vote. Perot said that if elected president he would "create an electronic town hall," where "with interactive television every other week, say, we could take one major issue, go to the American people, cover it in great detail, have them respond, and show by congressional district what the people want."[15] But the dangers of unmediated electronic direct democracy far outweigh the possible benefits. Allowing citizens to engage directly in policy making via instant, interactive television and computers brings us closer to pure plebiscitary democracy. Bypassing Congress, the parties, and the mainstream media to take issues directly to the people opens the door for a modern-day Caesar. It is easy to imagine the public becoming entranced by a talented demagogue selling the snake oil of the moment. Philip Roth's novel *The Plot Against America* makes one ponder the nation's susceptibility to sweet-sounding words that promote illiberal passions and undermine democracy's values.[16] The Perot idea is primed for abuse.

C. Wright Mills argued that the pattern of communication between leaders and citizens is critical in determining whether an institution is democratic.[17] While true democracy requires robust two-way communication between elites and citizens, mass communication goes from one to many, for example, Katie Couric or Anderson Cooper, beaming the news to millions of viewers sitting in their living rooms. The pattern of communication is, frankly, authoritarian. Still, despite its weaknesses, Perot's electronic town hall captured the imagination of millions of voters who yearn for a new way to be plugged into the political system.

TERM LIMITS

During the 1990s, term-limit fever swept the nation as twenty-two states jumped on the bandwagon—mostly via the initiative process. Frustrated by incumbent congressmen winning re-election more than 90 percent of the time, alienated from a political system increasingly professionalized, angry at legislators' cozy relationships with special-interest bank accounts, many voters bought the argument that term limits would re-establish a virtuous citizen-legislature.[18]

A democratic argument can be made for the fundamental idea behind term limits—rotation in office. The principle of rotation, taking turns ruling and being ruled, was fundamental to Aristotle's understanding of the relationship between equal citizens in a good polis.[19] However, in a nation of 300 million, rotating 435 House seats every six years is effectively the same as the current system, in which turnover occurs because House members voluntarily retire. Even if rotation does not help us meet Aristotle's standard, supporters argue that term limits will improve the behavior of legislators. Supporters expect term-limited legislators to be more courageous.[20] A second-stated goal is in tension with the first. The citizen-legislators are supposed to be more responsive to the public. No longer would representatives act like experts treating citizens as mere clients.[21] Both are worthy goals, but whether term limits will achieve them is suspect.

At present, the case against term limits is stronger than the argument in favor. There is no compelling reason to insist on 100 percent turnover in Congress every twelve years when 50 to 75 percent of the members of the House and the Senate are routinely replaced every decade because of voluntary retirement or defeat. And term limits alone will not change the "professional" nature of modern politics because, as Alan Ehrenhalt explains: "A politician whose public office requires the commitment of six months campaigning and a half a million dollars expended, and whose legislative work takes up three-quarters of every year, is a professional politician, whether he serves ten terms in office or is required to retire after three or four."[22]

Ironically, term-limited legislators may be less public-spirited than traditional politicians. Under term limits, the incentive to tackle complex policy questions diminishes; the lure is to do the quick splash, claim credit, and run for the next office.[23] Big, complex problems lie untended when term limits come to roost. No one is around long enough to work on them. That is the experience of the California Legislature, where the nation's most severe term limits have been in place since 1990.[24] In addition, lame-duck legislators tend to behave like seniors during the last semester of high school—their attention wanes. Unless the new legislators are retirees or independently wealthy, research shows they will naturally look ahead to their next career posting.[25] By contrast, running for re-election focuses the mind of the politician on pleasing his constituency. To paraphrase Hamilton, indefinite re-election encourages legislators to make their self-interest coincide with their duty.[26] Rather than term limits, what is needed is a commitment to make legislative districts more competitive. Iowa asks civil servants to draw the district lines without reference to incumbents or regional voting patterns. Five other states give redistricting authority to bipartisan commissions and other states may soon join the parade.[27]

Given the fact that the power of governors and presidents has grown during the twentieth century, it is important that we not make reforms that significantly weaken the legislative branch.[28] But term limits do just that. When we fill the legislature with newcomers, the advantage swings to strong chief executives, seasoned bureaucrats, and longtime lobbyists.[29] A key question about term limits is, Do term-limited legislators have sufficient time to become wise and effective leaders? The evidence says no. The speaker of the California Assembly from 1998 to 2000 was Antonio Villaraigosa, the current mayor of Los Angeles. *Los Angeles Times* capitol columnist George Skelton praised Villaraigosa for being a good legislative leader but said having only two years as speaker gave Villaraigosa very little time to learn from experience and show his full potential.[30] The most sensible and direct way to increase legislative turnover is to increase the electoral success of challengers.[31] It is a good thing to have people in the legislative branch who dedicate their professional lives to politics and public policy. As with any good baseball team, we want the state legislature and Congress to be a mix of experienced veterans and rookies.[32]

PARLIAMENTARY REFORM

One of the most basic questions of constitutional engineering is how to set up the executive and legislative branches. Do we retain the separation-of-powers doctrine on which presidential systems are based? Or do we shift toward a parliamentary system in which the legislative and executive branches are joined? Beginning with Woodrow Wilson, whenever Americans become frustrated by gridlock, they look wistfully across the Atlantic to Great Britain.[33] Starting with Watergate and continuing with divided government during the 1980s and 1990s, there have been scores of proposals suggesting that various elements of the British system be grafted onto our own.[34] The British parliamentary system has always had a very strong attraction for American political reformers. It appears responsive and effective; the American system is neither.

Too often, say critics, the outcome of our separation-of-powers system is division and gridlock. True, it is difficult to get things done in the American system; the U.S. Constitution has a distinct bias toward inaction. The president, the Senate, and the House, each independent of one another with separate electoral bases, have to come together. If the president is from one party and Congress is controlled by the other, how does anything get done? Important legislation does pass, but the process is slower than in Great Britain. In the United States, major legislation often takes years, sometimes decades, and the struggle wears down all involved. By contrast, in Britain, the party that wins the national election and holds majority power in the House of Commons can do whatever it wants (shocking as this may seem to Americans)—without concern for vetoes, checks, or judicial review.

The supposed advantages of the parliamentary system can be briefly summarized. In a parliamentary system, the party that wins the legislature also gains control of the executive branch. The party leader—a Tony Blair—not only holds a seat in Parliament but becomes prime minister. The prime minister then selects other legislators to form a cabinet—an executive committee of the legislature that then governs the nation. Because the legislative and executive branches are fused, the likelihood increases that the government will take action to solve the major problems of the day.

The perception that divided government (the president from one party and the Congress controlled by the other) puts important legislative business on the shelf is the main impetus for parliamentary reform. Some, however, challenge this impression. In *Divided We Govern*, Mayhew refutes the claim that divided government, when one party controls the presidency and the other controls Congress, automatically and necessarily, leads to inaction on important policy issues. Focusing on the period from 1947 to 1990, Mayhew discovered that important legislative enactments were about as numerous in the twenty-six years of divided government as they were during the eighteen years of unified government.[35] In the American case, divided versus unified government does not affect legislative output. Sometimes Congress and the president disagree, even when controlled by the same party, and often a skilled president can find common ground with the political opposition, especially if a preponderance of interest groups want legislation enacted.

A parliamentary system is great for the winners. However, the losing side of the national election feels the loss more deeply. By contrast, in the United States, voters could support the Gingrich revolution in Congress while keeping President Clinton in the White House. Because of the separation of powers and bicameralism, the American system allows for nuanced choice. Americans often say they want change, but how much, how fast, in what direction, and with what kind of understanding? Frustrating as the American system is, it has an advantage: Although it takes a long time to build a successful coalition across parties and between interest groups, it is difficult to reverse successful legislation. By contrast, parliamentary systems allow parties to govern without bipartisan support. The result is policy instability, which can be a real economic headache. In Great Britain, Labour and Conservative governments have taken turns nationalizing, denationalizing, nationalizing, and privatizing the steel industry. Might part of the reason for Britain's century-long economic decline be her parliamentary system? In addition, the parliamentary model does not protect minority rights nearly as well as the Madisonian system.[36] The United States has a very diverse population, and under the parliamentary model there is enormous potential for locking certain groups out of the political process.[37]

DEMOCRACY, ITALIAN STYLE

Another way to alter American politics is via the electoral system. In most of the world's democracies, citizens vote for the party (Conservative, Green, Liberal, Social Democratic, or the Polish Beer-Lovers Party—no kidding!) that best represents their political interests. Legislative seats are then allocated among the parties on the basis of the proportion of the total vote they receive. Each party whose popular vote percentage exceeds an established threshold qualifies for seats in the legislature.[38]

The great virtue of proportional representation systems is that they ensure that nearly all voters elect someone they want to represent them. There is much less "voting for the lesser of two evils." If it is true that proportional representation (PR) systems are so much fairer, why doesn't the United States switch? First, PR is a complex system that appears bizarre to many Americans used to the winner-take-all system.[39] Instead of sending one person to Congress from each House district, under PR the first-place party would send four or five representatives, the second-place party would send three or four candidates, and the third-place party might send one representative if it gained enough votes, say over 10 percent.[40] Second, fairness is not the only factor to consider when selecting an electoral system. Electoral systems interact with the rest of the political system, especially the party system, with this important consequence: winner-take-all systems foster two-party politics; proportional representation systems spawn multiparty democracy.

Fundamentally, two-party and multiparty systems lead to different styles of political culture and competition. Two-party systems have a moderating tendency on candidates and electorates, whereas multiparty systems encourage those with strong views to remain purists.[41] At bottom, as Harvard electoral expert Kenneth A. Shepsle points out, the choice is whether to encourage coalition building before or after the election.[42] In the Anglo-American system, various constituencies are forced to deal with one another before the election. The party that builds the broadest coalition—however odd—usually controls politics. Witness Franklin Roosevelt's New Deal coalition of big-city ethnics, the working class, and segregationist South, and President Reagan's coalition of traditional Republicans, neoconservative intellectuals, Christian right and pro-life forces, libertarians, and blue-collar Reagan Democrats.

Democracy Italian style, anyone? The choice between PR and the Anglo-American plurality system comes down to a preference for either representation or governance.[43] Under a PR system, it is highly unusual for a single party to win an absolute majority in the legislature. As a result, proportional representation and multiparty systems are notorious for instability. Italians change their government as often as teenage girls change clothes. In Israel, which also has a PR system, it is not unusual for a religious extremist party to hold the government hostage. The fracturing of representation leads to coalition governments made up of a number of parties, the smallest of which have an incentive to bolt and make a better deal with the opposition groups. Multiparty systems allow extreme views to flourish and discourage compromise—a necessary ingredient for successful democratic politics. True, many nations use proportional voting successfully. However, in an international era of ethnic and racial animosity, in a nation that is singularly diverse and pluralistic, we should exercise caution with a reform that could promote what Arthur M. Schlesinger Jr. calls the "disuniting of America."[44] There is one particular instance where proportional voting would make a great deal of sense. A strong case can be made for a proportional allocation of the Electoral College, whereby "whatever percentage of the popular vote a candidate wins in a particular state they win the same corresponding percentage of electoral votes for that state." Doing this would ensure that the quadrennial presidential contest was very much a national campaign, instead of a battle for a handful of swing states, as now is the case.[45] Such is the aim of the Campaign for a National Popular Vote. In this proposed reform "individual states would pledge themselves to an interstate compact under which they would agree to award their electoral votes to the national winner of the popular vote."[46]

It is relatively easy to point out the flaws of a winner-take-all system and, partially for this reason, PR enjoys a following among some intellectuals and journalists.[47] However, the case against PR goes beyond the inherent fragility of coalition governments. Many forces in American life contribute to fragmentation—mobility, ethnic diversity, individualism, and rapid economic shifts. Instituting proportional representation in the United States could well increase the factionalism and divisiveness already evident in American life. By contrast, our two-party system is one of those forces that binds us together. We may be frustrated with a two-party system, but it is a proven technique for bonding a cosmopolitan, multicultural people together. A key advantage of the Assembly reform is that it offers increased representation of minority voices but does not throw our Madisonian constitution out of alignment.

STRENGTHENING POLITICAL PARTIES

A final tactic—a perennial favorite with political scientists—is strengthening the political parties. But most of the public, agreeing with the founders and Progressive reformers, believes that political parties are something they would rather do without. Still, strong political parties unite divergent political groups, socialize people into politics, and provide politicians with an incentive to govern as well as campaign. Stronger, more disciplined parties could be a good thing, especially if they were less corrupt and more open than in the past. Stronger parties might well help us deal with the problem of size, counter the tendency toward consultant politics, and help promote more republican, participatory politics.

On the one hand, strengthening the parties so that they are once again vigorous state and local organizations appears unlikely. Our fragmented political system, individualistic culture, and fast-paced lifestyle make reversing the decay of the parties difficult.[48] It is no accident that today some Washington insiders think of national parties as rival groups of like-minded political consultants.[49] The grassroots entities of old—local organizations that mobilized and organized large numbers of people into politics in a disciplined manner, with common goals and an eye on controlling nominations and winning elections to a large slate of offices— have largely vanished because they no longer serve a necessary function. Consultants use money and technology to get people to the polls. No candidate is going to give up on direct mail. A grassroots organization is frosting on the cake. In the modern era, loyal party workers of the type who were crucial in days gone by are left high and dry unless they happen to live in a contested presidential state such as Ohio or Florida where parties go high tech and low tech in an effort to reach every voter.[50]

Today, only an activist minority work for the party, and few people vote the straight party ticket as in the old days. Modern Americans vote for the person as much as for the party. How anachronistic the following attitude from Postman's *Amusing Ourselves to Death* is:

> As a young man, I balked one November at voting for a Democratic mayoralty candidate who, it seemed to me, was both unintelligent and corrupt. "What has that to do with it?" my father protested. "All Democratic candidates are unintelligent and corrupt. Do you want the Republicans to win?" He meant to say that intelligent voters favored the party that best represented their economic interests and sociological perspective. To vote for the "best man" seemed to him an astounding and naive irrelevance. He never doubted that there were good men among Republicans. He merely understood that they did not speak for his class.[51]

On the other hand, parties remain important in Congress because they are necessary to organize political struggle within a legislature and, yes, the national party structures have a great deal more money and power than in the past. In the 1950s, political scientists banded together to call for "responsible parties."[52] Until recently, the parties had suffered a steady deterioration. But in the past decade, the power of the national parties has grown dramatically, and now the Republican Party functions *nationally* much like the powerful urban machines of yesterday. The inner circle at the top run the show, and the organization has the resources in terms of cutting-edge political knowledge, campaign finance dollars, and consultant expertise to "maintain partisan unity and power."[53]

As the political scientists of the 1950s hoped, the national parties have grown stronger, more cohesive, and more ideologically distinctive. But instead of competing in the middle of the spectrum, today's parties — again especially the Republican Party — focus on their most passionate and extreme members.[54] The power of the Republican right wing can veto a president's choice for the U.S. Supreme Court, as was the case with White House Counsel Harriet Miers in 2005. Strengthening the national parties was supposed to lead to responsible party government. What happened instead, Hacker and Pierson write, is :

> *irresponsible* party government. Parties (or at least one of them) increasingly have the power to act. But they have acted with the impunity that comes when such actions are not disciplined by accountability. A strong party system was supposed to have greatly increased the responsiveness of our political system. Instead, the growing concentration of economic and political resources and the growing use of innovative tools of backlash insurance (strategies and procedures party leaders use to keep quavering moderates in line and shield party loyalists against party retaliation by moderate voters) have left ordinary voters with limited sway over our nation's course.[55]

In sum, the major reforms discussed are either flawed or fail to do enough. Parliamentary reform and PR threaten to unbalance the Constitution. Term limits and Perot's version of e-democracy excite the public, but on inspection they turn out to be unrealistic panaceas that do more harm than good. And, finally, strengthening the political parties has not been the wonderful tonic its proponents sought.

Fortunately, there is a meaningful political reform that avoids most of these pitfalls. It would curb corruption and encourage civic virtue, improve prospects for deliberative democracy and political participation, and forge a bridge between the public and the political elite. Instead of being a reform based on partisanship, it follows Mayhew's advice that we start from the anti-party Progressive tradition and take it in a new direction.[56] The reform is the Assembly and the People's House—deliberative democracy with a representative twist.

9.
America and the World

What are the wider implications of blending participation and representation in the Assembly reform? How would the Assembly reflect and possibly change the wider society beyond the legislative arena? Here I focus on how the Assembly and the People's House would help us in regard to three specific challenges: cyber democracy, diversity and civic identity, and America's role in the world.

Many "wired world" enthusiasts want to push ahead with direct mass democracy. They would dispense with representative democracy and schedule mass plebiscites. Every week they would put a major issue to the voters and, from the comfort of their homes and with a single keystroke, citizens would vote electronically. Yet, simple-minded electronic democracy would be uninformed, emotional, bereft of deliberation, and subject to elite manipulation. It would harm, not help, American democracy.

Today, the Internet enables both advertisers and political consultants to customize their message for the individual Internet user. The result furthers the trend toward narrowly focused interest groups. Like-minded individuals congregate no matter what. On the Web, individuals build a sense of community around work, hobbies, and political passions, and electronic networks often mirror existing community organizations and friendships.

However, the Internet also accentuates a postmodern politics rich in fragmentation. A technology that allows the personalization of the news where people can create their own front page—"I only want up-to-the-minute stock news and health"—erodes a common culture. The Balkanization of the virtual public sphere may make it more difficult to forge a common identity and solve collective problems.[1] For twenty-first-century democratic politics to flourish we must blend the digital experience with face-to-face interaction. The Internet is best regarded as a power-packed supplement for traditional political interaction, not its substitute. As Robert Putnam writes in *Bowling Alone,* "Both the history of the telephone and the early evidence on Internet usage strongly suggest that computer-mediated communication will turn out to *complement,* not *replace,* face-to-face community."[2]

Given our technological capabilities and busy schedules, why bother gathering face to face? One reason is that a good deal of communication is nonverbal. Local assembly delegates would need to get to know each other, just as legislators do in Washington, DC, and state capitols. They need to size one another up to know who is blunt, fickle, sly, or stubborn as well as to gauge who is a quick study and who knows which issues best. Yes, some of these personal attributes come through online. But the experience is richer in person, and our minds gather more clues with which to make a judgment about other people.[3] Judgments about character are best made at arm's—not cable—length. Cyber friends are a good thing, but they can be shadowy figures. Think of watching a televised event in person; editing and the camera's narrow view often eliminate critical information that we would see "live" in person. Reporting any event, whether for television or print, is an art form in which the reporter and editor make choices about what the viewer or reader will see. The same goes for online interactions; only so much information is transmitted electronically.[4] In-person meetings guarantee greater personal knowledge for each Assembly delegate. True, each delegate would physically meet only the delegates from his or her local assembly and surrounding jurisdictions. Yet, this traditional interaction would ground the experience and cause delegates to think of themselves, not as isolated individuals, but as members of a particular political community participating with other political communities across the nation.

Assembly delegates would represent congressional districts with distinct personalities and would speak for a community bound by place and history. Simply driving or walking across town to an assembly meeting would remind people of who they are and where they live. Although the virtual Assembly would ask delegates to think of the larger picture and to escape a provincial outlook, it is important that representatives be connected to their own community.[5] Yes, we are all part of the extended world, but we all start from some specific place. Assembly meetings would be community gatherings where people will see neighbors and friends—akin to a civic church where people talk and share experiences.[6] The assembly would be one of those public spaces, such as the pub, the ballpark, the PTA meeting, the senior center, where people socialize outside of work and family.[7]

The logic of face-to-face meetings as the norm for the Assembly and the People's House follows from the physical proximity of a bounded geographic area and the nature of civic life. City halls immediately spring to mind as gathering places, but council chambers are often built with raised daises that separate the council members from everyone else. They have an administrative and executive bearing that is different than that required for debate among equal citizens. Schools, community centers, libraries, and businesses with large meeting areas are good places to assemble, but they are less than ideal because they send a subtle but strong message that politics is one of life's secondary activities. In the long run, meeting halls are needed that are specifically designed for public debate. We have specific places to sleep and work, shop and pray. Why not a *space* designed and dedicated for public discussion?

In one vision of the cyberspace political future, the Internet will power a political revolution of increased participation. For example, a virtual national assembly would provide a common ground to explore shared values while confronting and transcending our differences. On another view, the net effect of the marriage of the consultant era and the Internet will be to hyperlink us to democracy-as-marketing to the nth power. Consultants use computer analyses of hundreds of personal characteristics, including age, buying habits, charitable giving, family structure, favorite magazines, home ownership, and websites to determine how susceptible we are to persuasion and which pitch will most likely be appealing. "You know, if you own a Ford Explorer and you garden and like the outdoors and you're over 50, there might be a high likelihood that you care about tort reform," said one veteran Republican consultant.[8] The Internet is a new arrow in the consultant quiver.

Fortunately, it is possible to counterbalance this clinical, manipulative, technocratic style of politics with new institutions such as the Assembly that accentuate communal deliberative politics. Since the 1960s, high tech has favored consultants, not citizens. But the Internet has the potential of promoting the widespread sharing of information that may help us regain democratic control of our politics.[9] In person and online, the Assembly and the People's House would allow us to say to the delegates selected, "We want you to look out for our interests. Ask the questions that need asking. Keep the politicians honest. Remind the bureaucrats that they work for us. Keep us informed about the big issues and help us make informed choices."

AMERICAN CIVIC IDENTITY

As the computer revolution and the Internet transfigure American society, so immigration and intermarriage literally are changing the face of the United States. The most technologically advanced society in the world is also the most cosmopolitan; as it becomes ever more diverse, more attention must be given to the glue that holds it together. Awash in cultural pluralism, how does the United States maintain unity? Historically, one people have made one nation-state, so it has always been a question in some observers' minds how long the great cosmopolitan experiment can last.[10] The United States is unique among the world's states in the degree to which it is a multicultural society composed of many peoples—a "nation of nationalities," to use Horace Kallen's famous phrase.[11] Many other nations today are multicultural, but usually one ethnic or racial group dominates the rest. In the case of the United States, however, no single group—not even the British—permanently dominated society, and because of constant intermarriage, we are a very blended society. New Haven, Connecticut, offers a good example of this. Beginning with the Puritans and Yankees, the city welcomed successive waves of Irish, Italians, African Americans, and Puerto Ricans. Since the 1960s, each of the new groups (except Latinos) has seen one of its members become mayor. Across the nation, a similar pattern prevails. No one group has been able to determine for long the character of local—let alone national—government.

A uniquely cosmopolitan nation, the United States still needs a sense of community that is particularistic, not universal; concrete, not abstract. As

Americans, we share the commonality of having forefathers who came here for a better economic and political life. But just how is our identity unique? Being an American is not as easy as it seems.[12] The challenge of our politics is to "create unity without denying or repressing multiplicity." We have done this by keeping the government largely neutral in regard to cultural questions and group identity. When a person steps into the political realm, he or she is an equal citizen with everyone else. At the same time, every ethnic group is free to do as much organization, outreach, education, fundraising, and social service work as it wants. We understand that it is the responsibility of every communal group to carry its tradition forward.[13]

In the ancient Greek and Roman understanding of citizenship, the community had to be homogenous, and citizenship was the most paramount identity held by the individual. Ignoring this stricture, Americans have developed their own unique brand of patriotism. We often identify ourselves as Chinese Americans, Irish Americans, Mexican Americans, or any other nationality because citizens of the United States think of it as an addition to rather than a replacement of ethnic consciousness. Both identities can be equally important to the individual, and often the individual's emotional life is centered on his or her ethnic heritage.[14] But how do we maintain loyalty to the sum of the parts? The bond is politics and patriotism. In one sense, the "only thing we can share is the republic itself." Here the modern understanding of the republican ideas becomes critical to understanding America. On the one hand, we are not passionate republicans in the tradition of Rousseau, and we have flouted the historic republican dictates warning that diversity and large-scale politics will bring ruin. Still, we are not a neutral liberal state either. Walzer says the American citizen receives inconsistent instruction. "Patriotism, civility, toleration and political activism pull him in different directions."[15] The first and last require a kind of zeal whereas civility and tolerance undercut commitment.

As Ronald Dworkin explains, a liberal society is one in which people are free to follow their own dreams, and there is no consensus about the ends of life.[16] The society is, instead, united around a strong procedural requirement to treat people equally, and the government restricts itself to seeing that citizens treat one another fairly and that the state deals equally with all. This sort of politics is united around individualism, secularism, toleration, and a focus on private rewards. Our classic free-market, limited-government vision fits the bill. Yet, as Walzer notes, "It is a hard politics because it offers so few emotional rewards; the liberal state is not a home for citizens; it lacks warmth and intimacy."[17] And, partially because of this, those willing to use emotion and prejudice to organize political support often defeat the ideals of toleration and fairness. The harsh bigotry, racism and Jim Crow segregation against African Americans for the first half of the twentieth century, and the McCarthy red scare in the 1950s are obvious examples that scarred American life for decades.

Fortunately, liberal principles can be blended with civic republican passions. A key part of our unique style of politics is the ability to practice republican politics on two levels. The first is the wide variety of multicultural group identities caused by our hyphenated personal identities. In civil society, we can join a plethora of groups—some business, some religious, some ethnic, some recreational—and we find in these group experiences a communal feeling and group spirit that Rousseau celebrates in the small city-state. We enjoy an active communal life outside the political arena, yet because these groups help satisfy our craving for social interaction and activity toward a common goal, they carry a "republican" charge, so to speak. This is especially true for the ethnic groups.

The second level is our common life together in the political arena. Here we are loyal to our liberal democratic constitution, which allows us broad liberties and freedoms to follow our own path in social and economic life. In addition, we practice a republican politics that values and encourages participation. Ours is a limited and focused republicanism within the strictures of a philosophic liberalism that teaches toleration and a respect for individual rights in the face of majority will. This modern liberal-republican understanding helps explain why ethnic tensions do not normally get out of control in the United States. The Assembly and the People's House would be forums where we work out our complex understanding of citizenship as tolerance *and* passion, as civility *and* civic virtue. As Walzer explains:

> Politics can be opened up, rates of participation can be
> significantly increased, decision-making really shared, without a
> full-scale attack on private life and liberal values, without a reli-
> gious revival or cultural revolution. What is necessary is the ex-
> pansion of the public sphere. I don't mean by that the growth of

state power . . . but a new politicizing of the state, a devolution of state power into the hands of ordinary citizens."[18]

Americans have a remarkable capacity to develop their own rules of co-operation and solidarity. "The trick," Alan Wolfe writes, "is to find a way to trust them so that they will do it."[19] The Assembly and People's House gatherings provide such a way, as institutions that would act as bridges between civil society and government, combining aspects of both. It is often said that democracy is America's secular religion. A national network of local assemblies would be a common room, a sanctuary, where we could try, in Lincoln's words, to be influenced by the "better angels" of our nature. Would there be angry confrontations? Without a doubt. Disagreement is to be expected in a large pluralistic society such as ours. But just as people learn to get along on the job and on jury duty, so people, by and large, would learn the social norms necessary for the assemblies to function. A sense of membership and community would first be established in the individual wards—about the size of a city council district or an area slightly larger than that served by a neighborhood school. Ward democracy would allow groups that would not necessarily have a chance to elect a congressional representative a chance to have formal representation and a voice. For example, groups without great numbers in a particular community—for example Quakers, hunters, gays, Vietnamese Americans—might have one of their members selected as a delegate. They would gain a voice, a seat at the legislative table, yet because of their small numbers they would dominate neither the agenda nor the debate. In the People's House, groups that have been largely ignored politically because of small numbers or have suffered past discrimination would have a way to tell the rest of society about their group identity and pride as they forge a stronger connection to the greater whole. At the same time, the Assembly would help us move beyond identity politics. Such a move is inevitable as the United States becomes ever more cosmopolitan, intermarriage between ethnic and racial groups increases, and racial barriers erode.[20]

REPUBLIC OR EMPIRE?

Contemporary Americans are burdened with a special responsibility to take democracy seriously. How we practice democracy would not be so important if we were Chile or Latvia or Singapore. If it was 1890 and the Republicans and Democrats were squabbling about tariffs and the federal budget was $318,000 (versus an estimated $2.656 trillion in 2007) it would not matter to the degree that it does now.[21] But the United States is radically different than it was just over a century ago. And one of the most important changes is the influence, both subtle and profound, that the United States has on billions of lives beyond our borders. It is hubris to think that America alone is going to decide world peace and ecological survival, but to ignore our leadership role on questions of enormous import is to deny reality.

The Roman republic did not survive imperial ambition. Two millennia later, the United States faces the same dilemma. At the dawn of the twenty-first century, this modern nation-state is the world's only super power—a polite synonym for empire.[22] The question that confronts us is, What kind of empire do we wish to be? In principle, our commitment to democracy means that more than just the foreign policy elite share in the responsibility for our foreign policy and global involvement. At the end of the Cold War, the purpose of American foreign policy became an open question. It remains so today. I have stressed the importance of Machiavelli to American political thought and to the idea of active citizenship that informs the Assembly. It may be disquieting, but Machiavelli insisted that republics and conquest go together. Speaking of Rome, he wrote,

> If the republic had been more tranquil, it would necessarily have resulted that she would have been more feeble, and that she would have lost with her energy also the ability of achieving that high degree of greatness to which she attained . . . But as all human things are kept in a perpetual movement, and can never remain stable, states naturally either rise or decline . . . a precise middle course cannot be maintained.[23]

The exertion of American power abroad since 1945 and particularly since September 2001 makes this a crucial matter for public debate. Critical observers such as Chalmers Johnson believe the military industrial complex is far past the ability of the public to control it. At the end of *The Sorrows of Empire*, Johnson writes,

> There is one development that could conceivably stop this process of overreaching: the people could retake control of Congress, reform it along with the corrupt elections laws that made it into a forum for special interests, turn it into a genuine assembly of democratic representatives, and cut off the supply of money to the Pentagon and the secret intelligence agencies . . . At this late date, however, it is difficult to imagine how Congress, much like the Roman senate in the last days of the republic, could be brought back to life and cleansed of its endemic corruption.[24]

As citizens of the United States and the world, we face an array of difficult issues. The wave of democratization that swept the globe after the fall of the Berlin Wall has been accompanied by rising ethnic and religious strife from the Balkans to Indonesia. The 9/11 attacks made the threat of terror on a massive scale very real—not only to Americans but also to people around the world. The new global economy creates wealth, but the instant mobility of capital poses serious challenges for workers and national economies. And today, as the snows of Kilimanjaro melt, it is clear that the earth's 6.5 billion people—especially those in the affluent West—increasingly stress the earth's ecological balance. A few pressing issues—cloning, global warming, and nuclear proliferation—are questions not just of individual life and death but also of the survival of the species and planet as we know it. No previous generation had to face such issues.

Why should the average American—the engaged, intelligent person who might become a delegate to the Assembly—want to have a voice about the future of the world? Fundamentally, because it is not at all clear that the people who were experts on the Cold War have similar expertise on the emerging issues. New habits of thought and action are required to deal with very different threats and opportunities. Additionally, for democracy to be healthy, it is necessary to constantly challenge the very idea of expertise, delegation, and guardianship. An increased public awareness and voice is the best way to shake lethargic bureaucracies into action.

A telling case in point: Mary Schiavo, former inspector general of the U.S. Department of Transportation, says that during her tenure, the

Federal Aviation Administration resisted her recommendations for multi-billion-dollar fixes to the airport security systems: "They said that Pan Am 103 [which exploded over Lockerbie, Scotland, in 1988] cost $3 billion, and that if we had another Pan Am in 10 years, that would be cheaper than making all the changes I proposed. They said it just wasn't worth it because we had never had a major domestic terrorist incident, and no one would put up with security measures or pay for them."[25] Would increased citizen awareness have been able to goad the powers that be in the FAA, the executive branch, and the Congress into acting and thus prevent 9/11? Obviously, we will never know. But we do know that the Assembly would give citizens, acting in concert, powerful leverage to move the system.

Today, a small group dominates the discussion and direction of U.S. foreign policy. Academic heavyweights at first-tier universities, the editors of magazines such as *Foreign Affairs,* and newspaper columnists and editorial writers at papers such as the *New York Times* and the *Wall Street Journal,* members of the foreign policy committees in Congress and their staff, think tank partisans, and lawyers and bankers who specialize in international affairs, join the president's national security staff and top defense and state department officials to make up a core group of possibly 5,000 people. For most of these individuals, foreign policy is the career they have pursued since leaving college. Similar to British civil servants, their long-term involvement gives them institutional memory of both success and failure. We rely on those in the government to use their expertise to put policies into place and execute them.

But should the people who have the technical, instrumental knowledge also have nearly exclusive purview over discussions about the purpose, direction, and goals of American foreign policy? Of course, daring to ask such a question challenges the authority and autonomy of the foreign policy elite. The professionals are "realists" who know that foreign policy is complex and delicate and that the public lacks both the requisite knowledge and interest. The experts resist any tinkering with their power and autonomy by belittling the ability of the public to understand the subtleties and harshness of international relations. They liken the interference of democracy with their work to "powerful gusts of popular emotion rather than factual data about the international situation."[26]

During our life-and-death struggle with Hitler and the Soviet Union, it made sense that the educated public would watch and listen but not challenge the "wise men" making decisions. That lasted until the debacle of Vietnam. Since that time, a number of missions have shaken foreign policy's best and brightest. Episodes such as the Iranian hostage crisis, the sending of American troops into Lebanon, the Iran-Contra Affair, and the current occupation of Iraq stand out. Obviously, we need foreign policy experts directing our relations with other nations. Specialized knowledge is critical for making informed decisions on all matters of public policy. Yet, an engaged segment of the "aware" public exercising deliberative judgment could help the U.S. government make sound decisions on the major international issues facing the nation.

MEGA-ISSUES

What are examples of major issues where it is critical that the public be more informed and involved? Whether to fundamentally alter Social Security in the manner suggested by President George W. Bush was such an issue in 2005. During the mid-1990s, the two most important issues confronting the nation were President Clinton's health-care proposal and how and why America should be involved in the Balkans. Both were very complex issues; they were also issues of first-order importance that required the public's assent. Here we review those two debates.

Reforming the health care system in the manner proposed by President Clinton would have affected nearly everyone in the nation; whether to intervene with American troops in the former Yugoslavia was a life-and-death issue for the soldiers and their families. True, on both issues a large-scale, wide-ranging debate took place in the media, and numerous public opinion polls felt the public's pulse. But, as we know, polls cannot get at the deliberative judgment the mass public might have if the response were based on more than a smattering of information, spin, and gut instinct. The turning point in the health insurance debate came when powerful health-care companies and conservative opponents of the president devised a public campaign against the initiative based on characterizing the president's plan as "government health care" not "national health insurance." This was dishonest because Clinton's approach to reforming health care was market oriented. It was based on managed competition and allowing small firms to join cooperatives so that together they would have the buying power of large companies. Some liberals in Congress endorsed a government-run, single-payer system such as found in Canada and Europe. Clinton did not.

The health care industry and small businesses mounted a massive public relations campaign to defeat the president's plan. A key part of their success was a series of commercials featuring a middle-aged couple sitting on their front porch speaking about government bureaucrats. The "Harry and Louise" ads began with an announcer saying: "The government may force us to pick from a few healthcare plans designed by government bureaucrats." Louise: "Having choices we don't like is no choice at all." Harry: "They choose." Louise: "We lose." [27] This simplistic message helped turn public opinion—and eventually Congress—against the president's plan. In a follow-up article for *Atlantic Monthly,* James Fallows made a strong case against the conventional wisdom that the plan was too complex, too top-down, and too bureaucratic. He calls the failure of the Clinton health plan a "triumph of misinformation."[28]

In its issue forum presentations, the Kettering Foundation does a very good job of helping people see the three or four main approaches to an issue—whether energy or health care or prescription drugs. Of course, every policy issue has various levels of complexity. But it is not necessary for journalists and aware citizens to master the details in the same way that an administration or congressional staffer must. What citizens must grasp are the basic policy choices along with the arguments pro and con for pursuing them. In this endeavor, they are not unlike a president or a governor who must grapple with making decisions on multiple issues where he or she must rely on others for their expertise.

In Bosnia and Kosovo, the key to our involvement was the ghost of Vietnam and the desire of our leaders prior to 9/11 to minimize American casualties. In the early years of the Balkans tragedy, the United States was largely a passive bystander to the violent disintegration of the former Yugoslavia. At first, we turned a blind eye to Serbian atrocities.[29] Later, the bombing campaign launched by U.S. and NATO forces against Serbia after its invasion of Kosovo succeeded in toppling Slobodan Milosevic from power. Relying on technology and recoiling from the risk of casualties is understandable. Yet, President Clinton's options in the Balkans were restrained by the fear of mass public opinion raising up to challenge our involvement if even one American solider was killed. With a military budget soaring toward $500 billion, a volunteer army, and power projected around the world, the United States needs a better way to discuss when, where, and why we are willing to deploy the military and put our soldiers in harm's way.[30] The current commitment of American troops in Iraq and Afghanistan demands no less.

In both examples, the Balkans crisis and the health-care debate, experts, elites, and very attentive citizens understood the policy choices and what they entailed. By contrast, most of the public had only a vague understanding of the issues and what was at stake. Some scholars argue that such a low-cost approach to political knowledge is sufficient for voters.[31] This is Schumpeter's model of citizenship in which democracy depends primarily on the circulation of elites. On this theory, if voters elect George W. Bush, for example, and his program does not work, then they have the right to vote for a change in leadership in the next election. Not much else is required than this retrospective judgment. The basic question boils down to, "Are you better off than you were four years ago?" For the more sophisticated voters, the question grows to include, "Is the country better off than it was four years ago?"

True, few of us need to become experts on arms control or weapons of mass destruction. On many narrow issues, it makes sense for experts and those groups most interested in the outcome to dominate the policy decision. Yet, on major domestic and international issues the debate must necessarily be wider. It is on these larger issues where our current method of public debate is tragically simplistic and emotional. Powerful interests, bureaucratic cliques, and spin too often manipulate the discussion. The issues cry out for greater public awareness, sophistication, and, yes, involvement.

Conclusion: Taking Control

Democracy is not easy in a superpower nation where corporate marketing campaigns drive public passions and win-at-all-costs consultants dominate politics. With political success depending on large amounts of money and sophisticated interest groups calling the shots in state capitals and in Washington, DC, the political game will not change of its own accord. The dumbing down of the public culture (Walter Lippmann, Edward R. Murrow, and Ted Koppel be damned) continues, while personalized campaign messages and "the deliberate crafting of policy to distort public perceptions" push politics toward manipulation pure and simple.[1] Tocqueville worried about the future of democracy in a large, individual-obsessed, commercial republic; today a respected political observer frets about "a public besotted with the sensational . . . unable to engage in substantive argument."[2] Just as the Soviet Union imploded because of its own weight and corruption run amok, so could the United States. Although this is highly unlikely and the dynamics would be different, the end point of political decay would be the same—the collapse of the Communist era in Russia and the end of democracy, as we know it, in America. If this seems farfetched, it is worth pondering Tocqueville's dark prophecy: "I think the type of oppression which threatens democracies is different from anything there has ever been in the world before . . . Under this system the citizens would quit their state of dependence just long enough to choose their masters and then fall back into it."[3] The people would continue to grant popular consent, enjoy full consumer rights in the economy, but have less and less control over their political fate.[4] It is worth noting that Schumpeter's minimalist theory fits with Tocqueville's prophecy without complaint.

MINIMAL DEMOCRACY

Many political scientists and many citizens accept Schumpeter's model as the best we can do. For Schumpeter, the essence of democracy is political leaders acquiring "the power to decide by means of a competitive struggle for the people's vote."[5] In a world filled with conflict and violence, finding a method by which societal conflict can be settled peacefully is no small accomplishment. And a political system in which rulers are selected by competitive elections is one in which "citizens can get rid of governments without bloodshed."[6] Yet, Schumpeter not only rejected the classical ambitions of citizen participation, he also abandoned the claim that democracy is a legitimate form of government because it is representative of the people's wishes.[7] In Schumpeter's view, politicians vie for votes just as firms compete for consumers. As a result, democracy is not about representation; "it is about selling a product—government output—in exchange for votes."[8]

But what does a system of rotating elites, of competitive oligarchy to be blunt, have to do with "democracy," a system in which the people rule? Here we return to the liberal and civic republican understandings of politics. Following Locke, Schumpeter's achievement was to codify a peaceful "right to rebellion." Social peace is maintained because the losing set of elites agrees to accept the verdict of the ballot box and the people exercise the right to rebellion by rejecting one set of rulers and replacing them or, alternatively, affirming the rulers currently in place. But this understanding of democracy does not give us very much beyond the right to change the government. Of course, this is extremely important, especially if the government is inept and its failings so apparent (for example, urban riots and the Vietnam War in 1965 and Hurricane Katrina and the War in Iraq in 2005) that they cannot be ignored. But aren't leaders supposed to be responsive to the public? By Schumpeter's account yes, to the degree that one group of elites gains advantage over the other in appearing responsive. No, in the sense that democracy "as a method" of selecting ruling elites is not about participation or representation, it is about granting the power to act. Once chosen, there is no requirement that the leaders be responsive to the public. Once elected, they can do as they wish, if they have the power and political skill to do so.

One can make a good argument that this is precisely how President George W. Bush and Vice President Dick Cheney internalized their election victories in 2000 and 2004. To be sure, critics complain that the Bush administration has displayed a certain arrogance about governing, but such an attitude is perfectly in line with a minimalist understanding of democracy. Why be responsive? "We won the election, enough said." Such a reading helps explain why the Bush administration would ask Congress to pass a massive tax cut in which 36 percent of the cuts went to the richest 1 percent of Americans and a nearly identical percent went to the bottom 80 percent of the public. This at a time when the public ranked tax cuts as a relatively low priority and, when asked, the public said it preferred that programs for education, the environment, college loans, social welfare, transportation, and so forth be maintained rather than sacrificed for a tax cut that would primarily flow to the wealthy.[9] Of course, when a government governs as a faction, favoring one segment of the population over others, democracy is in trouble. This Madison well understood.

Minimal democracy is premised on an analogy between firms competing for market share and politicians vying for votes. But economic logic does not always apply to politics. When companies and organizations face decline, individuals have the options of exit, voice, and loyalty.[10] In the economic world, the exit option works because there are many other companies to work for and many other products to buy. But in the political world, exit is neither easy nor attractive. How many people want to emigrate? Voice, in terms of a powerful voice that politicians cannot ignore, requires that a political system be representative and responsive to public opinion. This requires a method of accounting for public opinion that captures, not top of the head reactions, but public judgment and a political system where interest groups and public opinion have ample opportunities to shape public policy outside of periodic elections. One scholar writes, "Elections are not enough for sustaining American-style democracy because elections are episodic, and therefore between elections, a president has four years and senators six years to make and implement policy before they are called to account in an election . . . in the twenty-first century . . . a great deal of damage—even a great deal of irreversible damage—can be done between elections."[11] Finally, there is loyalty. But where does loyalty get you if the ship is sinking?

PARTICIPATION AND LIBERTY

The contrast between Schumpeter's minimalist theory and the civic republican understanding of democracy is clear and distinct. In the minimalist account, the people have power only in the sense of being the final arbiter. By contrast, republican democracy is about the power that is created when people come together to debate and deliberate, as in a townhall meeting or a legislature, or to march in the street and demand change, as in the Velvet Revolution that put an end to the Soviet Empire. In republican democracy, it is the deliberation before the casting of the secret ballot that bestows legitimacy. Majority rule is a mechanism by which we stop debate and declare a winner based on the deliberation that went on before. In the consent theory of Locke (and Schumpeter), we can imagine solitary individuals casting ballots that are then aggregated and a choice announced. But people are social beings and although we physically appear as separate and distinct individuals, we are who we are because of the constant communication and social interaction that we share with others. For republicans, the essence of democracy is a group of citizens meeting together, talking, sharing ideas, exchanging views, and arguing passionately about their common future. The Athenian Assembly, the Roman Senate, the Magna Carta, the Mayflower Compact, the New England town meeting, the Constitutional Convention, and the Lincoln Douglas debates are examples that instruct and inspire.

Republicans believe in political participation as a good in its own right. But, just as important, they view public participation in politics as the ultimate bulwark against potential incursions on personal liberty. Civic republicans believe the best way to protect individual liberty is to band together as a group to make sure that the government does not become a threat. If the people are vigilant and strong, elites who might otherwise be tempted to violate their oath of office will have few opportunities to abuse their authority. We created liberal democracy with constitutional safeguards to protect minority and individual rights from abuse by simple majority rule. But constitutions are not enough. Liberty is at risk when the people are passive, fail to pay attention, and assume that their leaders will take care of things.

Individual liberty depends on the exercise of political liberty. Civic republicans, conscious of history and the pain involved when dark times descend, are vigilant about signs of corruption in the body politic. Standing with Machiavelli, they understand that liberty is best protected and best exercised by the people at large.[12]

TAKING CONTROL

Clearly, the United States suffers the twin perils of republican corruption—alienation and greed. "If class warfare is being waged in America, my class is winning," says Warren Buffett, number two on *Forbes'* list of the world's wealthiest people.[13] In the current political system, the voice of the affluent and the active is magnified. Rosenstone and Hansen, in the authoritative text on political participation in the United States conclude: "The thirty year decline of citizen involvement and the more recent decline of citizen involvement in government *has yielded a politically engaged class that is not only growing smaller but also less and less representative* of the American polity. In fact, the economic inequalities in political participation that prevail in the United States today are as large as the racial disparities in political participation that prevailed in the 1950s."[14] Early in the twenty-first century, our best hope for genuine democratic reform is to create practices and institutions that push back against consultant politics, the power of cold cash, and the ability of elites to manipulate and mislead mass public opinion. Building on the founders, the Assembly would give greater power and leverage to citizens, but without unbalancing the Constitution or radically changing the political system. By combining Madison and Jefferson in a creative synthesis, we can solve the dilemma of scale that bedevils large republics and take a giant step toward making popular sovereignty real. Having elections turn on mudslinging television advertisements and simplistic, misleading direct mail is an insult to everyone registered to vote.[15] Making *this* the central part of our democratic experience is a tragic mistake with profound implications. Our challenge is to go beyond today's nominal democracy and establish a political system that allows "the people" an *intelligent* voice in their government.

The Assembly aims to build a more deliberative democracy focused on achieving Madison's vision of civic majorities on the great issues of the day. The Assembly and the People's House would allow us to bridge the growing gulf that now separates the political class and the public at large, making it possible, finally, to grapple with the major questions that cannot be settled without a nod from the mass public. Every generation confronts new challenges but each must tend democracy's garden. Self-government is not something that we can leave to others. The reform presented here would engage people in the political process, confront upper-class faction, and help broad-based civic majorities find their voice. It would be a new and improved republic—one that the founders could recognize and one that we could be proud to pass on to those who follow.

It is indeed possible to expand our idea of republican government and involve more citizens in the act of governing. Extending representation downward in the political system, the Assembly reform asks a cross section of citizens to take a formal, deliberative role in setting national policy. That is the Assembly and the People's House in a nutshell. This step would both confront the dilemma of scale and help control corruption. Expanding representation would greatly reduce the ratio of electors to representatives and help construct civic majorities fostering the common good.

In addition, this is a democratic reform that does not fall victim to the easy critiques made of participatory democracy as naïve and romantic. Deliberative democracy with a representative dimension is no ode to Rousseau. Rather, what has been proposed is a modification of Madison and representative government. Self-styled realists who dismiss the Assembly reform as being idealistic and impossible probably would not have stood with Patrick Henry and the founders when they risked life itself for the chance to invent the world's first modern democratic republic. Granted, the United States will never be the participatory republic that some envision. But being realistic about the prospects for democracy in America does not mean we must accept Schumpeter's vision as the best we can attain. The Assembly would involve only a small fraction of the population at any one time. Yet imagine, for a minute, how different the United States would be if the Assembly was part of the political system and operated in a manner similar to what I have described.

In *Inventing the People,* Yale historian Edmund Morgan explains how the American founders substituted one fictional notion, "popular sovereignty," for another, "divine right of kings."[16] The Assembly and the People's House would make popular sovereignty less of a fiction and more of a reality. Today, we have the right to vote, meaning that we have an equal right to consent, the right to choose the elites who govern. By adding the Assembly to our representative structure of government, we would give every American the equal right to be chosen as a delegate to the Assembly and, if chosen in the delegate lottery, the equal right to speak in the Assembly (*isēgoria,* the most fundamental democratic right). If the People's House were to become a reality, every American citizen would know he or she had an equal chance to possibly exercise that precious right and take a turn in ruling the nation.

Democratic norms and values are important; so are institutions. They work hand in hand. If we want to improve public debate and encourage the "vigorous exchange of ideas and opinions" necessary for democracy to flourish, then institutions matter.[17] Apathy is sometimes a consequence of a nation's political institutions and thus, instead of being an immutable quality, can be changed. Simply because we observe patterns of behavior does not mean they are inevitable. The apathy we see, particularly in the less educated and less affluent, for example, may, in fact, be consequences of political institutions or the lack thereof.[18]

The basic institutional choices made three centuries ago by the inventors of representative government have rarely been questioned.[19] The Assembly reform challenges those choices and suggests a more democratic approach to representative government in America.

SIZE AND DEMOCRACY

The framers lived in a nation of 3 million people, which by Lincoln's generation had grown to 33 million. Neither group could have imagined the United States at the beginning of the twenty-first century with a population of 300 million.[20] The dilemma of scale is a difficult puzzle for modern democracy. Minimalist democracy and the direct mass democracy of the initiative and primary are the two widely prescribed "solutions." The Assembly reform charts a different path. Incorporating the ideas of deliberative democracy and the republican tradition, the Assembly offers an approach to modern democracy that is neither romantic nor cynical. It is ambitious, to be sure, yet realistic in what it asks of human psychology, motivation, and ability. It is a practical way of recovering and nurturing human scale in politics, as well as a method for creating a deliberative public opinion that could legitimately represent and stand for the American public at large.

In *On Revolution*, Arendt writes

> If the ultimate end of [the American] revolution was freedom and the constitution of a public space where political liberty could appear, the *constitutio libertatis*, then the elementary republics of the wards, the only tangible place where everyone could be free [where freedom to stand and to speak to one's fellow citizens exists], actually were the end of the great republic whose chief purpose in domestic affairs should have been to provide the people with such places of freedom and to protect them. The basic assumption of the ward system, whether Jefferson knew it or not, was that no one could be called happy without his share in public happiness, that no one could be called free without his experience in public freedom, and that no one could be called either happy or free without participating, and having a share, in public power.[21]

The Assembly would give every American citizen an equal chance to share in public power. To do so would be a great accomplishment and would re-establish the United States as the world's leading democracy.

THE SECRET OF AMERICAN PRAGMATISM

Being pragmatic is usually synonymous with being practical, accepting known constraints, and doing what is possible. Pragmatism, in this definition, is hard-headed business sense as opposed to dreamy idealism. Yet the philosophical definition of pragmatism combines practicality *with* vision.

At the dawn of the twentieth century, Dewey, Peirce, William James, and Herbert Mead articulated a middle position between abstract German idealism and British utilitarianism. For the American philosophers, the problem with Kant and Hegel was that their feet rarely touched the ground, whereas British thinkers were often so empirical that they accepted the world exactly as it was. Similar to the magical realism of Gabriel Garcia Marquez, the German philosophers sought to escape the strictures of life where reform and progress seemed permanently blocked by creating a dream world where idealism could triumph.[22] British thinkers were less abstract, more concrete. By contrast, they gave too little credit to the ways human imagination, experimentation, rebellion, and pure chance combine to create the current status quo. Reflecting on the American experience and personality, the pragmatists explored the middle ground between strict empiricism and ideal reflections of the mind. The genius of America is our ability to combine the two traits.[23]

In staking out a middle path between direct democracy and traditional representative government, the Assembly and the People's House follow an American tradition of inventiveness. As pragmatic idealists, Americans do not like being told something is impossible. Instead of accepting hard and fast dichotomies, we continually strive for synthesis. In the world of ideas, American democracy is built on a marriage of Lockean liberalism and civic republicanism. In our constitutional structure, the United States is a compound republic that combines a national government with strong states and Westminster majoritarianism with consensual protections. In the realm of public policy, the New Deal state built by Roosevelt is a marriage of Jefferson's devotion to democracy and Hamilton's desire for a strong interventionist state.[24] Continuing this tradition in the sphere of political representation, the assembly reform would weld Jefferson's ward-republics to Madison's representative framework.

Few of us are naturally contemplative; we are far too restless and energetic. "Life passes in movement and noise, men are so busy acting that they have little time to think,"[25] Still, both as individuals and as a society, we occasionally pull back to review our lives and reflect on what we could do differently. When we pause, we take the pragmatist's advice and use our minds to imagine what can be. The challenge, said Dewey, is to first "reconstruct" reality in our minds to bring it closer to our ideals and goals.

Then, instead of remaining solely in the realm of ideas, we must re-enter the stream of life and work to shape reality to our vision. First come ideas, then action. Thus, bit by bit, we remake the world according to our desires, goals, and ideals.

Pragmatic idealism runs deep in America. Robert F. Kennedy (borrowing from George Bernard Shaw) summarized this worldview when he said, "Some men see things as they are and say, 'why?' I dream of things that never were and say, 'why not?'"[26] In America, natural optimism and a belief that we can make things better unites with a desire to live in the here and now. The United States has always been a nation of practical idealists. We will need optimism, persistence, and practicality to reinvent representative government and save democracy in America.

Notes

INTRODUCTION

1. *It Could Always Be Worse,* A Yiddish folktale retold, including pictures, by Margot Zemach (New York: A Sunburst Book/Michael di Capua Books, Farrar, Straus and Giroux, 1976).

2. In 2000, according to the U.S. Census the population of the United States was 281.4 million people. By February 2006, the number had grown to more than 298.1 million people. http://www.census.gov/main/www/popclock.html (Accessed: 2/16/06).

3. That the broad public needs to engage in thoughtful discussion, especially on issues of magnitude, is made clear when one reads, for example, Michael Ignatieff's perceptive meditation on ethics in an age of terror. Michael Ignatieff, "Could We Lose the War on Terror?" *New York Times Magazine,* 2 May 2004, 46–94 and *The Lesser Evil: Political Ethics in an Age of Terror* (Princeton: Princeton University Press, 2004).

4. Headlines in 2006 included: "For Sale: Tom DeLay, Jack Abramoff, and Big Government Conservatism," *The New Republic,* 16 May 2006 and John Nichols, "Left Behind: DeLay Goes, But His Corrupt House Still Stands," *The Nation,* 24 April 2006. Headlines in 2005 included: "War, storms, leaks—and a growing array of ETHICAL CLOUDS. Dark Days for the Republican Party," *Newsweek,* 10 October 2005, 24–34, capitalization in original; Jonathan Chait, "Taking Sleaze to a New Level: DeLay and his successor are symbols of how today's Republican Party gains, and keeps, power," *Los Angeles Times,* 30 September 2005, B11, and Frank Rich, "In the Beginning There Was Abramoff," *New York Times,* 2 October 2005, Week in Review, 12.

5. See Alexis de Tocqueville, *Democracy in America* [1835, 1840] trans. George Lawrence, ed. J. P. Mayer (Garden City, NY: Doubleday Anchor, 1969).

6. In some places, party organizations were closed systems that gave little voice to rank-and-file citizens. This problem helped spark the 1960s movement for "participatory democracy."

7. Thomas E. Patterson, *The Vanishing Voter* (New York: Knopf, 2003), x.

8. "In presidential primaries over the last quarter century, turnout has peaked at a whopping 88 percent . . . The worst turnout in contested presidential primaries in the last 24 years was 70 percent." Faye Fiore, "Where Voting is a Primary Concern," *Los Angeles Times* (1 February 2000), A16.

9. Daniel Yankelovich, *Coming to Public Judgment: Making Democracy Work in a Complex World* (Syracuse: Syracuse University Press, 1991).

10. Neil Postman, *Amusing Ourselves to Death: Public Discourse in the Age of Show Business* (New York: Penguin Books, 1985), 69.

11. Thomas Friedman interview with Tim Russert on CNBC, 8 March 2003.

12. "During the past forty years the American electorate has become wealthier and vastly better educated. Moreover, electoral reforms have made voting easier (for eligible voters) than at any point since the late 1800s. According to models of voting behavior created by electoral scholars, these changes (all else being equal) should have raised voter turnout by five percentage points or more, to close to 70 percent. Instead, it has fallen, to around 50 percent." Don Peck, "The Shrinking Electorate," *Atlantic Monthly* (November 2002), 48.

13. Mary Ann Glendon, "Democracy's Discontent: America in Search of a Public Philosophy." *The New Republic* (1 April 1996), 39, emphasis added.

14. On the imperial presidency and its revival see Arthur M. Schlesinger Jr., "Bush's Thousand Days," *Washington Post* (24 April 2006), A17 and *The Imperial Presidency* [1973] with a New Introduction (New York: Houghton Mifflin, 2004), John W. Dean, *Worse Than Watergate* (New York: Warner Books, 2005) and Senator Robert C. Byrd, *Losing America: Confronting a Reckless and Arrogant Presidency* (New York: W. W. Norton, 2004).

15. Robert A. Dahl, *Democracy and Its Critics* (New Haven: Yale University Press, 1989), 338.

16. I am in agreement with Jacob S. Hacker and Paul Pierson who write, "Overwhelmingly, Americans say their form of government is the best in the world. Constitutional obstacles aside, the United States is simply not going to become a parliamentary democracy with clearer lines of electoral accountability. It is not going to elect national legislators using proportional representation (in which congressional seats are allocated according to the national party vote, not the results in any particular district). Reforms that fail to strike chords in our political heartstrings are not going to be popular destinations." Jacob S. Hacker and Paul Pierson, *Off Center: The Republican Revolution & the Erosion of American Democracy* (New Haven: Yale University Press, 2005), 190.

17. Michael Walzer, *The Company of Critics* (New York: Basic Books, 1988).

18. The progressive reformers were assisted by business interests that saw benefit in a more coherent, rational system of metropolitan administration. See

Samuel P. Hays, "The Politics of Reform in Municipal Government in the Progressive Era," *Pacific Northwest Quarterly* 55 (1964), 157–69.

19. Arthur M. Schlesinger Jr., *The Cycles of American History* (Boston: Houghton Mifflin, 1986) and E. J. Dionne Jr., *They Only Look Dead: Why Progressives Will Dominate the Next Political Era* (New York: Simon and Schuster, 1996). Dionne's "central assertion is that the United States is on the verge of a second Progressive Era," 11.

20. Given that my political sympathies are liberal, part of the argument I make for the Assembly reflects my ideological bent. However, a strong conservative could also make a convincing case for the Assembly idea.

CHAPTER ONE

1. *The World Almanac and Book of Facts 2004*, U.S. Population by the Official Census, 1790–2000 (New York: World Almanac Books, 2004), 370–71.

2. New Hampshire had a population of 1,235,786 in 2000 and 400 lower house representatives for a ratio of approximately 1 to 3,786. Vermont had a population of 608,827 in 2000 and 150 lower house representatives for a ratio of approximately 1 to 4,058. *Statistical Abstract of the United States 2000* (U.S. Census Bureau, 2000), Tables 18 and 387.

3. In California, each of the 40 members of the state Senate represents 846,791 constituents (according to the California State Senate Website) and the 80 members of the state Assembly have districts half as large.

4. See Edmund S. Morgan, *Inventing the People: The Rise of Popular Sovereignty in England and America* (New York: W. W. Norton, 1988), 74–75 and Bernard Manin, *The Principles of Representation* (Cambridge: Cambridge University Press), esp. Ch. 3.

5. Jack N. Rakove, *James Madison and the Creation of the American Republic,* (Glenview, IL.: Scott, Foreman/Little, Brown Higher Education, 1990), 78–79.

6. U.S. Census data cited by Robert D. Putnam, *Bowling Alone: The Collapse and Revival of American Community* (New York: Simon & Schuster, 2000), 206–07.

7. http://factfinder.census.gov/servlet/DTTable?_bm=y&-state=dt&ds_name=DEC_2000_SF1_U&-gc_url=010:00|52|64|72|84|85|88|&-CONTEXT=dt&-mt_name=DEC_2000_SF1_U_P001&-redoLog=false&-geo_id=01000US&-format=&-_lang=en

8. *Statistical Abstract of the United States 2002* (U.S. Census Bureau, 2002), Tables 1, 18, and 30; *The World Almanac and Book of Facts 1980* (New York: Newspaper Enterprise Association, 1980), United States—State Governments, 316–17.

9. Edmund Morris, *The Rise of Theodore Roosevelt* (New York: The Modern Library, 2001), "Prologue: New Year's Day 1907," xi–xxxiv.

10. *The World Almanac and Book of Facts 2004,* U.S. Population by the Official Census, 1790–2000, 370–71.

11. "U.S. Interim Projections by Age, Sex, Race, and Hispanic Origin," *U.S. Census Bureau,* 2004, Table 1a. Projected Population of the United States, by Race and Hispanic Origin: 2000 to 2050. http://www.census.gov/ipc/www/usinterimproj/

12. According to U.S. and World Population Clock, the world population is 6.498 billion. http://www.census.gov/main/www/popclock.html (Accessed: 2/16/06).

13. J. R. McNeill, *Something New Under the Sun: An Environmental History of the Twentieth-Century World* (New York: Norton, 2000), 282.

14. Ali Piano and Arch Puddington, eds. *Freedom in the World 2005: The Annual Survey of Political Rights and Civil Liberties* (New York: Freedom House, 2005), 5. "In 2004, 119 out of 192 countries (62 per cent) qualified as electoral democracies, two more than in 2003." The designation is based on whether the last major national election qualified under established international standards as "free and fair."

15. Conversation with the author.

16. Walter Lippmann, *Public Opinion* [1922] (New York: Free Press, 1965); Daniel J. Boorstin, *The Image: A Guide to Pseudo-Events in America* [1961] (New York: Vintage Books, 1987).

17. Robert A. Dahl and Edward R. Tufte, *Size and Democracy* (Stanford: Stanford University Press, 1973), 3.

18. Ibid. 2.

19. *Statistical Abstract of the United States: 2002,* Table No. 405. Number of Governmental Units by Type: 1952 to 2002.

20. Involvement in local government, jury duty, and free discussion are the chief instruments of public education and involvement recommended for citizens by Tocqueville and John Stuart Mill. See Tocqueville, *Democracy in America*; and John Stuart Mill, *Considerations on Representative Government,* edited with an introduction by Currin Shields (Indianapolis: Bobbs-Merrill, 1958), esp. ch. 15; and Dennis F. Thompson, *John Stuart Mill and Representative Government* (Princeton: Princeton University Press, 1976), 41.

21. The original Bill of Rights included twelve amendments. The eleventh was eventually ratified as the twenty-seventh amendment in 1992. The other that failed to be adopted when the first ten were ratified in 1791 deals with the size of the House of Representatives. It reads: "Article the first . . . After the first enumeration required by the first Article of the Constitution, there shall be one Represen-

tative for every thirty thousand, until the number shall amount to one hundred, after which the proportion shall be so regulated by Congress, that there shall be not less than one hundred Representatives, nor less than one Representative for every forty thousand persons, until the number of Representatives shall amount to two hundred; after which the proportion shall be so regulated by Congress, that there shall not be less than two hundred Representatives, nor more than one Representative for every fifty thousand persons."

22. Ross Baker, *House and Senate* (New York: W. W. Norton, 1989). In *Size and Democracy,* their cross-national empirical study on the effects of scale on modern democracies, Dahl and Tufte write: "As the membership of a parliament increases . . . discussion becomes more burdensome; participation in debate must be more and more severely restricted; delegation of authority to committees creates problems of coordination and collective control. The parliament, in short, becomes less and less capable of functioning as an assembly. *As a consequence, parliaments cannot be allowed to expand indefinitely.*" Dahl and Tufte, 80, emphasis added.

23. Democracy on a large scale has distinct advantages. Large democracies are better able to defend themselves from external threats. In addition, the size of a nation-state does not seem to have a direct effect on political participation and a sense of efficacy among citizens. This, however, depends on the amount of federalism and decentralization within a particular country. And size is a benefit in lowering the cost of dissent. The greater the number of members in a political system, the greater the chance a person in the minority will find allies and be able to organize effectively. On the other hand, the costs of participation rise when numbers get larger. The larger the scale, the less able is the average citizen to deal directly with his or her elected representatives and the more likely there will exist a large gap of knowledge between leaders and citizens. Dahl and Tufte, 13, 65, 87–91.

24. See Morris P. Fiorina, *Congress: Keystone of the Washington Establishment* (New Haven: Yale University Press, 1977).

25. Richard F. Fenno Jr., *Home Style: House Members in their Districts,* with a new foreword by John R. Hibbing (New York: Longman, 2003).

26. Roberto Michels, *Political Parties: A Sociological Study of the Oligarchical Tendencies of Modern Parties,* trans. E. Paul and C. Paul; intro S. M. Lipset. (New York: Collier Books, 1962).

27. See Dahl, *Democracy and Its Critics,* esp. ch. 19 "Is Minority Rule Inevitable?" 265–79. "Michels committed an elementary mistake in generalizing from political parties to the government of a polyarchal system . . . the theorists of minority domination discussed here had little or no experience with systems of competitive parties in countries with a broad suffrage or, certainly, with systematic analysis of competitive party systems." 276.

28. Jean M. Yarbrough, *American Virtues: Thomas Jefferson on the Character of a Free People* (Lawrence: University Press of Kansas, 1998), 111 and Robert A. Dahl, *Controlling Nuclear Weapons, Democracy versus Guardianship* (Syracuse: Syracuse University Press, 1985). See Manin, *Representative Government,* for the argument that the authors of the Constitution consciously chose representative government as an alternative to popular self-rule. On how the United States quickly moved away from an elitist understanding of democracy see Gordon S. Wood, *The Radicalism of the American Revolution* (New York: Vintage Books, 1991) and Robert H. Wiebe, *Self-Rule: A Cultural History of American Democracy* (Chicago: University of Chicago Press, 1995).

29. See Dahl, *Democracy and Its Critics.*

30. See Jane J. Mansbridge, *Beyond Adversary Democracy,* with a revised preface (Chicago: University of Chicago Press, 1983). Mansbridge provides a case study of an urban cooperative and a New England town run by direct democracy principles.

31. See James Miller, *"Democracy is in the Streets" From Port Huron to the Siege of Chicago* (New York: Simon & Schuster, 1987); Todd Gitlin, *The Twilight of Common Dreams: Why America Is Wracked by Culture Wars* (New York: Owl Book, Henry Holt, 1995) and *The Sixties: Years of Hope, Days of Rage* (New York: Bantam Books, 1987).

32. Robert A. Dahl, *After the Revolution?* (New Haven: Yale University Press, 1970) and David Brooks, *Bobos in Paradise* (New York: Simon & Schuster, 2000).

33. See Carole Pateman, *Participatory Democracy* (Cambridge: Cambridge University Press, 1970) and Mansbridge, *Beyond Adversary Democracy.*

34. Lippmann, *Public Opinion,* Part Eight "Organized Intelligence" and Fareed Zakaria, *The Future of Freedom* (New York: W. W. Norton, 2003), esp. Conclusion.

35. Dick Morris, *Behind the Oval Office: Winning the Presidency in the Nineties* (New York: Random House, 1997), 9.

36. News organizations poll the public on an astounding variety of subjects, from the president's credibility on weapons of mass destruction to whether Elvis is alive. But do the polls actually increase understanding or are they just noise? One expert says, "Asking people questions that they have no clue about and yet are willing to give you an answer . . . I think that's very unfortunate." When polled about a complex public issue, most people react with reflexive prejudice rather than thoughtful opinion. It is widely known that most Americans receive the majority of their news from television and that a person watching a national news program receives less information in 30 minutes than he or she

would receive reading the front page of a major newspaper. The increase in celebrity and entertainment news and the decline in viewership of the networks' nightly newscasts feed this information deficit." Quote is from Steve Farkas, senior vice president and director of research at the think tank Public Agenda quoted by Lori Robertson, "Poll Crazy," *American Journalism Review* (January/February 2003), 41–45.

37. Scott L. Althaus, *Collective Preferences in Democratic Politics: Opinion Surveys and the Will of the People* (New York: Cambridge University Press, 2003), 4. In this passage Althaus is referring to the era before polling when people looked to election results, the press, and interest groups to try to decipher what the public was thinking. But the quote, as I use it, fits with his main argument.

38. Ibid., 3.

39. Larry M. Bartels, "Is 'Popular Rule' Possible? Polls, Political Psychology, and Democracy" *Brookings Review* (Summer 2003), 12.

40. Specialists in public opinion have long tried to square relative ignorance with some sense of judgment. In a review article of the field, Donald Kinder and David Sears write, "Americans are indifferent to much that transpires in the political world, hazy about many of the principle players, lackadaisical regarding debates on policies that preoccupy Washington, ignorant of facts that experts take for granted" but go on to say that this "dreary recitation is no indictment." Others may not agree. Donald R. Kinder and David O. Sears, "Public Opinion and Political Action." in G. Lindzey and E. Aronson, eds., *Handbook of Social Psychology,* 4th ed. (New York, Random House, 1985), 664.

41. Samuel L. Popkin, *The Reasoning Voter: Communication and Persuasion in Presidential Campaigns* (Chicago: The University of Chicago Press, 1991), 16, 20.

42. Popkin quoting polling expert W. Russell Neuman from "Public's Knowledge of Civics Rises Only a Bit," *New York Times* (May 28, 1989), 31. This statement is a good summary of W. Russell Neumann, *The Paradox of Mass Politics: Knowledge and Opinion in the American Electorate* (Cambridge: Harvard University Press, 1986).

43. Popkin, *Reasoning Voter,* 69–70.

44. Popkin, *Reasoning Voter,* 102–14, 75.

45. John R. Zaller, *The Nature and Origins of Mass Opinion* (Cambridge: Cambridge University Press, 1992), 96.

46. "Communication, rather than taking place from the bottom up, from citizens to politicians via elections, movements, lobbying, polls, and so on, is from the top down: elites shape citizens' views on matters of public concern by framing them in persuasive ways or through sheer intensity of exposure." Ibid., 268.

47. Susan C. Stokes, "Pathologies of Deliberation," in Jon Elster ed., *Deliberative Democracy* (Cambridge: Cambridge University Press, 1998), 124, 126.

48. E. E. Schattschneider, *The Semi-Sovereign People* (New York: Holt, Rinehart and Winston, 1960) and Benjamin I. Page, "The Semi-Sovereign Public," in Jeff Manza, Fay Lomax Cook, and Benjamin I. Page, eds., *Navigating Public Opinion: Polls, Policy, and the Future of American Democracy* (New York: Oxford University Press, 2002), 325, 342.

49. Zaller, *Mass Opinion,* 8–9, 269.

50. Lawrence R. Jacobs and Robert Y. Shapiro, "Politics and Policymaking in the Real World: Crafted Talk and the Loss of Democratic Responsiveness," in Jeff Manza, Fay Lomax Cook, and Benjamin I. Page, eds., *Navigating Public Opinion: Polls, Policy and the Future of American Democracy* (Oxford: Oxford University Press, 2002), 55, and *Politicians Don't Pander: Political Manipulation and the Loss of Democratic Responsiveness* (Chicago: University of Chicago Press, 2000).

51. Ibid., 36.

52. Ibid., 45.

53. Wiebe, *Self-Rule,* p. 256. See Christopher Hitchens, "Voting in the Passive Voice: What Polling has Done to American Democracy," *Harper's* (April 1992), 45–52 for a similar analysis.

54. Many observers argue that questions of spending and taxes cannot be understood without being placed in the context of choices, priorities, and trade-offs. See John Mark Hansen, "Individuals, Institutions and Public Preferences over Public Finance," *American Political Science Review* 92 (1998): 513–31.

55. From the Truman Doctrine to Khrushchev's brash boasts and the Cuban Missile Crisis, from Vietnam and Nicaragua to President Reagan's speech about the "Evil Empire," the Cold War was the central fact of our existence. The ever-present danger of a nuclear holocaust made other dangers pale by comparison; the bomb backlit our minds. In John Updike's 1990 novel, *Rabbit at Rest,* an aging Roger "Rabbit" Angstrom speaks wistfully of the great struggle: "I miss it, the Cold War. It gave you a reason for getting up in the morning." John Updike, *Rabbit at Rest* (New York: Ballentine Books, 1990).

56. For one treatment of the shift in American political and legal thought from republican ideas to procedural neutralism see Michael J. Sandel, *Democracy's Discontent: America in Search of a Public Philosophy* (Cambridge: The Belknap Press of Harvard University Press, 1996).

57. We are all familiar with the basic elements of the democratic process: freedom to form and join organizations, freedom of expression, the right to vote, the right of political leaders to compete for support, alternative sources of information, all leading to the central democratic procedure of modern democratic

states—free and fair elections. Of course, the United States has always embraced these formal requirements. Yet such an operational definition ignores the ethical and substantive dimensions of democracy. Robert Dahl and Charles Lindblom coined the term "polyarchy" (control of leaders) for this set of basic political rights. See Robert A. Dahl and Charles E. Lindblom, *Politics, Economics and Welfare* (Chicago: University of Chicago Press, 1953), chs. 10–11; and Robert A. Dahl, *A Preface to Democratic Theory* (Chicago: University of Chicago Press, 1956), and *Polyarchy* (New Haven: Yale University Press, 1971).

58. True, Americans witnessed and took part in widespread democratic activism and protest during the Civil Rights and anti-war mobilizations of the 1960s. Yet, outside of vigorous decades such as this, elections and interest groups are the primary ways that modern Americans think about and practice democracy.

59. Joseph Schumpeter, *Capitalism, Socialism and Democracy* (New York: Harper and Row, 1942), chs. 20–22. Schumpeter's revision of democratic theory appears in a section entitled "Socialism and Democracy." This is no accident.

60. A European conservative, Schumpeter felt comfortable in a society dominated by an aristocratic, bourgeois elite; the "Tory democracy" of late nineteenth-century England was his political ideal. See Richard Swedberg, "Introduction, The Man and His Work," in *Joseph A. Schumpeter,* ed. Richard Swedberg (Princeton: Princeton University Press, 1991), 8, 13. Although his public position was that of a European conservative, Schumpeter's private politics were more reactionary. A biography of the Austrian-born Schumpeter revealed disturbing findings akin to the Paul de Man scandal. Schumpeter, it turns out, was an anti-Semite and a supporter of the war aims of fascist Germany and Japan. See Bernard Semmel, "Schumpeter's Curious Politics," *Public Interest* 106 (1992): 3–16; Robert Loring Allen, *Opening Doors: The Life and Work of Joseph Schumpeter* (New York: Transaction Books, 1991).

61. Schumpeter, 269.

62. Schumpeter, 284–85, emphasis added.

63. In attempting to simplify the cognitive problem facing the voter, Schumpeter reduces the complex political judgment required of a citizen to the more simple market choice required of a consumer. See Charles E. Lindblom, *Politics and Markets* (New York: Basic Books, 1977), ch. 10, esp. 134–36. Lindblom writes: "A number of contemporary democratic theories have borrowed the concept of preference from economic theory. Just as people have preferences for goods and services, they are considered to have preferences for leaders or for particular public policies . . . Yet the concept of preferences distorts the picture of polyarchy (and democracy)," 134. Volitions, by contrast, are complex judgments, and this is a better way of describing political thinking.

64. Following Schumpeter's lead, many American political scientists began to think about democracy primarily in procedural terms, and this way of defining democracy began to filter into journalism and everyday discussion. Important early examples of the procedural view are Dahl and Lindblom, *Politics, Economics and Welfare,* Dahl, *A Preface to Democratic Theory,* Robert A. Dahl, *Who Governs?* (New Haven: Yale University Press, 1961); Anthony Downs, *An Economic Theory of Democracy* (New York: Harper and Row, 1957); David Truman, *The Governmental Process* (New York: Knopf, 1951); Bernard Berelson, Paul Lazarsfeld, and William McPhee, *Voting* (Chicago: University of Chicago Press, 1954), ch. 14. Two important examples in the past twenty-five years are Robert A. Dahl, "Procedural Democracy," in Peter Laslett and James Fishkin, eds. *Philosophy, Politics, and Society,* 5th series (Oxford: Basil Blackwell, 1984) and William H. Riker, *Liberalism Against Populism: A Confrontation between the Theory of Democracy and the Theory of Social Choice* (San Francisco: W. H. Freeman and Company, 1982). Schumpeter's continuing influence can be seen in many works of contemporary political science including, for example, John Mueller, *Capitalism, Democracy and Ralph's Pretty Good Grocery* (Princeton: Princeton University Press, 1999) and Steven E. Schier, *You Call This an Election? America's Peculiar Democracy* (Washington, DC: Georgetown University Press, 2004).

65. "The principal theme of the new Cold War conservatism was the betrayal of the West by liberals, who were identified with the communists . . . The liberals never truly recovered from the early onslaught. They developed a *defensive flinch,* as if they had to prove their loyalty," Sidney Blumenthal, *Pledging Allegiance* (New York: Harper Collins, 1990), 8–9; emphasis added. The Civil Rights movement focused on civic equality but the War on Poverty failed, in part, because of a lack of consensus about the importance of economic equality as a democratic value. Here we can think of economic equality as a minimal economic floor akin to Western European nations and similar to the way John Rawls speaks of equality in *A Theory of Justice* (Cambridge: Harvard University Press, 1971).

66. As a nation, the United States is held together by political beliefs that go beyond a commitment to democratic procedures. Blending the liberal and republican traditions together into a cohesive whole, John Dewey argued that five values lie at the heart of the American democratic experience: liberty, equality, community, intelligence, and public good. These five values play a critical role in binding our large, heterogeneous, multicultured country into a single democratic community. In fact, we are Americans precisely because an overwhelming majority of us believe in and have adopted these democratic values as our communal ideals. In contrast to thinking about democracy solely as elections and the rotation of elites, Dewey argued that these values constitute "democracy as a way of life." See Robert B. Westbrook, *John

Dewey and American Democracy (Ithaca: Cornell University Press, 1991) and Kevin O'Leary, "John Dewey, Herbert Croly and Progressive Democratic Theory" unpublished dissertation, Department of Political Science, Yale University, 1989.

67. Louis Hartz, *The Liberal Tradition in America* (New York: Harcourt, Brace, 1955), 5.

68. By defining the terror threat of Al Qaeda as a "war" instead of the police emergency that it really is, President Bush has pushed us back into the ideological framework of the Cold War. See Michael Howard, "What's in a Name? How to Fight Terrorism," *Foreign Affairs* (January/February 2002), 8–13.

69. Two of the most important and influential books on participatory democracy are Pateman, *Participation and Democratic Theory* and Benjamin Barber, *Strong Democracy: Participatory Politics for a New Age* (Berkeley: University of California Press, 1984). Both authors are strongly influenced by Rousseau. Barber writes: "Representation is incompatible with freedom because it delegates and thus alienates political will at the cost of genuine self-government and autonomy," 145.

70. Jean-Jacques Rousseau, *On the Social Contract* [1762] with the *Geneva Manuscript and Political Economy* edited by Roger D. Masters, trans. by Judith R. Masters (New York: St. Martin's Press, 1978).

71. See "Introduction," Rousseau, *Social Contract,* Roger D. Masters ed., 17.

72. Rousseau, *Social Contract,* bk. III, ch. XV: On Deputies or Representatives, 102–03.

73. Writers who question whether Rousseau should be viewed as a democrat include Bertrand de Jouvenel, "Rousseau's Theory of the Forms of Government," in Maurice Cranston and Richard S. Peters eds., *Hobbes and Rousseau: A Collection of Critical Essays* (Garden City, NY: Anchor Books, 1972) and Judith Shklar, *Men and Citizens* (Cambridge: Cambridge University Press, 1969). Shklar finds two distinct utopias in his work, the spartan city and the patriarchal household, neither particularly democratic. Also for a champion of direct democracy, Rousseau leaves plenty to be done by magistrates and executives.

74. James Miller, *Rousseau: Dreamer of Democracy* (New Haven: Yale University Press, 1984). Miller gives us a portrait of the man and his writings that places the *Social Contract* in the context of Rousseau's work as a whole. This is important because the *Social Contract* alone does not reveal Rousseau's full democratic imagination and vision.

75. Rousseau, *Social Contract,* bk. III, ch. IV: On Democracy, 85.

76. Miller, 74.

77. Rousseau, *Social Contract,* 85.

78. The radical rejection of modern life can be seen clearly when one reads not only *The Social Contract* but also *The First and Second Discourses*.

79. Miller, 166.

80. Each of these three paths owes a debt to Rousseau. See Miller, 205.

81. See David Broder, *Democracy Derailed: Initiative Campaigns and the Power of Money* (New York: Harcourt, Brace, 2000).

82. Peter Schrag, "California, Here We Come: Government by plebiscite, which would have horrified the Founding Fathers, threatens to replace representative government," *Atlantic Monthly* (March 1998), 20–31.

CHAPTER TWO

1. Carl L. Becker, *The Declaration of Independence: A Study in the History of Political Ideas* [1922] (New York: Vintage Books, 1958); Bernard Bailyn, *The Ideological Origins of the American Revolution* (Cambridge: The Belknap Press of Harvard University Press, 1967), J.G.A. Pocock, *The Machiavellian Moment* (Princeton: Princeton University Press, 1975) and Gordon Wood, *The Creation of the American Republic, 1776–1787* (New York: Norton, 1969).

2. Philosophic liberals focus on rights, procedures, and the pluralist struggle between self-interested groups. In liberal thought, the substance and resources of politics comes from outside the political arena. As Michael Sandel points out, modern political thought is distinctive in holding that "government should be neutral on the question of the good life." Sandel, *Democracy's Discontent*, 7. By contrast, republican theory views the purpose of politics to be, in part, to cultivate the virtues and the character necessary for the continued existence of the republic.

3. Hartz, *Liberal Tradition*.

4. Cass R. Sunstein, The Enduring Legacy of Republicanism," in *A New Constitutionalism,* eds. Stephen L. Elkin and Karol Edward Soltan (Chicago: University of Chicago Press, 1993), 174–75.

5. See Quintin Skinner, "The Republican Idea of Political Liberty," in Gisela Bock, Quentin Skinner, and Maurizio Viroli eds., *Machiavelli and Republicanism* (Cambridge: Cambridge University Press, 1990), 293–309; Quentin Skinner, *Liberty Before Liberalism* (Cambridge: Cambridge University Press, 1998), Philip Pettit, *Republicanism: A Theory of Freedom and Government* (Oxford: Oxford University Press, 1999) and Maurizio Viroli, *Republicanism* (New York: Hill and Wang, 2002).

6. See Shapiro's argument that democracy is a "foundational" yet "subordinate" good. It is foundational because no more basic political commitment commands our allegiance, but also subordinate because there are many other goods that people pursue. Ian Shapiro, *Democracy's Place* (Ithaca: Cornell University Press, 1996), 109–36.

7. Hannah Arendt, *The Human Condition* (Chicago: University of Chicago Press, 1958) and Alasdair MacIntyre, *After Virtue* (Notre Dame, IN: Notre Dame University Press, 1981). Michael Sandel and Bernard Manin are two other influential scholars who look more to the Greeks than to the Romans for inspiration. There are aspects of Athenian democracy and the Roman republic on which we can draw, as I will in Chapter 4. But to say that politics is the highest and best good and to define virtue, as did Cicero, as the ability of political actors to put "justice, or the common good, before personal advantage" is overly ambitious. Cicero, *On Duties* (Cambridge: Cambridge University Press, 1991), 53, 59–60 cited in Iseult Honohan, *Civic Republicanism* (New York: Routledge, 2002), 34.

8. Hannah Arendt, *On Revolution* [1965] (New York: Penguin Books, 1977) argues that public happiness was a driving force behind the Revolution and that in Jefferson's original draft of the *Declaration* his phraseology was "the pursuit of life, liberty and *public* happiness," ch. 3.

9. Tom Holland, *Rubicon: The Last Years of the Roman Republic* (New York: Anchor Books, 2003), 4.

10. Sunstein, "Enduring Legacy of Republicanism," 180–81. Also see Herbert J. Storing, *The Complete Anti-Federalist,* 7 vols. (Chicago: University of Chicago Press, 1981), esp. vol. 1, "What the Anti-Federalists Were *For,*" "The Small Republic," 15–23, and the key texts by the most important Anti-Federalist writers: The Federal Farmer, Brutus, A [Maryland] Farmer, and The Impartial Examiner.

11. Ibid.

12. Holland, *Last Years of the Roman Republic,* xviii.

13. Ibid., xv, 11, 8.

14. Madison, *Federalist* 10, in Alexander Hamilton, James Madison, and John Jay, *The Federalist Papers,* Introduction by Clinton Rossiter (New York: New American Library, 1961).

15. Dahl and Tufte, *Size and Democracy,* 89.

16. Progressive reformers had reason to be concerned over elected officials skimming the public coffers dry. See *Plunkitt of Tammany Hall,* Introduction by Arthur Mann (New York: Dutton, 1963) and Lincoln Steffens, *The Shame of the Cities* (New York: Sagamore Press, 1957). Of course, straight-forward monetary corruption still exists. For example, "a tearful, trembling Rep. Randy "Duke" Cunningham (R-CA) resigned Monday after pleading guilty to receiving $2.4 million in bribes from military contractors and evading more than $1 million in taxes." Tony Perry, "Rep. Cunningham Pleads Guilty to Bribery, Resigns" *Los Angeles Times* (29 November 2005), A1.

17. For example, the numerous investigations into former House Majority Leader Tom DeLay's associates fall into this category.

18. William Greider, *Who Will Tell the People: the Betrayal of American Democracy* (New York: Simon & Schuster, 1992); Postman, *Amusing Ourselves to Death*; and Jedediah Purdy, *For Common Things: Irony, Trust and Commitment in America Today* (New York: Knopf, 1999).

19. Benjamin Ginsberg and Martin Shefter, *Politics by Other Means,* 3rd ed. (New York: W. W. Norton, 2002).

20. George F. Will, "The Veep and the Blatherskite: Perot's watery Caesarism may be a glimpse of what the 21st century has up its nasty sleeve," *Newsweek,* 29 June 1992, 72.

21. In fact, some argue that the crisis of democratic control of our public life has deepened since the global war on terror began. "The Bush doctrine converts us into the world's judge, jury and executioner—a self-appointed status that, however benign our motives, is bound to corrupt our leadership." Arthur Schlesinger Jr., "Good Foreign Policy a Casualty of War," *Los Angeles Times,* Sunday Opinion, 23 March 2003, p. M1.

22. David M. Ricci, *Good Citizenship in America* (Cambridge: Cambridge University Press, 2004), 254–55, 292.

23. Madison, *Federalist* 10, 78.

24. Tocqueville's phrase in *Democracy in America* gained contemporary currency with Robert Bellah et al., *Habits of the Heart* (Berkeley: University of California Press, 1985).

25. "They therefore do not raise objections to men pursuing their interests, but they do all they can to prove that it is in each man's interest to be good." Tocqueville, *Democracy in America,* bk. 2, part II, ch. 8, "How Americans Combat Individualism by the Doctrine of Self-Interest Properly Understood," 525–28.

26. A number of writers, including Robert Bellah, Barbara Ehrenreich, and Robert Putman, have commented on how American civic culture has become corrupt in just this way. Bellah et al., *Habits of the Heart*; Barbara Ehrenreich, *The Worst Years of Our Lives* (New York: Pantheon Books, 1990) and Putnam, *Bowling Alone.*

27. Dennis F. Thompson, "Mediated Corruption: The Case of the Keating Five," *American Political Science Review* 87 (1993): 269–81. The senators were Dennis DeConcini, Alan Cranston, John Glenn, Donald Riegle, and John McCain. Senator McCain, of course, has since become probably the single most important proponent of political reform in America.

28. *California Journal,* December 2004.

29. U.S. Census Bureau data. See Patterson, *The Vanishing Voter,* esp. ch. 1, "The Incredible Shrinking Electorate," quote from 4, and U.S. Census Bureau,

Statistical Abstract of the United States, 2002, Table No. 396 Resident Population of Voting Age and Percent Casting Votes—States: 1994 to 2000.

30. Jonathan Schell, the author of *The Time of Illusion* (New York: Vintage Books, 1976) on the Nixon era and *The Fate of the Earth* (New York: Avon Books, 1982) on the nuclear threat, asked this simple but profound question during the 1996 presidential election. See Jonathan Schell, "The Uncertain Leviathan," *Atlantic Monthly*, August 1996, 70–78.

31. Patterson, *Vanishing Voter*, 22.

32. Michael Kinsley, *Big Babies* (New York: Morrow, 1995).

33. Grieder, *Who Will Tell the People*, 18.

34. Adam Clymer, "The Body Politic: Nonvoting Americans and Calls for Reform Are Drawn Into Stark Focus in 2000 Races," *New York Times*, 2 January 2000, A1 and 20.

35. Ibid., 20.

36. Phone interview with Kim Alexander, president of the California Voter Foundation. See John Gaventa, *Power and Powerlessness: Quiescence and Rebellion in an Appalachian Valley* (Urbana: University of Illinois Press, 1980).

37. Commenting on how quiet the public was in the spring of 2006, *Los Angeles Times* columnist Steve Lopez wrote, "I don't know what the nation's leaders have to do to get people worked up. There was a time when the kind of news we've had recently, combined with the bloodbath in Iraq, would have sent throngs into the streets." Steve Lopez, "The Sound of Apathy Over War Resounds," *Los Angeles Times*, 14 April 2006, B1.

38. See Popkin, *Reasoning Voter* and W. Russell Neuman, *The Paradox of Mass Politics*.

39. V. O. Key, *The Responsible Electorate* (New York: Vintage Books, 1966), 7.

40. Patterson, *Vanishing Voter*, 84–85. Joan Didion, *Political Fictions* (New York: Knopf, 2001), 10–11.

41. Mark E. Warren, "What Can Democratic Participation Mean Today?" *Political Theory* 30 (2002), 681; and Pippa Norris ed., *Critical Citizens: Global Support for Democratic Government* (New York: Oxford University Press, 1999), esp. 1–27 and 257–72.

42. Ronald Inglehart, "Postmodernism Erodes Respect for Authority, But Increases Support for Democracy," in *Critical Citizens*, 236.

43. Norris, *Critical Citizens*, 27.

44. Dan Morain, "Wealth Buys Access to State Politics," *Los Angeles Times*, 18 April 1999, A1. In a state with 35 million residents, the *Times* found

that approximately 330 individuals, corporations, and political action committees dominated political contributions by giving $100,000 or more to state politics—about 60 percent of the estimated $500 million spent on campaigns in 1998.

45. The door was left open for Hamilton who, not content to secure a "natural aristocracy" of virtuous gentlemen, wanted to create "a new and unnatural one, an aristocracy of speculators and financiers," Morgan, *Inventing the People*, 286. For a more favorable view of Hamilton see Stanley Elkins and Eric McKitrick, *The Age of Federalism* (New York: Oxford University Press, 1993).

46. All of this is not to say that Hamilton was not a republican in the sense of looking out for the good of the nation. More than the other founders, he saw America's future as a commercial republic and great power. In Madison's eyes, the constitutional scheme of checks and balances made for a passive national government. But Hamilton wanted movement, and he sought to build an upper-class bias into the system by fostering close ties between financial interests and the new American state. In general, Hamilton sought a national government that would protect capitalist interests that, in turn, would support a strong American state. See Forrest McDonald, *Alexander Hamilton: A Biography* (New York: Norton, 1982).

47. Manin, *Representative Government*, 120.

48. The "inefficaciousness of his theories would, in his own eyes, be abundantly demonstrated by the triumph of Hamiltonianism." Forrest McDonald, *Novus Ordo Seclorum: The Intellectual Origins of the Constitution* (Lawrence: University Press of Kansas, 1985), 203.

49. Michael Lind, *The New American Nation* (New York: The Free Press, 1995), esp. chs. 4 and 5.

50. Kevin Phillips, *Wealth and Democracy: A Political History of the American Rich* (New York: Broadway Books, 2002), xv.

51. Ibid., xiii, emphasis in original.

52. Ibid., 324.

53. Senator Bill Bradley, Speech to the John F. Kennedy School of Government, Harvard University, 16 January 1996, quoted in Phillips, *Wealth and Democracy*, 405, 407.

54. David Cay Johnston, *Perfectly Legal: the Covert Campaign to Rig Our Tax System to Benefit the Super Rich—and Cheat Everybody Else* (New York: Portfolio/Penguin, 2003).

55. Phillips, *Wealth and Democracy*, 325.

56. Phillips, *Wealth and Democracy*, Ibid. President Bush's first tax cut resulted in a 43 percent cut for the top 1 percent of income earners. His 2003 tax cut gave the top 1 percent of America's income strata an average annual tax re-

duction of $45,000. The people in the middle 20 percent of the income distribution had their taxes cut by an average of a whopping $265. And the least fortunate 60 percent at the bottom of the income ladder got an annual tax break of $95. See Joe Conason, *Big Lie: The Right-Wing Propaganda Machine and How it Distorts the Truth* (New York: Thomas Dunne Books, St. Martin's Press, 2003), 26, 16.

57. Numbers from Phillips, *Wealth and Democracy,* xviii.

58. Ibid., 149, chart 3.19.

59. Paul Krugman using averages from table on 154 of Phillips, *Wealth and Democracy* (chart 3.23 "Up, Up and Away: The Rise of Top Corporate Executive Compensation, 1981–2000). Paul Krugman, "Plutocracy and Politics," *New York Times,* 14 June 2002, A35.

60. Lindblom, *Politics and Markets,* esp. chs. 12–14. In its review, *Business Week* wrote, "Lindblom argues his case with such clarity and objectivity as to endow his thesis with astonishing force." See Robert G. Magnuson, "Yes to Markets, No to Big Business," *BusinessWeek,* 26 December 1977, 17.

61. In addition to Lindblom, see the idea of "capital strike" in Fred Block, "The Ruling Class Does Not Rule: Notes on the Marxist Theory of the State," in *Revisiting State Theory: Essays on Politics and Postindustrialism* (Philadelphia: Temple University Press, 1987), 51–68.

62. Derek Bok makes note of this key point: "One of the worst features of citizen apathy is that it is spread so unequally throughout the population. In contrast to low-income people in Western Europe, poor and working-class Americans vote much less and care much less about public affairs than their better-educated, more affluent compatriots. It is no accident, then, that lower-income groups have received so little protection in the United States and lack basic safeguards and benefits, such as guaranteed access to health care and paid parental leave, that other advanced democracies granted long ago to all their citizens. Derek Bok, *The Trouble with Government* (Cambridge: Harvard University Press, 2001), 396–97.

63. The United States is the only Western industrial power without a working-class political party. One reason is the two-party system; another is race and ethnic conflict among blue-collar workers. A prime example was the Populist failure to unite Midwest farmers with East Coast ethnic workers in the 1890s. As a result, William McKinley crushed William Jennings Bryan in the pivotal 1896 presidential race, cementing Republican control of the presidency from Lincoln to Herbert Hoover—with Woodrow Wilson as the lone Democratic exception.

64. Michael Barone, *Our Country: The Shaping of America from Roosevelt to Reagan* (New York: Free Press, 1990).

65. See Thomas Byrne Edsall, *The New Politics of Inequality* (New York: Norton, 1984) and Lind, *Next American Nation.*

66. See Bolivar Lamounier, "Brazil: Inequality Against Democracy," in Larry Diamond, Juan J. Linz, and Seymour Martin Lipset, eds., *Volume Four, Democracy in Developing Countries: Latin America,* (Boulder, CO: Lynne Rienner Publishers, 1989), 111–57.

67. See a 1998 report by the Conference Board, a business-supported research group. Earlier studies showed class inequality increased markedly during the 1980s as low-income groups lost income and high-income groups gained. Taken together, the lowest quintiles had 15.5 percent of pretax family income in 1977 but dropped to 12.8 percent in 1989. The highest quintile began with 45.6 percent of pretax family income in 1977 and gained to 51.4 percent by 1989. Source: Congressional Budget Office tax simulation model, cited in *U.S. House Ways and Means Committee 1992 Green Book,* 1521.

68. Gregg Easterbrook, "Trading Up: There's Chaos in Seattle. Fabulous." *The New Republic,* 20 December 1999, 16.

69. Phillips, *Wealth and Democracy,* 322.

70. Jonathan Chait, "Special K: Why the Bush Administration is worse than DiIulio said," *The New Republic,* 30 December 2002 and 6 January 2003, 17.

71. Paul Glastris, "Vision Quest: How John Kerry can create jobs by taking on K Street," *Washington Monthly* (April 2004).

72. In this they follow John Rawls' trickle-down argument. See Rawls, *A Theory of Justice.* See also Gaventa, *Power and Powerlessness* and his argument that when people are economically oppressed and beaten down, they give up on political participation figuring the system is rigged and their side can never win.

73. Michael Walzer, *Spheres of Justice* (New York: Basic Books, 1983).

74. In a comment on Mickey Kaus's plea for civic equality, Christopher Lasch writes, "Social and civic equality presuppose at least a rough approximation of economic equality." See Christopher Lasch, "Introduction: The Democratic Malaise," *The Revolt of the Elites and the Betrayal of Democracy* (New York: W. W. Norton, 1995), 22; and Mickey Kaus, *The End of Equality* (New York: Basic Books, 1992). Rousseau, Jefferson, Tocqueville, Dewey, and Walzer all agree that democracy works better when there is a rough sense of economic equality. Trying to maintain some degree of economic equality among citizens was the reason Jefferson, together with Benjamin Franklin and Madison (in his later years), vigorously opposed Hamiliton and wanted to maintain a predominantly agrarian economy as long as possible. See Drew R. McCoy, *The Elusive Republic: Political Economy in Jeffersonian America* (New York: Norton, 1982). Civic republicans realize that the dramatic growth of economic inequality at the end of the 1990s, fueled by the sky-

rocketing stock market, fostered class envy and political impotence—qualities corrosive to a sense of democratic community. "Everyone's Getting Rich But Me," exclaimed a *Newsweek* cover story (5 July, 1999), making this sensation of being left behind palpable. The bubble of extravagant exuberance burst but the question of the uneasy relationship between unbridled capitalism and democracy remains. See Charles Lindblom, *The Market System: What It Is, How It Works, and What to Make of It* (New Haven, Yale University Press, 2001); and Kaus, *The End of Equality.*

75. Bok, *Trouble with Government,* 395.

76. Hacker and Pierson, esp. ch. 2 and Jacob S. Hacker and Paul Pierson, "Abandoning the Middle: The Bush Tax Cuts and the Limits of Democratic Control," *Perspectives on Politics* 3 (March 2005): 33–53.

77. On the deceptions behind the Iraq War see the series of columns written by Frank Rich in the *New York Times* Sunday editions during the summer and fall of 2005.

78. Zaller, *Mass Opinion,* 313, emphasis in original.

79. Wood, *Creation of the American Republic,* 429.

80. John P. McCormick, "Machiavellian Democracy: Controlling Elites with Ferocious Populism," *American Political Science Review* 95 (2001), 311 and Adam Przeworski, "Minimalist Conception of Democracy: A Defense," in Ian Shapiro and Casiano Hacker-Cordón, eds., *Democracy's Value* (Cambridge: Cambridge University Press, 1999): 23–55.

81. Jennifer Hochschild, roundtable discussion of Theodore Lowi, "Presidential Democracy in America," in *Political Science Quarterly,* Special Issue, 109 (1994), 425 and Dahl, *Controlling Nuclear Weapons.*

CHAPTER THREE

1. Madison, Hamilton and Jay, *Federalist Papers.*

2. Wood, *Creation of the American Republic,* 232.

3. Madison, *Federalist 52,* 327.

4. Michael Barone and Grant Ujifusa, *The Almanac of American Politics 1990* (Washington, DC: National Journal, 1989), 71.

5. See Wood, *Radicalism of the American Revolution* and Manin, *Representative Government.*

6. *Federalist* 10, p. 82, emphasis added.

7. The founders understood that the Constitution they worked so hard to create would include errors later generations would have to rectify. Hamilton concludes the final *Federalist,* 85, with Hume's advice to permit experience and new knowledge to correct the mistakes of those who attempt the founding of a

new nation. "To balance a large state or society, whether monarchical or republican, on general laws, is a work of so great difficulty that no human genius, however comprehensive, is able, by the mere dint of reason and reflection, to effect it." *Federalist* 85, 526–27, Hamilton quoting Hume, *Essays,* "The Rise of Arts and Sciences," vol. 1, 128.

8. Charles A. Beard, *An Economic Interpretation of the Constitution of the United States* (New York: Macmillan, 1913).

9. *Federalist* 10, 80.

10. *Federalist* 10, 79.

11. *Federalist* 10, 83, emphasis added.

12. *Federalist* 51, 325.

13. Samuel H. Beer, *To Make a Nation: The Rediscovery of American Federalism* (Cambridge: Belknap Harvard, 1993), 264.

14. Harrington is an odd character in the republican tradition. He is viewed by many, including John Pocock, as the great English republican—the writer most responsible for transmitting the republican ideas of the Italian city-states to the American founders. But while Harrington's institutions are republican, his basic understanding of politics is much more aligned with Hobbes than Machiavelli. Like Hobbes, his desire is for social peace and stability and "we see in Harrington's *Oceana*, no less than Hobbes's *Leviathan,* the abolition of the participatory basis of classical citizenship. In both cases the reason is the same: that this is what it takes to achieve peace. Unlike Hobbes, however, while abolishing the *substance* of participation Harrington does, throughout *Oceana*, preserve and ritualize the external appearance of it." Jonathan Scott, "The Rapture of Motion: James Harrington's republicanism," in Nicholas Phillipson and Quentin Skinner eds., *Political Discourse in Early Modern England* (Cambridge: Cambridge University Press, 1993), 151, emphasis in original.

15. Beer, *To Make a Nation,* 264.

16. Beer, Ibid., 267–77.

17. Joseph M. Bessette, *The Mild Voice of Reason: Deliberative Democracy and American National Government* (Chicago: University of Chicago Press, 1994), 106.

18. *Federalist* 10, 83–84.

19. Beer, *To Make a Nation,* 281, emphasis added.

20. Beer makes a strong case for this interpretation. See Beer, *To Make a Nation,* ch. 9, "Auxiliary Precautions." Samuel Kernell believes Madison was less attached to the idea of a separation of powers than generally believed and more willing to make use of pluralism to umpire political conduct. See "'The True Principles of Republican Government:' Reassessing James Madison's Political Science," in Samuel

Kernell ed., *James Madison: The Theory and Practice of Republican Government* (Stanford: Stanford University Press, 2003): 92–125.

21. *Federalist* 10, 82.

22. David Hume, "That Politics May Be Reduced to a Science," in *Philosophical Works,* eds. T. H. Green and T. H. Grose (London: Longmans, Green, 1875), vol. 3, 99–100.

23. Gary Remer, "James Harrington's New Deliberative Rhetoric: Reflections of an Anticlassical Republicanism," *History of Political Thought* 16 (1995), 536.

24. Manin, *Representative Government*, 1.

25. Wood, *Radicalism of the American Revolution*, 258.

26. Cass R. Sunstein, *The Partial Constitution* (Cambridge: Harvard University Press, 1993), xvi, quoting Madison.

27. Wood, *Creation of the American Republic*, 475, commas and emphasis added.

28. *Federalist* 63.

29. Beer, *To Make a Nation*, 280.

30. Bruce A. Ackerman, *We the People: Foundations* (Cambridge: Belknap Press of Harvard University Press, 1991).

31. Wood, *Creation of the American Republic*, 516, emphasis added.

32. Patrick Henry, in Debates III, 167, cited by Isaac Kramnick, "Editor's Introduction," Madison, Hamilton, and Jay, *The Federalist Papers* (New York: Penguin Books, 1987), 43. Richard Henry Lee in Wood, *Creation of the American Republic,* 516.

33. Sunstein, *Partial Constitution*.

34. Douglass Adair was the first historian to discover the connection between Madison and Hume. Douglass Adair, "That Politics May Be Reduced to a Science: David Hume, James Madison, and the Tenth Federalist," [1957] *Fame and the Founding Fathers, Essays of Douglass Adair,* ed. Trevor Colbourn (New York: W. W. Norton, 1974), 93–106.

35. David Hume, "Idea of a Perfect Commonwealth," [1752] in *Essays: Moral, Political and Literary* edited with a foreword, notes, and glossary by Eugene F. Miller (Indianapolis: LibertyClassics, 1985), 512–29.

36. Hume, "Idea of a Perfect Commonwealth," 527.

37. Hume, Ibid., 516–17, emphasis and [London] added.

38. James Harrington, *Oceana* [1656] in *The Political Works of James Harrington,* edited with an introduction by J. G. A. Pocock (Cambridge: Cambridge University Press, 1977); Pocock, "Historical Introduction," *The Political Works of James Harrington,* 1–152, and Manin, *Representative Government*, 67–70.

39. Hume, "Idea of a Perfect Commonwealth," 522–23.

40. Hume, Ibid.

41. Beer, *To Make a Nation,* 269.

42. Mancur Olson, *The Logic of Collective Action* (Cambridge: Harvard University Press, 1965) and "The Second Coming," in William Butler Yeats, *Selected Poems and Three Plays* (New York: Macmillan, 1966).

43. On Lockean liberalism see John Locke, *Second Treatise of Government* (New York: New American Library, 1965), esp. section 6, *A Letter Concerning Toleration* (Indianapolis: Bobbs-Merrill, 1955); Becker, *Declaration of Independence;* Hartz, *Liberal Tradition in America* and Rogers M. Smith, *Liberalism and American Constitutional Law* (Cambridge: Harvard University Press, 1985). On civic republicanism see Arendt, *On Revolution;* Bailyn, *Ideological Origins of the American Revolution;* Wood, *Creation of the American Republic;* Pocock, *Machiavellian Moment;* and Paul Rahe, *Republics: Ancient and Modern* 3 vols. (Chapel Hill: University of North Carolina Press, 1994).

44. See Garrett Ward Sheldon, *The Political Philosophy of Thomas Jefferson,* (Baltimore: The Johns Hopkins University Press, 1991) esp. ch. 3 and Honohan, *Civic Republicanism.*

45. Thomas Jefferson, *Notes on Virginia* [1781] "Query XIX: The Present State of Manufacturers, Commerce, Interior and Exterior Trade?" in *The Life and Selected Writings of Thomas Jefferson* edited, and with an introduction by Adrienne Koch and William Peden (New York: The Modern Library, 1944), 278–79.

46. See Lance Banning, "Jefferson's Ideology Revisited: Liberal and Classical Ideas in the New American Republic," *William and Mary Quarterly* 43 (1986): 3–19; McCoy, *Elusive Republic;* and Joyce Appleby, *Capitalism and a New Social Order: The Republican Vision of the 1790s* (New York: New York University Press, 1984).

47. Thus, although it is a mistake to cast Jefferson as only a republican, it is also misleading to say that Jefferson's liberal commitments "drive him outside [the republican] tradition." See Don Herzog, "Some Questions for Republicans," *Political Theory* 14 (1986), 483.

48. See Sean Wilentz's critical review of David McCullough's *John Adams.* Sean Wilentz, "America Made Easy: McCullough, Adams, and the decline of popular history," *The New Republic,* 2 July 2001, 35–40. "Above all, he (Adams) never shook off the classical understanding of politics as the incorporation of distinct social interests." 40.

49. Jean Yarbrough, "Republicanism Reconsidered: Some Thoughts on the Foundation and Preservation of Representative Government," *Review of Politics* 41 (1979), 87 and Yarbrough, *American Virtues,* esp. ch. 4 "Civic Virtue, Statesmanship, Self Government," 102–152.

50. Sheldon, *Political Philosophy of Thomas Jefferson,* 86.

51. Arendt, *On Revolution*, 232, 235.

52. Arendt, *On Revolution*, 136.

53. Thomas Jefferson to John Taylor, 26 May 1810, in *Jefferson Writings*, 1227.

54. Ibid., 1226

55. Thomas Jefferson to Samuel Kercheval, 12 July 1816, in *Jefferson Writings*, 1399.

56. Thomas Jefferson to Joseph C. Cabell, 2 February 1816, in *Jefferson Writings*, 1380.

57. Thomas Jefferson to John Taylor, 28 May 1816, in *Jefferson Writings*, 1392.

58. Arendt, *On Revolution*, 251.

59. Arendt, *On Revolution*, 253. Obviously, there is a degree of hyperbole in this statement. Americans do participate in the political arena in a variety of ways. See Sidney Verba, Kay Lehman Schlozman, and Henry E. Brady, *Voice and Equality: Civic Voluntarism in American Politics* (Cambridge: Harvard University Press, 1995) and Putnam, *Bowling Alone*, 45.

60. Sunstein writes about the importance of deliberation in liberal republican thought. See Cass R. Sunstein, "Interest Groups in American Public Law," *Stanford Law Review* 38 (1985): 29–87 (republished as "The Enduring Legacy of Republicanism" cited above) and "Beyond the Republican Revival," *Yale Law Journal* 98 (1988): 1539–1590 and *Partial Constitution*. Sandel has articulated the republican position from a communitarian perspective. See Sandel, *Democracy's Discontent*. Skinner, Pettit, and Viroli are major voices of the Cambridge School of republican scholarship, which stresses the idea of political liberty. See Skinner, "The Republican Idea of Political Liberty," Skinner, *Liberty Before Liberalism*; Pettit, *Republicanism: A Theory of Freedom and Government* and Viroli, *Republicanism*. McCormick puts forth an argument for an energetic populism he calls "Machiavellian democracy." See John P. McCormick, "Machiavelli Against Republicanism: On the Cambridge School's 'Guicciardian Moments'" *Political Theory* 31 (2003): 615–43 and "Machiavellian Democracy," 297–13.

61. See McCormick, "Machiavelli Against Republicanism" and "Machiavellian Democracy."

62. Herzog, "Some Questions for Republicans."

63. Gurpreet Rattan, "Prospects for a Contemporary Republicanism," *The Monist* 84 (2001), 122.

64. Nicholas Buttle, "Republican Constitutionalism: A Roman Ideal," *Journal of Political Philosophy* 9 (2001): 331–49 and Timothy O'Hagan, "Review of Pettit's Republicanism," *Journal of Applied Philosophy* 15 (1998), 212–15.

65. Viroli, 61.

66. Rawls, *Theory of Justice* and Milton and Rose Friedman, *Free to Choose* (New York: Avon Books, 1979).

67. Tocqueville, 305–15.

68. Isaiah Berlin, "Two Concepts of Liberty," *Liberty: Incorporating Four Essays on Liberty*, ed. Henry Hardy (Oxford: Oxford University Press, 2002), 169.

69. Berlin, 176–77. "Liberty in this sense is not incompatible with some kinds of autocracy, or at any rate with the absence of self-government. Liberty in this sense is principally concerned with the area of control, not with its source . . . Freedom in this sense is not, at any rate logically, connected with democracy or self-government."

70. Pettit, 9.

71. Honohan, *Civic Republicanism*, 67. "Seeing it is known that whereas the greatest bashaw is a tenant, as well of his head as of his estate, at the will of his lord," James Harrington, *The Commonwealth of Oceana and a System of Politics*, ed. J. G. A. Pocock (Cambridge: Cambridge University Press, 1992), 20.

72. This paragraph of examples draws extensively on Viroli, 35–36. In ancient times, Viroli writes, house slaves were "often perfectly free to do what they want, either because their master is far away or because he is kind or foolish, but who are also subject to his arbitrary will, since he can punish them harshly if he chooses."

73. Viroli, 40, emphasis in the original.

74. Skinner, 1990, 308.

75. Harrington, *Commonwealth of Oceana*, 20.

76. Rawls, of course, builds his argument without an appeal to natural rights and argues that the republican tradition is compatible with political liberalism. See both *Theory of Justice* and *Political Liberalism* (New York: Columbia University Press, 1993).

77. Viroli, 8–10.

78. Geoffrey Pridham, *Hitler's Rise to Power: The Nazi Movement in Bavaria, 1923–1933* (New York: Harper Torch Book, 1974).

79. Tocqueville, however, did not neglect the dark side of the American democracy. See his incisive portrait of the injustice inflicted against black slaves and Native Americans. Tocqueville, *Democracy in America*, esp., 316–63.

80. Philip Pettit, "Reworking Sandel's Republicanism," *Journal of Philosophy* 95 (1998), 85; Skinner, 1990, 304.

81. O'Hagan, 214.

82. Sandel, *Democracy's Discontent*.

83. MacIntyre, *After Virtue*, 220.

84. See Albert O. Hirschman, *The Passions and the Interests: Political Arguments for Capitalism Before Its Triumph* (Princeton: Princeton University Press, 1977).

85. See William Galston, "Defending Liberalism," *American Political Science Review* 76 (1982), 629. Quoted in Jeffrey C. Isaac, "Republicanism vs. Liberalism? A Reconsideration" *History of Political Thought* 9 (1988), 357.

86. Karl Marx, "On the Jewish Question," in *The Marx-Engels Reader,* ed. Robert C. Tucker (New York: Norton, 1971), 33. Emphasis in original. Quoted in Isaac, "Republicanism vs. Liberalism?" 357.

87. Cary J. Nederman, "Rhetoric, reason and republic: republicanisms—ancient, medieval, and modern," in James Hankins ed., *Renaissance Civic Humanism: Reappraisals and Reflections* (Cambridge: Cambridge University Press, 2000): 247–69.

88. See note 14 on Harrington's relationship to Hobbes and his rejection of classical participation.

89. The parliament of Oceana, Harrington's vision of England as his idealized state, is bicameral with an elitist senate made up of 300 members who debate and a popular assembly or "prerogative tribe" consisting of 1,050 members who, by majority vote, decide. Harrington is emphatic that debate only takes place in the senate, stipulating that anyone who dares introduce debate in the popular assembly shall be executed. As Gary Remer writes, "For Harrington, popular debate merits nothing less than the death penalty." Anyone who dares speak up is silenced—literally. Remer, "James Harrington's New Deliberative Rhetoric," 535–36.

90. Madison, *Federalist* 63.

91. Nederman, pp. 263–64. See also Mark Hulliung, *Citizen Machiavelli* (Princeton: Princeton University Press, 1983).

92. Nederman, 267.

93. See Herzog, "Some Questions for Republicans."

94. "The ideals of active citizenship that once so moved Thomas Jefferson, have passed out of fashion. Too stern, too humorless, too redolent of cold showers. Nothing, in our aggressively postmodern age, could be more of a turn-off than the classical. Heroworshiping the Romans is *so* nineteenth century." Holland, *Rubicon,* xvi, emphasis in original.

95. Skinner, 304.

96. John Ferejohn, "Pettit's Republic," *The Monist* 84 (2001), 94.

97. For a powerful critique of social choice theory and the claim that the public good cannot exist see Gerry Mackie, *Democracy Defended* (Cambridge: Cambridge University Press, 2003).

98. Robert E. Goodin, *Reflective Democracy* (New York: Oxford University Press, 2005).

99. Shelley Burtt, "The Politics of Virtue Today: A Critique and a Proposal, *American Political Science Review* 87 (1993), 365. "Classical republicans . . . addressed themselves primarily to an ambitious elite whose private interests (a desire for power and prestige) were, indeed, at odds with the republicans' hope for a free polity."

100. Burtt, 367. Writers who fall in this camp include John Dewey, *The Public and Its Problems* [1927] (Athens, Ohio: Swallow Press, n.d.), Stephen L Elkin, *City and Regime in the American Republic* (Chicago: University of Chicago Press, 1987), Ricci, *Good Citizenship in America* and Goodin, *Reflective Democracy.*

101. Viroli, *Republicanism,* 55, 54.

102. MacIntyre, *After Virtue,* 220.

103. "If all Men are born Free, how is it that all Women are born slaves?" Mary Astell, *Reflections upon Marriage,* 1706 Preface, xi, in Patricia Springborg ed., *Mary Astell, Political Writings* (Cambridge: Cambridge University Press, 1996) and Patricia Springborg, "Republicanism, Freedom from Domination, and the Cambridge Contextual Historians," *Political Studies* 49 (2001): 851–76.

104. Pettit, *Republicanism,* 277. Also see Honohan, *Civic Republicanism,* 61–62.

105. Not withstanding a quip by Mort Saul about the 1960 presidential race between Kennedy and Nixon. "Today we have 150 million people and the top two contenders for president are Kennedy and Nixon. At the start of the republic, we had 3 million people and luminaries such as George Washington, Thomas Jefferson, Alexander Hamilton, James Madison, Benjamin Franklin and a host of others. Do you know what this proves? It proves Darwin was wrong!"

106. Judith Shklar, "Montesquieu and the new republicanism," in Bock, Skinner, and Viroli, eds., *Machiavelli and Republicanism,* 277.

107. Niccolò Machiavelli, *The Prince and the Discourses,* ed. Max Lerner (New York: Random House, 1950), *The Discourses,* ch. 5, 122.

CHAPTER FOUR

1. Manin, *Representative Government,* 8, 237.

2. Pateman, *Participation and Democratic Theory,* Peter Bachrach, *The Theory of Democratic Elitism: A Critique* (Boston: Little, Brown and Company, 1967), Peter Bachrach and Aryeh Botwinick, *Power and Empowerment: A Radical Theory of Participatory Democracy* (Philadelphia: Temple University Press, 1992), Barber, *Strong Democracy,* Mansbridge, *Beyond Adversary Democracy.*

3. I discuss deliberative democracy in Chapter 7.

4. Harrington is key because he was one of the first to think in terms of representative government versus direct participation. His innovation was to cut the tie between republicanism and the city-state.

5. McCormick recommends Machiavelli's *Discourses* as a model for controlling elites. See McCormick, "Machiavellian Democracy"

6. On the shift from party politics to consultant politics see Sidney Blumenthal, *The Permanent Campaign* (Boston: Beacon Press, 1980), especially the introduction; Alan Ware, *The Breakdown of Democratic Party Organization 1940–1980* (Oxford: Clarendon Press, 1985); Alan Ehrenhalt, *The United States of Ambition: Politicians, Power, and the Pursuit of Office* (New York: Times Books, 1991); David Menefee-Libey, *The Triumph of Campaign-Centered Politics* (New York: Chatham House, 1999); and Joe Klein, *Politics Lost: How American Democracy Was Trivialized by People Who Think You're Stupid* (New York: Doubleday, 2006).

7. I am indebted to Paul Glastris, *Washington Monthly* editor-in-chief and former speechwriter for President Clinton, for helping me think about the Assembly.

8. See Adair, *Fame and the Founding Fathers,* and Ernest Becker, *The Denial of Death* (New York: Free Press, 1973), on the importance of being a hero in one's own life.

9. Bok points out why the encouragement of intelligent participation is important. "As the public presses for more referenda and congressional leaders turn increasingly to opinion polls to help them decide how to vote on a pending bill, misinformation and ignorance promise to have more harmful effects on the policy-making process than in the past . . . there is every reason to believe that popular opinion tends to improve not only with better information but also with greater attention and effort on the part of the people and more opportunities for deliberation to test ideas and hear new facts and arguments." Bok, *Trouble with Government,* 381–84.

10. One version of Fishkin's idea would improve the presidential nominating process. A national sample of the voting-age population would be flown to one site—say Chicago or Austin, Texas—to meet with presidential candidates of both major parties. These individuals would meet in small groups with the candidates and after several days they would be polled on their views of both the candidates and the issues. The program could be broadcast on national television to allow the broader public to watch and make judgments. A second version of Fishkin's idea is what Ackerman and Fishkin call Deliberation Day. They suggest the United States institute a national holiday two weeks prior to the national election, a day set aside for political discussion. See Bruce Ackerman and James Fishkin, *Deliberation Day* (New Haven: Yale University Press, 2004). I discuss *Deliberation Day* in Chapter 5.

11. Fishkin, *Democracy and Deliberation,* 1. Deliberative Polling® is a trademark of James S. Fishkin.

12. Fishkin, 4, emphasis in original.

13. Shapiro, "Elements of Democratic Justice," 602.

14. Ned Crosby is an early innovator in experimenting with forms of random sample forums. In Minnesota, he developed the Center for New Democratic Processes to promote the use of the Citizen Jury deliberation process. In an analogy to a jury, as opposed to a regular public opinion poll, a citizen jury hears evidence and argument and then deliberates about the best course of action. Similar to the NIF program, Crosby has conducted numerous citizen jury projects on local, state, and federal issues. See Ned Crosby, "Citizen Juries: One Solution for Difficult Environmental Questions," in Ortwin Renn, Thomas Webber, and Peter Wiedeman eds., *Fairness and Competence in Citizen Participation: Evaluating Models for Environmental Discourse* (Boston: Kluwer Academic Publishers, 1995).

15. "The political ignorance of the American voter is one of the best-documented features of contemporary politics." Larry M. Bartels, "Uninformed Votes: Informational Effects in Presidential Elections," *American Journal of Political Science* 40 (1996), 194.

16. Shapiro, "Elements of Democratic Justice," 603

17. After studying efforts at health care reform dating back to President Harry Truman, Senator Wyden became convinced that early public involvement is crucial for success. He argues that if the public gains a basic knowledge of what is being proposed it will be more difficult for powerful special interests to derail the effort. The Wyden-Hatch bill starts with the public by sponsoring a national health care dialogue with hearings and meetings in hundreds of communities, conducted under the auspices of a twenty-six-member Citizen Care Working Group.

18. Section 1014 of the Medicare Prescription Drug, Improvement, and Modernization Act of 2003, "Health Care That Works For All Americans: Citizens Health Care Working Group."

19. Joel B. Finkelstein, "Bill Aims for Public to Drive Health Reform," *American Medical News,* 9 December 2002.

20. Matthew Miller, "Ron Wyden's Healthy Idea," *Tribune Media Services,* 23, October 2002.

21. Its name in final passage is the Hatch-Wyden Amendment. With Republicans controlling both houses of Congress and Senator Hatch the second-ranking Republican on the Senate Finance Committee and the chair of the Judiciary Committee, this sort of change in nomenclature might be expected.

22. Assembly members Joe Canciamilla (D-Pittsburg) and Keith Richman (R-Northridge) introduced ACA 28, the Citizens Assembly on Electoral Reform Act of 2006, in January 2006.

23. Lind, "A Radical Plan to Change American Politics."

24. Madison, *Federalist 58*, emphasis added.

25. See Yankelovich, *Coming to Public Judgment.*

26. People who are knowledgeable about a subject—be it politics or fashion or music—often influence others. Katz and Lazarsfeld call this "two-step flow" communication. Elihu Katz and Paul Lazarsfeld, *Personal Influence* (Flencoe, Illinois: Free Press, 1955).

27. The meetings would be open to the public and interested citizens could attend and listen, but would not participate unless the moderator asked for question or comments from the audience.

28. This is similar to the function that the Council of 500 played in Athenian democracy.

29. See Josiah Ober, *Mass and Elite in Democratic Athens: Rhetoric, Ideology and the Power of the People* (Princeton: Princeton University Press, 1989) and *The Athenian Revolution: Essays on Ancient Greek Democracy and Political Theory* (Princeton: Princeton University Press, 1996), ch. 3 "Public Speech and the Power of the People in Democratic Athens."

30. Frank M. Bryan, *Real Democracy: The New England Town Meeting and How it Works* (Chicago: University of Chicago Press, 2004) and "Direct Democracy and Civic Competence: The Case of the Town Meeting," in Stephen L. Elkin and Karol Edward Soltan, eds., *Citizen Competence and Democratic Institutions*, (University Park: The Pennsylvania State University Press, 1999), 198.

31. Manin, *Representative Government,* 17.

32. While the regular delegate position would be unpaid, except for a small meeting stipend, an argument can be made that fifty people selected to serve on the national steering committee should receive a salary comparable to that paid senior legislative staff. Serving on the Assembly steering committee would be a demanding job that would require at least a part-time and often a full-time commitment by individuals. The performance of the steering committee would be crucial to the working of the People's House, and it is important that these individuals be able to focus on their public duties without worrying about how to pay their bills. Also because the steering committee would constitute the leadership of the People's House, it is important to assure the integrity and honesty of these delegates when they are the focus of lobbying efforts by various interest groups.

33. On these issues see Cass R. Sunstein, "The Law of Group Polarization," *Journal of Political Philosophy* 10 (2002), 175–95 and Michael Rabinder James, *Deliberative Democracy and the Plural Polity* (Lawrence, Kansas: University Press of Kansas, 2004).

34. Goodin, *Reflective Democracy.*

35. Mill, *Representative Government*, 78–79.

36. This paragraph draws on the language about a stratified random sample used by California Assemblymen Joseph Canciamilla (D) and Keith Richman (R) in their proposal for a Citizens' Assembly (ACA 28). Press Release: January 26, 2006, "Canciamilla and Richman Announce Legislation to Establish a California Citizen Assembly" from Assembly member Joseph Canciamilla's office.

37. Dahl's criteria for inclusion: "The demos must include all adult members of the association except transients and persons proved to be mentally defective." Dahl, *Democracy and Its Critics*, Ch. 9, 129. On illegal immigrants see Peter H. Schuck and Rogers M. Smith, *Citizenship without Consent* (New Haven: Yale University Press, 1985) and Walzer, *Spheres of Justice*, Ch. 2 on guest workers.

38. Manin, *Representative Government,*, 13.

39. Akhil R. Amar, "Choosing Representatives by Lottery Voting," *Yale Law Journal,* 93 (1984) 1287 citing 419 U.S. 522 (1975) striking down under the Sixth and Fourteenth Amendments Louisiana's exclusion of women jurors.

40. Dahl, *Controlling Nuclear Weapons*, 88. He conceives of these policy juries as having only advisory powers and no binding effect on the relevant executive or legislative body.

41. Dahl, *Democracy and Its Critics*, 97–99.

42. To correct this common misperception see Ober, *Mass and Elite in Democratic Athens.*

43. Manin, *Representative Government*, 24.

44. M. I. Finley, *Democracy Ancient & Modern*, revised ed. (New Brunswick, NJ: Rutgers University Press, 1985), 54.

45. James Wycliffe Headlam, *Election by Lot at Athens* [1891] (Cambridge: Cambridge University Press, 1933), 2. This remains one of the best studies about the use of lot in ancient Athens.

46. Aristotle, *The Politics*, ed. Stephen Everson (Cambridge: Cambridge University Press, 1988), VI, 2, 1317b, 42–43.

47. Manin, *Representative Government*, 29–30.

48. Aristotle, *The Politics,* IV, 9, 1294b, 8–11.

49. The nation's leading expert on congressional elections writes, "The minimum price tag for a competitive House campaign under average conditions today is probably closer to $700,000; every one of the thirty-seven challengers who defeated

incumbents from 1996 through 2002 spent more than that amount." Gary C. Jacobson, *The Politics of Congressional Elections,* 6th ed. (New York: Pearson Longman, 2004), 44.

50. Aristotle, *The Politics,* IV, 4, 1290b, 1–4.

51. Mogens Herman Hansen, *The Athenian Democracy in the Age of Demosthenes,* trans. J. A. Crook (Norman: University of Oklahoma Press, 1999), 236

52. Headlam, 32 drawing on Aristotle, *The Politics,* IV, 4, 1292, 10–20.

53. Manin, *Representative Government,* 236–38.

54. Living in a world where the predominant form of government is liberal democracy, we all know what representative democracy is. But representation is a tricky philosophical subject. To begin, the word's etymological origin gives us the meaning, re-presentation, a making present again. As Pitkin writes, "Representation means the making present of something which is nevertheless not literally present." Rousseau, for one, famously argued that political representation is just not possible. The classic question facing all elected officials is whether a representative should do what her constituents want, and be bound by instructions from them, or should she be free to act, as seems best to her, in pursuit of their welfare. In the first, representatives attempt to mirror or reflect the opinions of their constituents. For the second view, Edmund Burke famously argued that representation is trusteeship, an elite caring for others or guardianship. He argued that a representative should be devoted to the constituent's interests, but not their opinions. Hanna Fenichel Pitkin, *The Concept of Representation* (Berkeley: University of California Press, 1967), 8, 114, 145, 176.

55. Manin, *Representative Government,* 129.

56. Ibid., 116.

57. Ibid., 129.

58. The Anti-Federalists, on this reading, clearly rejecting the Burkean elitist position while not fully adopting the mirror position explained in note 54, above.

CHAPTER FIVE

1. Finley, *Democracy Ancient & Modern,* 36.

2. The odds would be more favorable still because 6,500 would be the total population of the ward, as 1/100th of the congressional district, but the total number of adult citizens could range anywhere from 3,000 to 6,000 depending on whether the particular demographics of the area were young or old.

3. At the same time, we would not have to worry about the passions of direct democracy overpowering the system. The People's House would be part of a

constitutional structure in which checks and balances and a judicial branch stand ready to curb excesses of passion and irrationality.

4. Viroli, *Republicanism*, 27.

5. Such a regime would be based on "an institutional mix of popular representation and direct popular participation, as well as a political culture driven by an active rather than passive sociopolitical orientation." McCormick, "Machiavellian Democracy," 311.

6. For a critique of contemporary politics driven by the uninformed populism of regular opinion polls see Zakaria, *The Future of Freedom*, esp. 166–67.

7. Glendon, "Democracy's Discontent."

8. Jonathan Rauch has written a perceptive analysis of the process of "demosclerosis." See Jonathan Rauch, *Government's End: Why Washington Stopped Working* (New York: PublicAffairs, 1999).

9. Lasch, *The Revolt of the Elites*, 11–12, emphasis added.

10. Focused less on an equality of rights and more on equality of interaction, the Assembly would be a vehicle that puts a robust, energetic, assertive understanding of democracy into practice. Wiebe, *Self-Rule*, 252–53.

11. The Assembly would not bring about the "participatory society" that some dreamed of in the 1960s but it would provide a way for people to participate—with or without local strong parties. On "participatory democracy" see Pateman, *Participation and Democratic Theory* and Barber, *Strong Democracy*. For sympathetic critiques see Gitlin, *The Twilight of Common Dreams*; and Miller, *"Democracy is in the Streets."*

12. Lippmann, *Public Opinion*.

13. Abraham Lincoln, "Address to the Young Men's Lyceum of Springfield, Illinois," (Jan. 27, 1838) *Speeches and Writings 1832–1858*, edited by Don E. Fehrenbacher (New York: Library of America, 1989), 28–37.

14. Jürgen Habermas, "Struggles for Recognition in the Democratic Constitutional State," in Charles Taylor's *Multiculturalism*, edited and introduced by Amy Gutmann (Princeton: Princeton University Press, 1994), 113.

15. Yankelovich, *Coming to Public Judgment*.

16. Nelson W. Polsby, "Legislatures," in Philip Norton ed., *Legislatures* (New York: Oxford University Press, 1990), 129–47

17. See Woodrow Wilson, *Congressional Government* [1885] (New York: Meridian Books, 1956).

18. A number of contemporary writers stress the Tocquevillian theme of community connections and the need for a strong sense of civil society. See Alan Wolfe, *Whose Keeper?: Social Science and Moral Obligation* (Berkeley: University of California Press, 1989); Bellah, *Habits of the Heart*; Robert D. Putnam, *Bowling*

Alone and *Making Democracy Work: Civic Traditions in Modern Italy* (Princeton: Princeton University Press, 1993), and Michael J. Sandel, *Liberalism and the Limits of Justice* (Cambridge: Cambridge University Press, 1982). Michael Walzer, who favors these goals just as strongly, has written an insightful essay on how modern mobility makes traditional understandings of community difficult, if not impossible, in the modern world. See Michael Walzer, "The Communitarian Critique of Liberalism," *Political Theory* 18, 6–23, esp. his discussion of the "Four Mobilities."

19. Steven J. Rosenstone and John Mark Hansen, *Mobilization, Participation and Democracy in America,* 2nd ed. (New York: Longman, 2003), 1–2.

20. Ibid., 230.

21. Ibid., 228.

22. Jack L. Walker Jr., *Mobilizing Interest Groups in America* (Ann Arbor: University of Michigan Press, 1991).

23. Robert E. Goodin, "Institutionalizing the Public Interest: The Defense of Deadlock and Beyond," *American Political Science Review* 90 (1996), 341. Dewey writes, "Every officer of the public, whether he represents its as a voter or a stated official, has a dual capacity." Dewey, *Public and Its Problems,* 76.

24. Schattschneider, *Semi-Sovereign People.*

25. Madison, *Federalist* 10, 83.

26. What about the susceptibility of these mini-legislators to interest group lobbyists and the power of cold cash? This could be a danger if the delegates were chosen by election because organizations with far-flung and highly motivated memberships, such as the National Education Association (NEA), the American Association of Retired Persons (AARP), and National Rifle Association (NRA), could mobilize volunteers for campaigns even if fund-raising was limited to the district. Assembly delegates selected by lot would need neither money nor election volunteers. And if a delegate were to take payments from outside groups, this is the type of corruption that the local press excels at ferreting out. When delegate Sally Jones takes expensive vacations and shows up driving a new Mercedes-Benz, eyebrows are sure to be raised.

27. See Dahl, *Who Governs?*

28. See Dahl, *Preface to Democratic Theory,* esp. 132–33, 150; and Dahl, *Who Governs?* For a critique of interest group pluralism see Theodore Lowi, *The End of Liberalism,* 2nd ed. (New York: W.W. Norton, 1979).

29. Lowi, *End of Liberalism,* 59.

30. See David M. Brady and Craig Volden, *Revolving Gridlock: Politics and Policy from Jimmy Carter to George W. Bush,* 2nd ed. (Boulder, Colorado: Westview Press, 2006), 204–07 and John Mark Hansen, *Gaining Access: Congress and the Farm Lobby, 1919–1981* (Chicago: University of Chicago Press,

1991). As Brady and Volden note, Hansen offers a more subtle analysis showing that elected representatives want information about how different policy choices will affect them politically. Over time, the groups that provide the best information gain and maintain the best access to the legislator's thinking.

31. Hugh Heclo, "Issue Networks and the Executive Establishment," in Anthony King, ed., *The New American Political System,* (Washington, DC: American Enterprise Institute, 1978).

32. See Stockman, *Triumph of Politics* (New York: Avon Books, 1987) and the process of "demosclerosis" described by Rauch in *The End of Government.*

33. Jeffrey Birnbaum and Alan Murray, *Showdown at Gucci Gulch: Lawmakers, Lobbyists and the Unlikely Triumph of Tax Reform* (New York: Vintage Books, 1988).

34. One reason this happened is that interest groups spring to life after the major legislation has been passed and the agencies established. Interest groups are not so much a cause as a consequence of the growth of government, and, in particular, the expansion of the federal bureaucracy. Walker, *Mobilizing Interest Groups.*

35. Rauch, *Demosclerosis: The Silent Killer of American Government* (New York: Times Books, 1994), 135. (This is Rauch's earlier version of *The End of Government.*)

36. Rauch, *Government's End,* 153, 148.

37. Zakaria, *The Future of Freedom,* 177.

38. "Democsclerosis" (the clogged arteries of government) harms the aims of both political parties. Rauch writes: "For conservatives, demosclerosis means that there is no significant hope of scraping away outmoded or counterproductive liberal policies, because nothing old can be jettisoned. For liberals, it means that there is no significant hope of using government as a progressive problem-solving tool, because the method of trial and error has broken down. For politicians, it means tinkering on the margins of public policy. For the public, it means living with an increasingly dysfunctional government, one that gradually turns itself into a sort of living fossil." Rauch, *Government's End,* 163.

39. Dionne, *They Only Look Dead,* 285.

40. Often, the question of whether a particular measure makes it to a floor vote has less to do with its substantive merits than the bill's usefulness as a pawn in a larger legislative chess game. See William Muir Jr, *Legislature: California's School for Politics* (Chicago: University of Chicago Press, 1982).

41. In Chapter 7, I discuss deliberative democracy but not all democratic theorists land in the republican or deliberative camp. Dahl, for example, probably the most influential democratic theorist currently writing and one of the leading political scientists of his generation, can be read as favoring democracy as a fair aggre-

gation of enlightened preferences rather than deliberation based on public reasons. Dahl's books, from *Politics, Economics, and Welfare* (1953) with Charles Lindblom where they first outlined their idea of polyarchy, to *A Preface to Democratic Theory* (1956), to *Who Governs?* (1961), to *After the Revolution?* (1970), to *Polyarchy: Participation and Opposition* (1971), to *Dilemmas of Pluralist Democracy* (1982), to *Democracy and Its Critics* (1989) and, most recently, *How Democratic Is the Constitution?* (2001), as well as his many articles, have had a strong influence on contemporary political science. See Robert A. Dahl, *Toward Democracy: A Journey, Reflections: 1940–1997*, two vols. (Berkeley: Institute of Governmental Studies Press, University of California, Berkeley, 1997).

42. Jack Knight and James Johnson, "Aggregation and Deliberation: On the Possibility of Democratic Legitimacy," *Political Theory* 22 (1994), 280.

43. Ibid., 282.

44. David Miller writes, "deliberative democracy has the resources to attenuate the social choice problems faced by the political community." David Miller, "Deliberative Democracy and Social Choice," in David Estlund, ed., *Democracy* (Oxford: Blackwell Publishers, 2002)

45. James Fishkin makes this point responding to Shapiro's critique of deliberative democracy. See James Fishkin, "Defending Deliberation: A Comment on Ian Shapiro's 'The State of Democratic Theory,'" *Critical Review of International Social and Political Philosophy* (8) 2005, 71–78.

46. Dewey, *Public and Its Problems*, 207, quoted in Knight and Johnson, "Aggregation and Deliberation," 277, emphasis in original.

47. Robert Westbrook, "Pragmatism and Democracy: Reconstructing the Logic of John Dewey's Faith," delivered at a conference entitled "The Revival of Pragmatism," City University of New York, 4 November 1995. Quoted in Eric Alterman, *Who Speaks for America? Why Democracy Matters in Foreign Policy* (Ithaca: Cornell University Press, 1998), 172.

48. Bok, *Trouble with Government*, 212, emphasis and parentheses added.

49. Two recent institutional proposals also merit mention. In *By Popular Demand*, John Gastil argues that we should link deliberative democracy to the election process. He proposes that random sample citizen panels issue summary conclusions about the different issues studied and that these reports be made available to the voting public. If voters were as conscientious as members of the League of Women Voters this would be a good idea. However, as a real-world reform, this proposal would likely prove burdensome and of limited efficacy because many sample ballots are already large, and voters find themselves barraged at the end of campaigns. Many voters already look to their newspaper's editorial page for insight into ballot propositions, issues, and candidates. It is unclear whether voters of moderate or low sophistication

would do anything with the new information. John Gastil, *By Popular Demand: Revitalizing Representative Democracy through Deliberative Elections* (Berkeley: University of California Press, 2000). In *Deliberative Democracy in America,* Ethan J. Leib argues that we should create a fourth branch of government where randomly selected citizens would debate and vote on issues that now go to the initiative process. His popular branch of government consists of a Fishkin-type Deliberative Poll of approximately 500 randomly selected individuals considering one issue at a time. The result, Leib believes, would be an improved version of the initiative and referendum process championed by the Progressives. I agree with Leib's goal of connecting intelligent deliberation to actual government decision making. However, his particular model is problematic for three reasons. First, the random sample methodology asks the participation of very few citizens. In fact, it is a bit strange to think of a random sample of 500 people as constituting a popular branch of government. By contrast, the reform I suggest asks for the participation of more than 40,000 citizens on a regular basis. Second, Leib insists that participation be mandatory for those selected. Given the rebellious nature of American political culture, this is highly unlikely. Third, the small number of participants debating, and deciding, matters of great importance raises the distinct possibility that lobbying pressures will skew the deliberative outcome and thus violate some of the basic normative goals of deliberative democracy. As a defense against this danger, Leib feels compelled to insist on near absolute privacy for participants. It is hardly Leib's intent, but readers will view his unfortunate combination of compulsion and anonymity as police state democracy. His proposal for how we should integrate deliberative democracy into our constitutional structure is very much at odds with the American tradition of publicity, transparency, and a positive desire for fame that the founders thought critical for democracy's success. While Leib's intent of going beyond Dahl and Fishkin is well-founded, his suggested model is flawed. Ethan J. Leib, *Deliberative Democracy in America: A Proposal for a Popular Branch of Government* (University Park, PA: The Pennsylvania State University Press, 2004).

50. Letter from Michael Walzer to author. Althaus, *Collective Preferences in Democratic Politics,* 101.

51. Ackerman and Fishkin, *Deliberation Day,* 3.

52. Ibid., 33, emphasis in original.

53. Ibid., 21.

54. Shapiro, *The State of Democratic Theory,* 25.

55. Ackerman and Fishkin, *Deliberation Day,* 12, 164, 171.

56. Jane Mansbridge has written a cautionary tale about the unsuccessful attempt to make the Equal Rights Amendment part of the Constitution. Jane J. Mansbridge, *Why We Lost the ERA* (Chicago: University of Chicago Press, 1986).

57. Robert A. Dahl, "The Pseudodemocratization of the American Presidency," *The Tanner Lectures on Human Values,* vol. 10 (Salt Lake City: University of Utah Press, 1988), 52, emphasis added.

58. Ibid., 58–59.

59. And by providing a legitimate institutional channel for the intense activism of exceptional decades and nurturing grassroots participation in periods of normal politics, the Assembly and the People's House would help cure American politics of its periodic excessive oscillations between "democracy in the streets" and apathetic withdrawal. See James A. Morone, *The Democratic Wish: Popular Participation and the Limits of American Government,* rev. ed. (New Haven: Yale University Press, 1998) and Miller, *"Democracy Is in the Streets."*

60. *The 9/11 Commission Report: Final Report of the National Commission on Terrorist Attacks upon the United States,* Authorized Edition (New York: W. W. Norton, 2004); and Maura Reynolds, "Bush Supports 9/11 Panel Not on Details: He would keep proposed intelligence czar separate from the White House and limit the post's budget powers," *Los Angeles Times* (3 August 2004), A1.

61. These three examples (international trade, electric grid legislation, and the highway bill) are drawn from actual legislation in Congress in 2004—and are given a creative twist. Based on the Wednesday, 4 August 2004, "Marketplace" report on national public radio by John Dimsdale entitled "Workin' Nine to Five" that focused on how the spirit of legislative procrastination in Congress often has major economic consequences. http://marketplace.publicradio.org/shows

62. On why such a report would be alarming see Jonathan Rauch, "The New Old Economy: Oil, Computers and the Reinvention of the Earth," *Atlantic Monthly* (January 2001), 35–49. Rauch explains how technology is now expected to stretch oil reserves well into the future.

63. Thomas Friedman makes the argument that the United States should institute a tax that fixes the pump price at $3.50 to $4 a gallon—no matter whether the OPEC price rises or falls. See Thomas L. Friedman, "The New 'Sputnik' Challenges: They All Run on Oil," *New York Times* (20 January 2006) and "Gas Pump Geopolitics," *New York Times* (28 April 2006).

64. I am indebted to Steve Thomas for this example.

CHAPTER SIX

1. Charles O. Jones, *The Presidency in a Separated System* (Washington, DC: Brookings Institution Press, 1994), 294, quoted in Keith Krehbiel, *Pivotal Politics: A Theory of U.S. Lawmaking* (Chicago: University of Chicago Press, 1998), 20.

2. Brady and Volden, *Revolving Gridlock,* 208, 203, 202.

3. See David R. Mayhew, *Divided We Govern: Party Control, Lawmaking, and Investigations, 1946–2002*, 2nd ed. (New Haven: Yale University Press, 2005). Quote is from Krehbiel, *Pivotal Politics*, 52–53.

4. This is a major concern in contemporary political science as seen in the work by George Tsebelis. See George Tsebelis, *Veto Players: How Political Institutions Work* (Princeton: Princeton University Press, 2002), "Veto Players and Law Production in Parliamentary Democracies: An Empirical Analysis," *American Political Science Review* 93 (1999), 591–608, "Decision Making in Political Systems: Veto Players in Presidentialism, Parliamentarism, Multicameralism and Multipartyism," *British Journal of Political Science* 25 (1995), 289–325.

5. Tsebelis, "Veto Players and Law Production," 593.

6. Tsebelis, *Veto Players*, 7–8.

7. Ibid., 14.

8. Here Tsebelis's research agrees with that of Krehbiel and Brody and Volden.

9. Ibid., 157.

10. Krehbiel, *Pivotal Politics*, 47.

11. William H. Riker, "The Justification of Bicameralism," *International Political Science Review* 13 (1992), 101.

12. Ibid.

13. Dahl, *Democracy and Its Critics*, 135–62.

14. John Ferejohn, "Instituting Deliberative Democracy," in Ian Shapiro and Stephen Macedo eds., *Designing Democratic Institutions* (New York: New York University Press, 2000), 87.

15. Keith Poole and Howard Rosenthal, *Congress: A Political-Economic History of Roll Call Voting* (Oxford: Oxford University Press, 1997).

16. Kenneth Arrow, *Social Choice and Individual Values* [1951] (New Haven: Yale University Press, 1963), Duncan Black, *The Theory of Committees and Elections* (Cambridge: Cambridge University Press, 1958). Consider three voters with preferences over three issues. If X can defeat Y, Y can defeat Z, and Z can defeat X, then "pairwise voting can lead to an endless cycle." Dennis C. Mueller, *Public Choice* (Cambridge: Cambridge University Press, 1979), 39.

17. Riker, "Justification for Bicameralism," 113, emphasis and parentheses added.

18. Brady and Volden, *Revolving Gridlock*, 3.

19. Krehbiel, *Pivotal Politics*, 94, emphasis in original.

20. Ibid., 99.

21. Here I draw on Tom Geoghegan's argument about the Senate. Tom Geoghegan, "The Infernal Senate: The Real Source of Gridlock," *The New Republic*, 21 November 1994: 17–23, and *The Secret Lives of Citizens* (Chicago: University

of Chicago Press, 2000), ch. 4, "In the Gridlock Archipelago," 62–78. See also Francis E. Lee and Bruce I. Oppenheimer, *Sizing Up the Senate: The Unequal Consequences of Equal Representation* (Chicago: University of Chicago Press, 1999).

22. Geoghegan, *The Secret Lives of Citizens,* 76–77.

23. Goodin, "Institutionalizing the Public Interest," 333.

24. Terry M. Moe, "Political Institutions: The Neglected Side of the Story," *Journal of Law, Economics, and Organization* 6 (1990), 240.

25. Riker, "Justification for Bicameralism," 114–15.

26. Goodin, "Institutionalizing the Public Interest," 333, 334.

27. Goodin, Ibid., 339 drawing on Brian Barry, *Political Argument* (London: Routledge & Kegan Paul, 1965), emphasis added.

28. Goodin, Ibid., 340

29. Ian Shapiro, *The State of Democratic Theory* (Princeton: Princeton University Press, 2003), 30.

30. See Robert A. Dahl, *How Democratic Is the American Constitution?* (New Haven: Yale University Press, 2001), 144–45.

31. In terms of scale, but not equity, it is probably a healthy thing that people can get elected to the U.S. Senate in states such as Maine and Idaho and rise to positions of power, as was the case with former Senate Majority Leader George Mitchell and the late Senator Frank Church, chair of the Senate Foreign Relations Committee, for example, without having to be incredibly focused, ambitious, driven, and with strong ties to money, as is certainly the case in large states such as Texas, California, Illinois, and New York. Powerful senators from small states have the opportunity to mix with average voters when they spend time on their home turf. Mitchell and Church are examples of senators who were admired by constituents and colleagues alike for their common touch, thoughtfulness, and humanity.

32. Case in point, Orange County, California, is famous for its conservative politics. Five out of six congressional seats are held by Republicans, all of them conservative. Few realize that there are more Democrats in Orange County than in San Francisco, a locale justly famous for its liberal politics. Up against 600,000 Republicans, the 450,000 Orange County Democrats have nary an impact on the House of Representatives. Their votes make a difference when it comes to statewide races for U.S. Senate and governor, but in the House of Representatives their votes—and their voices—go missing. A similar situation exists with all congressional minorities, wherever their district.

33. Geoghegan, "The Infernal Senate."

34. See Richard N. Rosenfeld, "What Democracy? The Case for Abolishing the United States Senate," *Harper's Magazine* (May 2004), 35–44.

35. Hacker and Pierson, *Off Center: The Republican Revolution & the Erosion of American Democracy* and Dionne, *Why Americans Hate Politics* discuss the tendency of the partisans to push for extreme policies that have little, if any, backing from the center of the electorate. E. J. Dionne Jr., *Why Americans Hate Politics* (New York: Simon & Schuster, 1991).

36. Richard E. Neustadt, *Presidential Power and the Modern Presidents* (New York: The Free Press, 1990) and Arthur M. Schlesinger Jr., *The Imperial Presidency* [1973] with a new introduction (Boston: Houghton Mifflin, 2004).

37. Theodore J. Lowi, *The Personal Presidency: Power Invested, Promise Unfulfilled* (Ithaca, NY: Cornell University Press, 1985).

38. Goodin, Ibid., 39.

39. Madison, *Federalist* 51, 325.

40. Brady and Volden, *Revolving Gridlock*, 208–09.

41. Joshua Cohen, "Deliberation and Democratic Legitimacy," [1989] in James Bohman and William Rehg, eds., *Deliberative Democracy: Essays on Reason and Politics* (Cambridge: The MIT Press, 1997), 84, emphasis added.

42. Ackerman and Fishkin, *Deliberation Day*, 12, 164, 171.

43. James Surowiecki, *The Wisdom of Crowds: Why the Many are Smarter Than the Few and How Collective Wisdom Shapes Business, Economies, Societies, and Nations* (New York: Anchor Books, 2005), xiv, xvii.

44. An example from the financial world; the worst-performing investment clubs are those where people socialize and think alike while the best-performing groups are composed of people who "do not see each other much and welcome dissent." Cass R. Sunstein, "Mobbed Up. (The Wisdom of Crowds: Why the Many are Smarter Than the Few and How Collective Wisdom Shapes Business, Economies, Societies and Nations) (Book Review)." *The New Republic* (28 June 2004): 40.

45. Surowiecki, *Wisdom of Crowds*, 71–72, 267–68.

46. Ibid., 267.

47. Sunstein, "Mobbed Up." DNA example borrowed.

48. Ackerman and Fishkin, *Deliberation Day*, 4.

49. Dahl, *Controlling Nuclear Weapons*.

50. Cass R. Sunstein, "Deliberative Trouble? Why Groups Go to Extremes," *Yale Law Journal* 110 (2000), 107.

51. Sunstein, "The Law of Group Polarization," 191.

52. Sunstein, "Deliberative Trouble?" 105.

53. In June 1999, the citizens of Los Angeles voted to reform the city's charter and in so doing endorsed setting up a network of neighborhood councils. On the East Coast, community boards have been in place for more than twenty-five

years in New York City. Other cities with neighborhood council systems include Birmingham, Alabama; Dayton, Ohio; Portland, Oregon; St. Paul, Minnesota; and San Antonio, Texas. See Jeffrey M. Berry, Kent E. Portney, and Ken Thomson, *The Rebirth of Urban Democracy* (Washington, DC: The Brookings Institute, 1993).

54. Interview with Raphael J. Sonenshein, executive director, Appointed Charter Reform Commission, City of Los Angeles.

55. The number comes from the Irvine Unified School District in Southern California.

56. Thomas Jefferson, letter to William Charles Jarvis, (28 September 1820) *The Writings of Thomas Jefferson,* ed. Paul L. Ford (New York: G. P. Putnam's Sons, 1899), vol. 10, 161.

CHAPTER SEVEN

1. Ian Shapiro, "Elements of Democratic Justice," *Political Theory* 24 (1996), 582, emphasis added.

2. C. Wright Mills, *The Power Elite* (New York: Oxford University, 1956), 298–99.

3. Arendt, *The Human Condition,* Dewey, *Public and Its Problems,* Jürgen Habermas, *Between Facts and Norms,* trans. William Rehg (Cambridge: The MIT Press, 1996).

4. Nancy Fraser, "Rethinking the Public Sphere: A Contribution to the Critique of Actually Existing Democracy," in Craig Calhoun, ed., *Habermas and the Public Sphere* (Cambridge: The MIT Press, 1992), 110–11. On the distinction between the market and the forum see Jon Elster, "The Market and the Forum: Three Varieties of Political Theory," in Jon Elster and Aanund Hylland, eds., *Foundation of Social Choice Theory* (New York: Cambridge University Press, 1986), 3–33.

5. Jürgen Habermas, *The Structural Transformation of the Public Sphere* [1962] trans. Thomas Burger (Cambridge: The MIT Press, 1989).

6. Immanuel Kant, *Foundations of the Metaphysics of Morals* and *What Is Enlightenment?* Translated with an introduction by Lewis White Beck (New York: Liberal Arts Press, 1959), 83. "[M]an's inability to make use of his understanding without direction from another."

7. Habermas, *Structural Transformation,* 104.

8. Habermas, *Structural Transformation,* 176

9. Bernard Manin, "On Legitimacy and Political Deliberation," *Political Theory* 15 (1987), 345, 351–52.

10. Ibid., 352, emphasis in original.

11. Jon Elster, "Introduction," in Jon Elster, ed., *Deliberative Democracy* (Cambridge: Cambridge University Press, 1998), 5.

12. On periods of creedal passion see Samuel P. Huntington, *American Politics: The Promise of Disharmony* (Cambridge: Belknap Press of Harvard University Press, 1981) and Ackerman, *We the People*. Some writers see this democratic wish as irrational. It is not. Instead, the republican spirit is central to the American democratic experience. See Marone, *The Democratic Wish*.

13. Dionne, *They Only Look Dead*, 253 and Lasch, *Revolt of the Elites*, 170–71. In *Revolt of the Elites* see especially "Introduction: The Democratic Malaise," ch. 6 "Conversation and the Civic Arts" and ch. 9 "The Lost Art of Argument."

14. John Dewey, *Democracy and Education* (New York: The Free Press, 1966), 158–59.

15. Hannah Arendt, *On Violence* (San Diego: Harcourt Brace Jovanovich, 1969).

16. Dahl, *Democracy and Its Critics*, chs. 8–9.

17. Cohen, "Deliberation and Democratic Legitimacy."

18. Habermas, *Facts and Norms*, 276 and *Legitimation Crisis* (Boston: Beacon Press, 1975), 108

19. Cohen, "Deliberation and Democratic Legitimacy," 74.

20. Jane Mansbridge, "Everyday Talk in the Deliberative System," in Stephen Macedo, ed., *Deliberative Politics* (Oxford: Oxford University Press, 1999), 225 quoting Habermas, *Structural Transformation* [1962].

21. Some deliberative theorists, such as Habermas and his followers, depart from the civic republican tradition by giving priority to language informed by logic and reason while relegating rhetoric and emotional language to a nonrational sphere. Here I side with Iris Marion Young, "Communication and the Other: Beyond Deliberative Democracy," in Seyla Benhabib, ed., *Democracy and Difference* (Princeton: Princeton University Press, 1996) and Benedetto Fontana, Cary J. Nederman, and Gary Remer, "Introduction: Deliberative Democracy and the Rhetorical Turn," in *Talking Democracy: Historical Perspectives on Rhetoric and Democracy* (University Park, PA: The Pennsylvania State University Press, 2004), 4–11.

22. Mansbridge, "Everyday Talk," 225–26.

23. Cohen, "Deliberation and Democratic Legitimacy," 75

24. On the dangers of looking too hard for consensus and ignoring possible conflict see Christopher F. Karpowitz and Jane Mansbridge, "Disagreement and Consensus: The Importance of Dynamic Updating in Public Deliberation," in John Gastil and Peter Levine, eds. *The Deliberative Democracy Handbook: Strategies*

for Effective Civic Engagement in the 21st Century (San Francisco, CA: Jossey-Bass, A Wiley Imprint, 2005): 237–53.

25. Peter Bachrach and Morton S. Baratz, "Two Faces of Power," *American Political Science Review* 56 (1962), 947–52, "Decisions and Nondecisions: An Analytical Framework," *American Political Science Review* 57 (1963): 632–642, Steven Lukes, *Power: A Radical View* (London: Macmillan, 1974), Gaventa, *Power and Powerlessness.*

26. Ian Shapiro, "Optimal Deliberation?" in *The Journal of Political Philosophy* 10 (2002), 199.

27. Sunstein, *Partial Constitution,* esp. 19–24.

28. This is what former California Senate Democratic leader John Burton said when speaking about Governor Arnold Schwarzenegger during his first year in office. Ann E. Marinow, "Governor Seeking Budget Compromise," *San Jose Mercury News* (23 April 2004).

29. John Dewey, *The Quest for Certainty* (New York: Minton, Balch, 1929), 262.

30. Madison, *Federalist* 42, 268, quoted by Bessette, *Mild Voice of Reason.*

31. John Rawls, *Political Liberalism,* 226, 243.

32. Sunstein, *Partial Constitution,* 19–20.

33. Young, "Communication and the Other," 122.

34. Shapiro, "Optimal Deliberation?" 211.

35. John Rawls, *Political Liberalism* (New York: Columbia, 1993), xxv, 45–46.

36. See Amy Gutmann and Dennis Thompson, *Why Deliberative Democracy?* (Princeton: Princeton University Press, 2004) for one of the best expositions about why deliberative politics is important. More than most theorists, Gutmann and Thompson are careful to discuss the intersection between deliberation and concrete public policy. See also Amy Gutmann and Dennis Thompson, *Democracy and Disagreement* (Cambridge: The Belknap Press of Harvard University Press, 1996).

37. Shapiro, "Elements of Democratic Justice," 581.

38. Barber, *Strong Democracy,* 145–46.

39. See Jon Elster, "Introduction," *Deliberative Democracy,* 8

40. Michael Walzer, "Deliberation, and What Else?" in Stephen Macedo, ed., *Deliberative Politics* (Oxford: Oxford University Press, 1999), 67. Walzer continues: "There is not a setting in the political world quite like the jury room, in which we don't want people to do anything *except* deliberate."

41. See Lynn M. Sanders, "Against Deliberation," *Political Theory* 25 (1997), 362, 370.

42. Young, "Communication and the Other," 124, 128–31.

43. Dahl, *After the Revolution?* 79–88.

44. Hanna Pitkin and Sara Shumer, "On Participation," *Democracy* 2 (1982), 50.

45. Fraser, "Rethinking the Public Sphere," 134.

46. Mansbridge, "Everyday Talk," 212.

47. "In a nutshell, a public sphere adequate to a democratic polity depends upon both the quality of discourse and the quantity of participation." Craig Calhoun, "Introduction: Habermas and the Public Sphere," in Craig Calhoun, ed., *Habermas and the Public Sphere* (Cambridge: The MIT Press, 1992), 2.

48. Explaining, expanding, and defending democracy as "a way of life" lies at the heart of Dewey's career as America's greatest philosopher. See Westbrook, *John Dewey and American Democracy,* and O'Leary, "John Dewey, Herbert Croly and Progressive Democratic Theory." More generally see Alan Ryan, *John Dewey and the High Tide of American Liberalism* (New York: W.W. Norton, 1995). For a recent appreciation of Dewey as a deliberative theorist see Jason Kosnoski, "Artful Discussion: John Dewey's Classroom as a Model of Deliberative Association," *Political Theory* 33 (2005): 654–677.

49. Dewey, *Public and Its Problems,* 15–16.

50. Dahl, *Who Governs?*

51. Arendt, *Human Condition,* 200 and Arendt, *On Violence,* 44.

52. Sometimes democracy is "as much about opposition to the arbitrary exercise of power as it is about collective self-government." Shapiro, "Elements of Democratic Justice," 582.

53. John R. Hibbing and Elizabeth Theiss-Morse, *Congress as Public Enemy: Public Attitudes Toward American Political Institutions* (New York: Cambridge University Press, 1995), 18, cited in Mueller, *Capitalism, Democracy and Ralph's Pretty Good Grocery,* 179.

54. See Frank Michelman, "Law's Republic," *Yale Law Journal* 97 (1988): 1493–1537 and Sunstein, "Beyond the Republican Revival."

55. Schattschneider, *Semi-Sovereign People,* 71.

56. Madison's vision of civic majorities "operating above the fray of private interests" is similar to Dewey's argument that third parties are essential when deciding public issues. They are two different ways of talking about the same phenomenon. The quote is from Sunstein, *Partial Constitution,* 20.

57. Madison, *Federalist 51,* 325.

58. Beer, *To Make a Nation,* 276, emphasis added.

59. Richard Kraut, review of Bernard Yack, The Problems of a Political Animal: Community, Justice, and Conflict in Aristotelian Political Thought (Berkeley:

University of California Press, 1993) *Political Theory* (August 1995), 548, emphasis added.

60. Gaventa, *Power and Powerlessness,* 42.

61. Gaventa, 13–16. See also Bachrach and Baratz, "Two Faces of Power," Lukes, *Power: A Radical View,* and Stokes, "Pathologies of Deliberation."

62. Sunstein, *Partial Constitution.*

63. Shapiro, "Optimal Deliberation?" 199.

64. Important critiques include Walzer, "Deliberation, and What Else?"; Ian Shapiro, "Enough of Deliberation: Politics Is about Interests and Power," in Stephen Macedo, ed., *Deliberative Politics* (Oxford: Oxford University Press, 1999); Sanders, "Against Deliberation"; Stokes, "Pathologies of Deliberation"; and Iris Marion Young, "Activist Challenges to Deliberative Democracy," *Political Theory* 29 (2001): 670–90.

65. Shapiro follows Walzer on this point. See Shapiro, *The State of Democratic Theory.*

66. Walzer, "Deliberation, and What Else?" 67, emphasis in original.

67. Dewey, *Public and Its Problems,* 209.

68. Dewey, *Public and Its Problems,* 146.

69. Machiavelli, *Discourses,* Ch. 5, 121–22.

CHAPTER EIGHT

1. Arend Lijphart, *Democracies: Patterns of Majoritarian and Consensus Government in Twenty-One Countries* (New Haven: Yale University Press, 1984).

2. For example, Brookings Institution scholar James Sundquist argues for a set of modest reforms including four-year House terms, team (party) ticket, and campaign finance reform. See James L. Sundquist, *Constitutional Reform and Effective Government* Revised ed. (Washington, DC: The Brookings Institution, 1992).

3. See David Osborn and Ted Gaebler, *Reinventing Government* (New York: Plume Books, 1993) and Albert Gore's report on streamlining the Federal Government, *From Red Tape to Results: Creating a Government that Works Better and Costs Less: Executive Summary: The Report of the National Performance Review,* (Washington, DC: The Review, 1993). On campaign finance reform see *The Constitution and Campaign Finance Reform: An Anthology,* Frederick G. Slabach, ed. (Durham, NC: Carolina Academic Press, 1998); David Donnelly, Janice Fine, and Ellen S. Miller, *Money and Politics* (Boston: Beacon Press, 1999); E. Joshua Rosenkranz, *Buckley Stops Here: Loosening the Judicial Stranglehold on Campaign Finance Reform,* Report of the Twentieth Century Fund Working Group on Campaign Finance Litigation (New York: The Century Foundation

Press, 1998); Anthony Corrado et al., *The New Campaign Finance Sourcebook* (Washington, DC: The Brookings Institution, 2005) and Andrew C. Geddes, "Campaign Finance Reform After McCain-Feingold: The more speech—more competition solution" *Journal of Law and Politics* 16 (2000): 571–637.

4. James Q. Wilson, *Bureaucracy: What Government Agencies Do and Why They Do It* (New York: Basic Books, 1989). See also Sylvia Nasar, "The Bureaucracy: What's Left To Shrink?" in *New York Times* (11 June 1995), Section 4, 1.

5. See David Frum, "The Elite Primary," *Atlantic Monthly* (November 1995), 22–36. There are a plethora of proposals to change the role of money in politics. Most recently, the McCain-Feingold reform effort won an uphill battle to become law. See, for example, Lind, *Next American Nation,* 311–14 and proposals by former U.S. Senator Bill Bradley and former Interior Secretary Bruce Babbitt. All proposals must grapple with current Supreme Court rulings that equate money with free speech, in particular the 1976 Supreme Court decision in the *Buckley v. Valeo* case that prohibited caps on campaign spending. All serious proposals require the Supreme Court to rethink its position. On *Buckley v. Valeo* see E. Joshua Rosenkranz, *If Buckley Fell: A First Amendment Blueprint for Regulating Money in Politics* (New York: The Century Foundation Press, 1999).

6. Jonathan Rauch, "Give Pols Free Money, No Rules, How to Repair America's Campaign Finance System, Part 1" *U.S. News & World Report* (29 December 1997–5 January 1998), 54.

7. Bruce Ackerman and Ian Ayres, *Voting with Dollars: A New Paradigm for Campaign Finance* (New Haven: Yale University Press, 2002). Ackerman and Ayres' proposal is worth considering, as is Sunstein's suggestion that the Supreme Court fundamentally change its views on what constitutes political speech. See Cass R. Sunstein, *Democracy and the Problem of Free Speech* (New York: The Free Press, 1995).

8. F. Christopher Arterton, *Teledemocracy* (Newbury Park: Sage Publications, 1987), 194.

9. The initiative process is poorly suited to make complex policy trade-offs. Most often, initiatives ask voters to raise or lower taxes without regard to what programs will be cut as a result. Benjamin Barber suggests a two-stage referendum process to deal with this problem. See Barber, *Strong Democracy,* 281–89.

10. Bruce E. Cain, Sara Ferejohn, Margarita Najar, and Mary Walther, "Constitutional Change: Is It Too Easy to Amend our State Constitution?" in Bruce E. Cain and Roger G. Noll, eds., *Constitutional Reform in California: Making State Government More Effective and Responsive* (Berkeley: Institute of Governmental Studies Press, University of California, 1995), 281.

11. Public affairs do not have much salience with the mass public, except on highly emotional issues. Yet, it is exactly these issues that are often handled better by a legislative body. See Thomas Cronin, *Direct Democracy* (Cambridge, Harvard University Press, 1985), 158; and John Ferejohn, "Reforming the Initiative Process" in *Constitutional Reform in California*, 319.

12. Initiatives often become ugly but effective wedge issues. California's Proposition 187 (concerning illegal immigration) remains the prime example. Not wanting to get blamed for California's deep recession in the early 1990s, Governor Pete Wilson was able to use the Anglo backlash against illegal immigration as a way of ensuring his reelection in 1994.

13. George Gallup Sr., interview, Jan. 10, 1984; quoted in David D. Schmidt, "United States Direct Democracy in Perspective: The Case for the Initiative and Referendum (Paper presented at the American Political Science Association Meeting, Washington, DC, September 1986), 9. Cited in Cronin, *Direct Democracy*, 158.

14. See Broder, *Democracy Derailed: Initiative Campaigns*.

15. James W. Robinson, ed., *Ross Perot Speaks Out* (Rocklin, California: Prima Publishing, 1992), 66 (20 February 1992 speech).

16. Philip Roth, *The Plot Against America* (New York: Houghton Mifflin, 2004).

17. Mills, *The Power Elite*, 303–04.

18. However, the drive for term limits appears to be more about political power than good government. The energy and resources of the movement came overwhelmingly from conservative groups aiming to win seats in Congress and state legislatures. For Republicans, term limits were a powerful weapon in their fight to wrestle control of the House of Representatives from the Democrats and dethrone Assembly Speaker Willie Brown in California. Republican officeholders suddenly lost interest in term limit reform once they won control of the House in 1994. See Thomas Mann, "The Wrong Medicine: Term Limits Won't Cure What Ails Congressional Elections," *The Brookings Review* (Spring 1992), 23.

19. Aristotle, *The Politics*, III, 1, 1275a. The citizen is defined by his participation in the power of judgment and the power of command.

20. They speak of citizen-legislators who view service in the Congress or state legislature as a temporary departure from their regular career and who "will deal with the tough challenges that face this country." Former Senator Fred Thompson, (R-Tennessee), testimony on term limits for members of Congress, presented before the Subcommittee on the Constitution, Federalism and Property Rights of the Senate Judiciary Committee, on 25 January 1995, in *Congressional Digest* (April 1995), 108.

21. Professor Mark P. Petracca, University of California, Irvine, testimony on term limits for members of Congress, presented before the Subcommittee on the Constitution, Federalism and Property Rights of the Senate Judiciary Committee, on 25 January 1995, in *Congressional Digest* (April 1995), 118.

22. Ehrenhalt, *The United States of Ambition*, xxii–xxiii.

23. See David R. Mayhew, *Congress: The Electoral Connection* (New Haven: Yale University Press, 1974).

24. Assembly members are limited to three two-year terms and state Senators are limited to two four-year terms. See Kevin O'Leary, "Time's Up: Under Term Limits, California's Legislative Engine Sputters," *American Prospect* (17 December 2001), 30–33.

25. A study of Costa Rica, the only democracy with experience with term limits, refers to this as the "last-term problem." Because "ambitious legislators will cater to those who control future career opportunities," we can expect shirking of duties and outright corruption in the last term. John M. Carey, *Term Limits and Legislative Representation* (Cambridge: Cambridge University Press, 1996), 25.

26. Alexander Hamilton, *Federalist*, 72.

27. "Congressional Redistricting: How to Rig an Election," *The Economist*, 25 April 2004; California Governor Arnold Schwarzenegger made redistricting by a panel of retired judges a top priority of his administration's top goals, but the initiative he supported was defeated in 2005.

28. Most Americans do not appreciate the fact that the United States has the strongest legislative branch in the world. As Senator Patrick Moynihan once remarked: "The United States is the one nation in the world with a *real* legislative branch. Individuals elected to Congress and the state legislatures take ideas and transform them into law. These "transformative legislatures" exist because of the powers given to Congress in the Constitution. See Polsby, "Legislatures," 129–47.

29. Congressional scholar Norman Ornstein explains: "I am not surprised that most special interests oppose term limits; they have invested a lot in learning how to take advantage of the current system . . . But I have absolutely no doubt that, before long, the interests would have more leverage, not less, over a Congress consisting of inexperienced newcomers." Norman J. Ornstein, resident scholar, American Enterprise Institute, testimony on term limits for members of Congress, presented before the Subcommittee on the Constitution, Federalism and Property Rights of the Senate Judiciary Committee, 25 January 1995, in *Congressional Digest* (April 1995), 117.

30. George Skelton, "We'll Never Know How Good Speaker Could Have Been," *Los Angeles Times* (17 March 2000), A3. A six-year term limit on state assembly members may seem reasonable until we factor in the need for legislative

leaders to actually have time to lead. At the state level, term limits of, say, 10 years would give politicians the time to gain and use political power within the legislature. Yet, for supporters of term limits, 10 years sounds like an eternity.

31. Two reforms are needed. First, reduce the need for money by making public airways available to candidates. Second, provide public financing and other campaign financing reforms to level the playing field between incumbents and challengers. Public financing is not popular with the voters, but it is actually a better solution than term limits. Public financing would serve to weaken the current preoccupation of all politicians with the next campaign and how to pay for it. We want to curb the permanent campaign and encourage a focus on governing. The cost of public financing of congressional contests is low considering the great benefit of stopping the fund-raising circus. If $500,000 were put aside for each congressional district, more in expensive metropolitan areas, less in low-cost rural contests, each major party candidate would have $250,000 to spend running for office and communicating with the voters. Half a million dollars times 435 Congressional districts comes to $217 million; truly small change in the U.S. budget. A cost-benefit analysis says do it now. The actor and political activist Warren Beatty champions this cause, as does journalist Alan Ehrenhalt. See Ehrenhalt, *The United States of Ambition*, xxiii, and conversations with the author.

32. See O'Leary, "Time's Up."

33. Woodrow Wilson, *Congressional Government*.

34. See William S. Livingston, "Britain and America: The Institutionalization of Accountability," *Journal of Politics* 38, no. 4 (November 1976): 879–94; Lloyd N. Cutler, "To Form a Government," *Foreign Affairs* 59 (1980): 126–43; Committee on the Constitutional System, *A Bicentennial Analysis of the American Political Structure* (Washington, DC: Committee on the Constitutional Structure, 1987); James Sundquist, *Constitutional Reform and Effective Government*; and Mickey Kaus, "The Madison Curse," *The New Republic* (31 May 1993), 4.

35. Mayhew, *Divided We Govern*.

36. A final disadvantage of the parliamentary system is that it would not bring a distant public closer to politics. Power is more centralized in the British system, as both a majority of Parliament and the public take a distinct back seat (back bench being the British term) to the Cabinet in policy making.

37. R. Kent Weaver, "Are Parliamentary Systems Better?" *Brooking Review* (Summer 1985), 17.

38. For lucid, nontechnical arguments supporting proportional representation and multiparty reform see Michael Lind, "A Radical Plan to Change American Politics," *Atlantic Monthly* (August 1992), 73–83; Douglas Amy, *Real Choices/New Voices: The Case for Proportional Representation in the United States* (New

York: Columbia University Press, 1993) and Steven Hill, *Fixing Elections: The Fail-ure of America's Winner Take All Politics* (New York: Routledge, 2002).

39. For an example, see Kathleen Bawn, "Representing Representation in California: Checks and Balances without Gridlock," *Constitutional Reform in California,* 129–62.

40. There are alternative ways to set up a PR system. Steven Hill suggests "combining three adjoining districts into one three-seat district elected by propor-tional representation" with a 25 percent victory threshold. He says such districts in the South would likely elect a black liberal Democrat, a white conservative Re-publican, and a moderate centrist of either party. See Hill, *Fixing Elections,* 289.

41. There are strong electoral pressures on candidates in two-party systems to converge on the "median ideal voter," Downs, *Economic Theory of Democracy.*

42. Kenneth A. Shepsle and Mark S. Boncheck, *Analyzing Politics: Ratio-nality, Behavior and Institutions* (New York: W. W. Norton, 1997), 190.

43. Kenneth A. Shepsle, "Representation and Governance: The Great Leg-islative Tradeoff," *Political Science Quarterly* 103 (1988), 461–84.

44. Arthur M. Schlesinger Jr., *The Disuniting of America: Reflections on a Multicultural Society* (New York: W. W. Norton, 1992).

45. Hill, *Fixing Elections,* 23–27. Hill argues that this method comes clos-est to guaranteeing majority rule and "better ensure that the Electoral College vote matches the national popular vote."

46. Hendrick Hertzberg, "Count 'Em," *The New Yorker,* 6 March 2006, 27.

47. Hill provides a catalog of sins. Writers who look favorably on propor-tional representation include Hedrick Hertzberg, Michael Lind, and Lani Guiner.

48. Mayhew, *Congress: The Electoral Connection* and Ware, *The Break-down of Democratic Party Organization 1940–1980.*

49. In 1950, the Committee on Political Parties of the American Political Sci-ence Association published a famous report of its recommendation for improving the party system. See Report of the Committee on Political Parties, "Toward a More Responsible Two-Party System," *American Political Science Review,* 3, Supplement (1950); E. E. Schattschneider, *Party Government* (New York: Farrar and Rinehart, 1942) and Austin Ranney, *The Doctrine of Responsible Party Government* (Ur-bana: University of Illinois Press, 1962). Democratic pollster Guy Molyneux de-scribed the national Democratic Party of the 1990s as a party of political consultants. "Insofar as there is a Democratic Party, it is a network of thirty to forty political consultants. They have the institutional memory and commitment." From John B. Judis, *The Paradox of American Democracy: Elites, Special Interests and the Betrayal of the Public Trust* (New York: Pantheon Books, 2000), 8.

50. With the 2004 presidential contest expected to be extremely close, both parties mounted extensive grassroots operations in key battleground states. Matt Bai discussed the blending of the new politics with the old in "The G.O.P. Ground War: The Republicans Have Built a New Type of Political Machine, Designed to Win Battleground States Out in the Newly Minted Exurbs—Where the Crucial Voters Are Thought to Be." *New York Times Magazine,* 25 April 2004, 42 ff.

51. Postman, *Amusing Ourselves to Death,* 133.

52. Report of the Committee on Political Parties, "Toward a More Responsible Two-Party System."

53. Hacker and Pierson, Off Center, 9, and ch. 5, The Republican Machine. "More than ever, American politics is being driven from the top," 135.

54. Ibid., 186–87.

55. Ibid., 187–88.

56. See the contrast between the British and American systems in the concluding pages of Mayhew, *Congress: The Electoral Connection,* and David R. Mayhew, *Placing Parties in American Politics* (Princeton: Princeton University Press, 1986).

CHAPTER NINE

1. Cass R. Sunstein worries about these issues in *Republic.com* (Princeton: Princeton University Press, 2001) and "The Law of Group Polarization," 185–86.

2. Putnam, *Bowling Alone,* 179, emphasis in original.

3. See Clifford Geertz, *Interpretation of Cultures* (New York: Basic Books, 1973) about the importance of "thick description"; and Thomas L. Friedman, "Brave New World," *New York Times* (22 September 2000). Friedman writes about the Japanese craze known as DoCoMo—a small, colorful, palm-held cell phone, with a tiny screen that provides both voice connections and wireless Internet access. He writes that the Japanese urban fad is a "glimpse at America's future." One mother told Friedman, "I deeply deplore the situation. My son is 17 and he seems to have a girlfriend, but I'm not so sure, because it seems that they don't meet each other so much, they usually communicate over the e-mail. There are so many things you can learn from human physical contact, but this younger generation is losing these interpersonal skills."

4. For instance, irony and subtle humor are often better communicated in person than in written form. This sort of nuanced communication is critical in a group process such as the People's House where members are building coalitions and looking for support for their positions.

5. Stephen Doheny-Farina, *The Wired Neighborhood* (New Haven: Yale University Press, 1996). "A community is bound by place, which always includes complex social and environmental necessities. It is not something that you can easily join. You can't subscribe to a community as you subscribe to a discussion group on the net," 37.

6. See James Q. Wilson on the importance of social or solidarity incentives to group success. James Q. Wilson, *Political Organizations* (New York: Basic Books, 1973).

7. Ray Oldenburg, *The Great Good Place: Cafes, Coffee Shops, Community Centers, Beauty Parlors, General Stores, Bars, Hangouts, and How They Get You Through the Day* (New York: Paragon House, 1989).

8. Stephen Doyle, "The Very, Very Personal is the Political," 45.

9. See Andrew L. Shapiro, *The Control Revolution: How the Internet Is Putting Individuals in Charge and Changing the World We Know* (New York: A Century Foundation Book, 1999). On the Internet revolution and how it has shaken, in particular, the Democratic Party, see Jerome Armstrong and Markos Moulitsas Zúniga, *Crashing the Gate: Netroots, Grassroots, and the Rise of People-Powered Politics,* foreword Simon Rosenberg (White River Junction, Vermont, Chelsea Green Publishing Co., 2006).

10. Michael Walzer, *What It Means to Be an American* (New York: Marsilo, 1992). This section draws from Walzer's insightful essays.

11. Horace M. Kallen, *Culture and Democracy in the United States* (New York: Boni & Liveright, 1924).

12. Appeals to universal principles—such as human rights—are intellectually unassailable but often lack emotional resonance. Group identity and sense of belonging seem to be psychologically critical for human beings; if we want to inoculate ourselves against prejudice, it is important to fashion democratic ways for people to belong. See Rogers M. Smith, *Civic Ideals: Conflicting Visions of Citizenship in U.S. History* (New Haven: Yale University Press, 1997). This is one of the major lessons that Smith draws in this penetrating study of American history.

13. Walzer, *What It Means to Be an American,* 63–66.

14. Ibid., 45.

15. Ibid., 98, 95.

16. Ronald Dworkin, "Liberalism," in Stuart Hampshire, ed., *Public and Private Morality,* (Cambridge: Cambridge University Press, 1978); and Rawls, *Theory of Justice.*

17. Walzer, *What It Means to Be an American,* p. 96.

18. Ibid., 99.

19. Wolfe, *Whose Keeper?*

20. One of the most poignant aspects of the terrorist attack on the World Trade Center was the international cast of the buildings' residents—including the famed Windows on the World restaurant on the 107th floor. The restaurant's whole morning shift—seventy-nine workers—disappeared with that tower's collapse. The workforce was a miniature United Nations including dishwashers from Ghana, busboys from Ecuador, and cooks from Bangladesh. They were Americans who had come from Brazil, Columbia, Egypt, Ivory Coast, Pakistan, the Philippines, Poland, Uruguay, and Yemen. National Public Radio report (20 September 2001) and Steven Greenhouse, "A Showpiece's Survivors Wonder What to Do Now," *New York Times* (21 September 2001), B12.

21. Sources: Historical Statistics of the United States and a March 2004 budget resolution passed by the U.S. Senate. www.gpoaccess\usbudget gives the total as $2.656 trillion for fiscal year 2007.

22. True, we have no colonies, but an empire is how we are perceived by those nations swamped by our wake. Neocolonialism is the new form that colonialism has taken, varying in degree by the particular Third World nation at issue and its various economic and political relationships with more powerful nations and multinational corporations. For a classic study see Colin Leys, *Underdevelopment in Kenya: The Political Economy of Neo-Colonialism, 1964–1971* (Berkeley: University of California, 1974).

23. Machiavelli, *The Discourses,* bk. 1, ch. 6, 127–29 and Hulliung, *Citizen Machiavelli,* 5.

24. Chalmers Johnson, *The Sorrows of Empire: Militarism, Secrecy, and the End of the Republic* (New York: Metropolitan/ Owl Book, 2004), 312.

25. Michael Hilzik et al. "How Did Hijackers Get Past Airport Security?" *Los Angeles Times,* (23 September 2001), A15.

26. Adam Ulam, former director of Harvard's Russian Research Center, cited in Alterman, *Who Speaks for America?,* 8.

27. Haynes Johnson and David S. Broder, *The System: The American Way of Politics at the Breaking Point* (Boston: Little, Brown, 1996), 205–07.

28. James Fallows, "A Triumph of Misinformation: Most of what everyone 'knows' about the demise of healthcare reform is probably wrong—and more importantly, so are the vague impressions people have of what was really in the Clinton plan," *Atlantic Monthly* (January 1995), 26–37. Bok agrees, saying the health care "debate left the public in a high state of confusion . . . the public felt that it knew *less* about the issues after they were fully debated than it did in the early months after Mr. Clinton first unveiled his plan." Bok, *Trouble with Government,* 377–378, emphasis in original.

29. David Halberstam, *War in a Time of Peace: Bush, Clinton and the Generals* (New York: Scribners, 2001).

30. United States Department of Defense 2006 Discretionary Budget Authority, $419.3 billion, Budget of the United States Government, Fiscal Year 2006 (Washington, DC: U.S. Government Printing Office, 2005), 83.

31. Anthony Downs, *Economic Theory of Democracy.*

CONCLUSION

1. Hacker and Pierson, "Abandoning the Middle," 33. Jacobs and Shapiro in *Politicians Don't Pander* and "Politics and Policymaking in the Real World," develop their theory by looking at the Clinton White House.

2. Joe Klein, "The Culture War Is Really a Culture Circus," *Time* (8 March 2004), 25.

3. Tocqueville, *Democracy in America,* vol. 2, part 4, ch. 6, "What Sort of Despotism Democratic Nations Have to Fear," 691, 693.

4. In Don Herzog's book on consent theory, *Happy Slaves,* he considers whether it is possible to alienate one's freedom to choose to become a "happy slave." Don Herzog, *Happy Slaves: A Critique of Consent Theory* (Chicago: University of Chicago Press, 1989), ix–xii.

5. Schumpeter, *Capitalism, Socialism and Democracy,* 269.

6. Przeworski, "Minimalist Conception of Democracy: A Defense," 23, citing Karl Popper, *The Open Society and Its Enemies* (London: Routledge and Kegan Paul, 1962).

7. Ian Shapiro and Casiano Hacker-Cordón, "Promises and Disappointments: Reconsidering Democracy's Value," in Ian Shapiro and Casiano Hacker-Cordón, *Democracy's Value,* 4

8. Ibid.

9. See Hacker and Pierson, "Abandoning the Middle," 33, 38. Hacker and Pierson argue that the disconnect between the public and the Bush White House and GOP-led Congress is a cause for concern. I agree, but such concern must be based on a different understanding of democracy than the one offered by Schumpeter. Hacker and Pierson summarize their argument thus: "By attacking the foundations of republican government—the accountability of politicians to ordinary voters for what they do in office—the new Republican machine threatens American democracy itself." Hacker and Pierson, *Off Center,* book jacket.

10. Albert O. Hirschman, *Exit, Voice and Loyalty* (Cambridge: Harvard University Press, 1970).

11. Demetrios James Caraley, "Complications of American Democracy: Elections Are Not Enough," *Political Science Quarterly,* 120 (2005), 399–400.

12. As Machiavelli observed, the people have less motive to subvert liberty and less desire to dominate others than do the elite. "One should always confide any deposit to those who have the least desire of violating it." Machiavelli, *The Discourses,* bk. 5, 121.

13. Buffett's annual letter to shareholders of Berkshire Hathaway Inc., March 2004.

14. Rosenstone and Hansen, *Mobilization, Participation, and Democracy in America,* 248, emphasis added.

15. See Hill, *Fixing Elections,* for his disturbing description of the 1998 U.S. Senate race in New York between Democrat Charles Schumer and Republican Alfonse D'Amato. 148–49.

16. Morgan, *Inventing the People.*

17. Lasch, *The Revolt of the Elites,* 10.

18. Jack L. Walker, "A Critique of the Elitist Theory of Democracy," *American Political Science Review,* 60 (1966): 285–95, 391–92 and Joel D. Aberbach, Frank R. Baumgartner, Thomas L. Gais, David C. King, Mark A. Peterson, and Kim Lane Scheppele, "Foreword," in Jack L. Walker, *Mobilizing Interest Groups in America,* ix. This might "be changed through the patient and deliberate building and amending of institutions by enlightened leaders." On quiescence and apathy see Gaventa, *Power and Powerlessness.*

19. Manin, *Representative Government,* 3.

20. The U.S. Census Bureau projects the nation's population will be 308 million in 2010. "U.S. Interim Projections by Age, Sex, Race, and Hispanic Origin," *U.S. Census Bureau,* 2004, Table 1a. Projected Population of the United States, by Race and Hispanic Origin: 2000 to 2050. http://www.census.gov/ipc/www/usinterimproj/

21. Arendt, *On Revolution,* 255.

22. Gabriel Garcia Marquez, *One Hundred Years of Solitude* (New York: Harper Perennial Library, 1998).

23. For lucid statements of this understanding of American pragmatism see John Dewey, *Reconstruction in Philosophy* [1920] (Boston: Beacon Press, 1957) and *The Quest for Certainty.*

24. See Croly, *The Promise of American Life.*

25. Tocqueville, *Democracy in America,* 642.

26. George Bernard Shaw, *Pygmalion* (New York: Pocket Books, 1989).

Acknowledgments

Many people helped bring about this book. One does not become an author without inspiration. Three of my teachers stand out as being particularly gifted in conveying excitement about intellectual ideas. In high school, I was fortunate to be a student of Marilyn Whirry, a future national teacher of the year: at UCLA, classes with Richard Sklar sparked my interest in political science: and at Yale Graduate School, Charles Lindblom was a model of intellectual rigor and pushing ideas. At Yale, Rogers Smith introduced me to John Dewey and American political thought, while David Mayhew and Robert Dahl deepened my knowledge of American politics and democratic theory. In particular, Lindblom's enthusiastic reaction to the manuscript encouraged me to press ahead. If this book is worthy, it is in part due to his comments and the example he set as a teacher and scholar. Teaching through their books, Lindblom, Christopher Lasch, Arthur Schlesinger Jr., and Michael Walzer are models of what scholarship and good writing are all about.

Friends and colleagues Oliver Avens, Roger Boesche, Alan Heslop, David Menefee-Libey, Dan Mazmanian, Mark Petracca, and Jack Pitney read early drafts and helped me focus my ideas. Professor Mayhew's comments and those from anonymous reviewers were of great assistance in making the book stronger. My thanks for their time and insight. Bill Boyarski, Tony Day, and the late Art Seidenbaum were wonderful mentors at the *Los Angeles Times*. Reporting for the *Times* as well as a year as a CORO Foundation Fellow gave me invaluable grounding in the world of practical politics. Students at UCLA, Claremont Graduate University, Claremont McKenna College, and UC Irvine provided stimulation and feedback. When I was busy pursuing my journalistic career at the *Pasadena Star-News* and the *Los Angeles Times,* Mazmanian suggested that I become a visiting scholar at the Claremont Graduate University. At UC Irvine, I am particularly grateful to Russ Dalton and William R. Schonfeld, the immediate past and current directors of the Center for the Study of Democracy, respectively, and Dean Barbara Anne Dosher for inviting me to be a research fellow. Both the Claremont Colleges and the University of California, Irvine are wonderful institutions that make serious scholarship possible.

As a fellow writer and journalist, I am fortunate to have worked with Steve Thomas at *OC Metro Magazine* and Larry Wilson at the *Pasadena Star-News* and to have Scott Martelle of the *Los Angeles Times* as a neighbor, friend, and fellow author. While editor of *OC Metro Magazine,* the regional magazine for Orange County, California, I got the idea of running a magazine series on the People's House during the 2000 presidential primaries. Steve Churm, Craig Reem, and Sonia Chung were enthusiastic in their support.

Over time, I have shared the idea of the Assembly with a number of journalists and writers. In the early stages, Jack Miles told me I had a book, and Jim Fallows offered advice and graciously read several drafts. Together, they helped speed me on my way. At different times, Jonathan Alter, Eric Alterman, Thomas Geoghegan, William Greider, John Judis, Robert Kuttner, Jonathan Rauch, Jonathan Schell, Ronald Steel, and the late John Jacobs of the *Sacramento Bee* expressed interest and offered encouragement for which I am grateful. *Washington Monthly* Editor-in-Chief Paul Glastris and *Governing* Editor Alan Ehrenhalt deserve special thanks. On meeting in Washington, DC, Glastris quickly understood my description of the People's House and encouraged me to develop the Assembly as an intermediate step with immediate political relevance. Alan has offered encouragement since the early stages of the project.

Barbara Abell, Elizabeth Lund, Heidi Lyons, and Vicki Ronaldson went beyond the call of duty when assisting with copyediting and preparing the manuscript. At Stanford University Press, Amanda Moran, Margaret Pinette, Puja Sangar, and Tim Roberts have been enthusiastic about the project and a pleasure to work with. Thanks also go to Jared Smith for his assistance with the manuscript.

Friends and family are essential for authors. Jim Bernstein, Peter Blasini and Nancy Yedlin, Steve Colome and Kathy Lottes, Jane Lappin and Jeff Griffiths, Margaret and Scott Martelle, Antonio Morawski and Francoise Schmutz, and Suzanne and Barry Ross have been great friends for years, as have Jim Schoning and Velma Sun Fletcher of the CORO Foundation family. My sister Kerry, my parents Charlene and Phil O'Leary, my brother-in-law Steve Robinow, and my wife's parents, Larry and Ricky Robinow, all have been wonderfully encouraging. The same is true of Mortimer Herzstein and Bob and Priscilla Herzstein.

My family has lived with this book from the beginning. My daughters, Allison and Rebecca, grew older, taller, and more accomplished as I wrote. Shrewd political observers and activists, I hope they think it has been worth the effort. And finally to my wife, Lita Robinow, to whom the book is dedicated, I am beyond grateful. Lita has been incredibly supportive of me and of this project. Having worked and fund raised for politicians, she married a political scientist and journalist. Having a writer as a spouse or family member is not always easy. More than she knows, I appreciate my wife's good humor and patience. Now the ideas can be shared with others, and I can return to family and friends.

Index

Abramoff, Jack, 38, 123
Ackerman, Bruce, 62, 128–29, 186, 247*n*10
Aggregation, 125–26, 165, 254*n*41
Alienation, 17
Al Qaeda, 6
Alterman, Eric, 255*n*47
Althaus, Scott, 22, 128
American empire, 3, 26–28, 203–209, 210–211
American Revolution, 34–35, 79
American tradition of democracy, 8, 11, 12, 230*n*66. *See also* Founding of United States
Anti-Federalists, 36–37, 62, 85, 111–12
Apathy, 38, 40, 43, 51–52, 56–57, 216
Arendt, Hannah, 36, 72–73, 78, 87, 161, 167, 175, 217, 233*n*8
Aristotle, 34, 51, 110, 111, 177, 188
Armstrong, Jerome, and bloggers and the Internet revolution, 272*n*9
Arrow, Kenneth, 126, 143
Articles of Confederation, 55, 61, 62
Assemblies (local): community building in, 119, 203; conduct of, 90, 100; moderators of, 100; regional groups of, 102–3
Assembly (national), 89–91, 159; and aggregation of interests/preferences, 125–26; and American tradition, 11; collective intelligence in, 153–55; communication in, 102–3; compensation for delegates of, 159, 249*n*32; cost of, 158–59; educational function of, 103–4; impact of, 89, 114; influence of, on public, 156; Internet and, 7, 87–89, 200; issues versus personality in, 158; jury as model for, 90, 108–9, 159; and law, 118; legislative, not bureaucratic, character of, 158; opposition to, 95–96, 131; overview of, 8; personality versus issues in, 158; polarization in, 156–57; political knowledge of delegates in, 99–100; polling of, 90–91; possibility of, 94–96, 130; predecessors of, 92–94; as public opinion, 87, 89, 95; purpose of, 95, 159; and repre-

sentation, 7–8, 10, 95, 120, 179; responsibility of individuals in, 159; selection of delegates for, 87, 89, 104–9, 179; service in, 11; spaces for, 199; versus special interests, 119–24; staff (administrative/technical) for, 159; steering committee for, 89, 249*n*32; technological advances and, 68; term limit for, 89; as weak public, 174. *See also* Assemblies (local); Assembly reform; Athenian Assembly
Assembly reform: and American tradition, 8, 12; benefits of, 10–11, 115, 132–33, 214–18; corruption and, 214; imaginative projection of, 133–38; Madison and Jefferson synthesized for, 88, 218; overview of, 7–9, 87–88; political neutrality of, 13; and popular sovereignty, 216; practicality of, 113–14, 217–18; promoting, 130–32; stages of, 8–9. *See also* Assembly (national); People's House
Athenian Assembly, 11, 100–101, 103, 106–7, 109–11, 163
Atlantic Monthly, 208
Authoritarianism, 173, 188
Ayres, Ian, 186

Bailyn, Bernard, 35
Balkans, involvement in, 208–9
Barone, Michael, 49, 56, 237*n*64
Bartels, Larry, 22–23
Beard, Charles, 57–58
Beer, Samuel H., 62, 66, 177
Belgium, 183
Bentham, Jeremy, 76
Berlin, Isaiah, on negative liberty, 74–77
Bessette, Joseph, 59–60, 169–70
Bicameralism, 65, 142–43, 191
Black, Duncan, 126, 143
Blumenthal, Sidney, on Cold War conservatism, 230*n*65
Bobos, 21
Bok, Derek, 52, 127
Boorstin, Daniel, 17
Boxer, Barbara, 70